KV-317-932

Japan's Great Stagnation and Abenomics

Japan's Great Stagnation and Abenomics

Lessons for the World

Masazumi Wakatabe

JAPAN'S GREAT STAGNATION AND ABENOMICS
Copyright © Masazumi Wakatabe, 2015.

All rights reserved.

First published in 2015 by PALGRAVE MACMILLAN® in the United States—a division of St. Martin's Press LLC, 175 Fifth Avenue, New York, NY 10010.

Where this book is distributed in the UK, Europe and the rest of the world, this is by Palgrave Macmillan, a division of Macmillan Publishers Limited, registered in England, company number 785998, of Houndmills, Basingstoke, Hampshire RG21 6XS.

Palgrave Macmillan is the global academic imprint of the above companies and has companies and representatives throughout the world.

Palgrave® and Macmillan® are registered trademarks in the United States, the United Kingdom, Europe and other countries.

ISBN: 978-1-137-43884-3

Library of Congress Cataloging-in-Publication Data

Wakatabe, Masazumi.
  Japan's great stagnation and abenomics : lessons for the world / Masazumi Wakatabe.
      pages cm
  Includes bibliographical references and index.
  ISBN 978-1-137-43884-3 (hardback)
      1. Japan—Economic conditions—21st century.   2. Japan—Economic policy—21st century.   3. Monetary policy—Japan.   4. Finance—Japan.   5. Stagnation (Economics)   I. Title.
  HC462.95.W3435 2015
  330.952—dc23
                                                                      2014042336

A catalogue record of the book is available from the British Library.

Design by Amnet.

First edition: April 2015

10 9 8 7 6 5 4 3 2 1

Contents

List of Tables and Figures

Tables

Figures

Preface

This is a book mainly about the past of the Japanese economy, but I hope it will help readers to understand the present and the future. Japan has experienced more than a decade of stagnation since 1990, and many of the subsequent decades have been dubbed as the "Lost Decade" or the "Lost Two Decades." In this book, I use the term Great Stagnation to designate the long stagnation of the Japanese economy. The stagnation is remarkable in its duration, now spanning almost three decades, and it is creating political, economic, and social problems. Once Japan was seen as the best performer in the world, but it is now seen as the department store of economic problems. But there is an ongoing, new development in the Japanese economy, initiated by Prime Minister Shinzo Abe. The new policy package, commonly known as Abenomics, has generated a lot of attention for the Japanese economy. However, to understand the significance and possible future of Abenomics, it is essential to understand Japan's Great Stagnation.

Again, this book is mainly about the Japanese economy, but I hope it will also inform readers about some aspects of the world economy. Since 2007, the world economy has experienced one of the biggest economic and financial crises in history. Since then, the world economy has been struggling to recover from this crisis, now known as the Great Recession. So far, the U.S. economy has been doing better than others have, but even in the United States, there is an ongoing discussion of the secular stagnation, and the possibility and fear of a Japan-like long stagnation has not yet completely disappeared. Rather, the European economies, with the notable exception of Germany, have been experiencing a sluggish recovery. It is true that the Great Recession and Japan's Great Stagnation have similarities and differences, but one can learn from another's experiences; particularly, the rest of the world can learn from Japan to avoid "Japanization," that is, becoming like Japan and having the problems that Japan has had and is still having.

This book is primarily about the economy and economics, but it is also about politics, society, and people. Japan was once hailed as the great country: there was a book titled *Japan as Number One* (Vogel 1979). It was exaggerated even back then, but Japan had a more than decent economic performance and enjoyed a fairly equal income distribution. Then, with the economic stagnation, politics and society have begun to change as well. I would not say that the old Japan was good: on the contrary, it was problematic. But compared with other economies that have been affected by the asset price boom and the subsequent collapse but that have a widely different culture or set of institutions from each other, Japan's stagnation has been too long to justify, and it has been long enough to change many of the better aspects of the society.

The literature on Japan's Great Stagnation is already voluminous. For instance, Japan's *Keizai shakai sogo kenkyusyo* (Economics and Social Research Institute of the Cabinet Office; ESRI) has published an 11 volume large-scale study on the subject (Naikakufu keizaishakai sogo kenkyusho 2009, 2011).[1] So why should I add another book on the subject? The reason has something to do with my frustration and profession. I am a historian of economic thought by profession, but as a Japanese economist, or rather as a Japanese citizen, I have been puzzled by the poor performance of the Japanese economy since 1990. Presumably, the majority of academic economists, in Japan or anywhere, are not interested in the current topics. I was no exception. It was when I began teaching an introductory economics course at Waseda University that I first took a look at several contemporary accounts of the economy: I thought that I, as a teacher, was obliged to comment on the current economic issues to motivate students. It was 1997, which became the pivotal year for Japan's Great Stagnation. Back then, I was astonished by the confusion and fierceness of the controversies surrounding Japan's Great Stagnation, and I started to follow the controversies. Later, I came to realize that those economic controversies are an important and integral part of Japan's Great Stagnation. A lot of explanations or stories have been advanced regarding the causes and remedies of the Great Stagnation, but people understand the economy through their preconceptions: economists are no exception, with the difference being economists' use of "models." Moreover, these preconceptions and models could dictate economists' actions, which in turn could influence their outcomes. In the case of Japan, those economic controversies reveal exactly what Japanese economists have been thinking during the crisis. As a historian of economic thought, I have been struck by how little Japan's Great Stagnation has been analyzed from that perspective. Therefore, I felt there was something I could contribute.

In this book, I refer to many Japanese sources whose translation is solely my responsibility.

Acknowledgments

As always, the book is a joint product of many people's generosity and help. I would like to thank Kikuo Iwata, now deputy governor of the Bank of Japan; Koichi Hamada, professor of economics emeritus at Yale University; and Nakahara Nobuyuki, former member of the Monetary Policy Committee of the Bank of Japan from 1998–2002. They are my mentors and guides. I would also like to thank the people at the Workshop on the Showa Depression headed by Iwata: Seiji Adachi, Yutaka Harada, Yasuyuki Iida, Goushi Kataoka, Muneyoshi Nakamura, Hideki Nakayama, Asahi Noguchi, Yoichi Takahashi, Hidetomi Tanaka, and Koiti Yano. They are my intellectual fellow travelers.

In writing the book, I have greatly benefited from the generosity, hospitality, and intellectual community of the Center on Japanese Economy and Business, Columbia Business School. I am grateful to Hugh Patrick, David Weinstein, Caroline Hasegawa, and Ryoko Ogino. The actual production owes a great deal to the editorial team at Palgrave Macmillan. My deepest thanks go to Leila Campoli, Sarah Lawrence, and Jamie Armstrong.

I appreciate the following institutions for giving me permission to reproduce their materials: Gaskuhuin Daigaku Keizai Gakkai for Figures 4-1 and 4-4 to 4-8, and the Bank of Japan for Figure 5-1.

A work like this needs good libraries and funding. I would like to thank the Waseda University and Columbia University Libraries. Financial assistance from the Japanese Society for the Promotion of Science (Grant No. 25380257) is greatly appreciated.

Last, but not the least, I would like to thank my wife Atsuko. She has constantly encouraged and supported my life and work. The book would not exist without her.

CHAPTER 1

Introduction: Once It Happened in Japan

I. Introduction

As the world economic crisis continues, people are turning to the Japanese example. Japan was one of the best macroeconomic performers in the world until 1990. Then Japan experienced the bursting of the asset price boom, a financial crisis, and more than a decade of deflation and stagnation. The Japanese episode, known as the Great Stagnation, received much attention during the 1990s and the early years of the 2000s, but the onset of the current crisis invigorated a renewed interest in that episode. Some commentators are even worrying about the Japanization, or Japanification, of the Western countries.[1] The prime example was the lead article in the July 30–August 5, 2011, issue of *The Economist*. Aptly titled "Turning Japanese," the article featured U.S. President Barack Obama and German Chancellor Angela Merkel wearing Japanese kimonos. The image the news magazine tried to convey was the sense that United States and European political leaders are marred with the same problems as their Japanese counterparts: a lack of leadership, incoherent policy initiatives, and the resultant prolonged stagnation.[2] Paul Krugman, the most vocal critic of macroeconomic policy as it is currently practiced all over the world, remarked several times that he should apologize to the Japanese because the Americans were not doing better than the Japanese were. His so-called apology was mere rhetoric for this master debater, but his reference to Japan is more substantial.[3]

Then, for most people, everything changed suddenly, or so it seemed. Shinzo Abe, the Liberal Democratic Party (LDP) politician and the prime minister of Japan from 2006 to 2007, emerged as the leader of the LDP once again and won the general election in December 2012. He has initiated a new policy package, commonly known as "Abenomics." This entails three pillars, or "three arrows" in Mr. Abe's terminology—that is, the "bold monetary policy," the "flexible fiscal policy," and the "growth strategy." The yen has immediately depreciated since November 14, 2012, when former Prime Minister Yoshihiko Noda announced that the general election would be held, thus virtually securing Abe's succession as the next prime minister. In addition, the stock market has soared. In February 2013, Abe appointed Haruhiko Kuroda as the new governor of the Bank of Japan (BOJ). Kuroda subsequently launched the "quantitative and qualitative easing (QQE)" on April 4, 2013, doubling the amount of base money within two years, to achieve a 2 percent inflation rate. The government has also budgeted for increased public spending. The early signs were promising: economic growth has resumed, and deflation has been receding. The real gross domestic product (GDP) growth rate for the first quarter of 2014 exceeded the 6.9 percent annualized rate, and the unemployment rate decreased to 3.7 percent, according to data released in July 2014.[4] However, the government raised the consumption tax from 5 percent to 8 percent in April 2014, in the name of fiscal consolidation. The data for the second quarter of 2014 showed that the GDP has plunged to negative 6.9 percent, and the data for the third quarter of 2014 recorded that the GDP has further decreased by negative 1.9 percent. The Japanese economy is again in danger of returning to a recession.

What happened in Japan's Great Stagnation? What caused it, and what lessons can the world learn from it? What is Abenomics? What is it trying to achieve, what is the likelihood of success, and what lessons the world can learn from Abenomics? These are all important questions, but to answer these questions, this book focuses mainly on the history of the economic controversies and debates during the Great Stagnation. Since any policy is related to—though not necessarily based on—certain ideas, an investigation into the relationship between ideas, policy, and outcomes is required to better understand the policymaking process. David Laidler, a renowned monetary economist and historian of economic thought, argued that, as economics assumes, every economic agent has a "model" of how the economy works, and policymakers must also have models, however crude or unsystematic a "model" may be. Therefore, the historians of economic thought can shed a light on the policymaking process by examining the models that policymakers have (Laidler 2003). Hamada and Noguchi (2005) argued that the policymakers of two deflationary episodes in Japan, the Great Depression era and the 1990s, were largely misled by "misconceived ideas," an erroneous understanding of the economy. Moreover, a cross-country comparison between economic ideas in Japan and those in the West would reveal not only similarities and differences in policy responses but also similarities and differences in ideas. As Fourcade's (2009) comparative analysis of the developments in the

United States, Great Britain, and France showed, economic ideas have been situated in cultural, institutional, and historical contexts. One may pursue a similar line of research in comparisons between economics in Japan and economics in the Western countries, highlighting the cultural and institutional characteristics of the Japanese economics academia (Wakatabe 2014a).

Yet one may discern similarities across countries as well as differences. During the debate, there have been several points of contention. Macroeconomic stabilization has been advocated, criticized, dismissed, and resurrected, while liquidationist thinking or macroeconomic policy nihilism—the belief that an inflationary boom should be followed by a deflationary recession, so the best remedy to recession is to "let things run the natural course," which is a nonintervention policy—has been returned to the policy discussion. With deflation and deflationary expectations persisting, the role of monetary policy became the center of the discussion, while professional economists were divided on the efficacy of monetary policy. As the recession became prolonged, a number of economists turned their eyes on the structural factors, proposing a wide variety of remedies in the name of "structural reforms," while these structural factors explanations changed over the course of the controversy. Furthermore, during the crisis, discussions became heated and emotionally charged, contributing to the policy paralysis in Japan.

The next section of the chapter overviews what happened during Japan's Great Stagnation. Main economic and social indicators show that the Japanese economy has a sluggish economic record and disturbing social trends. Section III sets out the theoretical perspective of the book in detail. It is my contention that events, ideas, and policies interact with each other and that "bad" economic ideas have grave consequences on performance. The last section offers a brief tour of the book.

II. Japan's Great Stagnation at a Glance

We start with the three most important figures in economics, the real GDP growth rate, the unemployment rate, and the inflation rate. Figure 1-1 shows Japan's real GDP growth rate: before 1990, Japan achieved an average growth rate that was around 4 percent during the 1980s, but the growth rate declined to less than 2 percent during the 1990s and even less in the first decade of the 2000s.

It has sometimes been claimed that on a per capita basis, the growth rate of the real GDP in Japan has not been as poor as has been commonly assumed. For example, Masaaki Shirakawa, a former BOJ governor, contended: "Japan's real GDP growth rate has declined and growth has been subdued compared to other developed countries. However, comparing the average real GDP

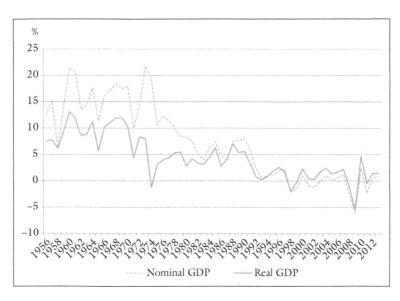

Figure 1-1   Japan's Real and Nominal Growth Rates from 1956 to 2014

Note/Source: The 1956–1980 data are from the 68 System of National Accounts settled in 1998 (with 1990 as the base year). The 1981–1994 data are from the 93 SNA settled in 2009 (with 2000 as the base year). The 1995–2012 data are from the 93 SNA settled in 2012 (with 2005 as the base year). Data from the Cabinet Office.

growth rate per capita over the past ten years, Japan's growth rate is almost the same as other developed countries. Moreover, Japan is highest in terms of real GDP growth rate per working-age population" (Shirakawa 2012, 7).[5] But the comparison is misleading because this does not account for the unused resources: the unemployed people, in particular. The more appropriate way is to take a look at the output gap: as Figure 1-2 shows, after 1993, the Japanese economy has had a constant output gap, averaging around 2 percent, with the exceptions of brief intervals in 1997 and 2007–2008. In other words, the Japanese economy might have performed better than was generally assumed by economists, but it could have performed even better if these unused resources had been utilized fully. Admittedly, the concept of the output gap and its estimation method are not without their problems.[6] Indeed, some economists argue strongly against the use of the concept of the output gap, but arguing against the output gap implies that Japan's Great Stagnation has been purely a long-term phenomenon in that all prices, including wages, have been adjusted fully. This has become a contentious matter in controversies during the Great Stagnation period, as we see in Chapter 3.

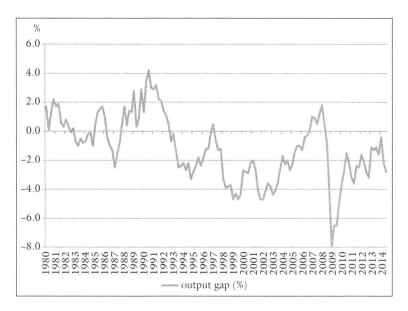

Figure 1-2 Output Gap (%) from 1980 to 2014
Source: Data from the Cabinet Office.

Historically, Japan has been known for its "low" unemployment rate, and it is still "low" by international standards, but it has increased since the 1990s, reflecting the output gap during the same period since the 1990s. It should also be noted that the Japanese official figure is somewhat misleading because the government subsidizes firms to keep employers, a system known as *koyo chosei jyosei kin* (employment adjustment subsidy). The exact magnitude varies: the government estimates that the system reduced at least 1 percentage point in 2009 when the unemployment hit the record high of 6.5 percent (Naikakufu 2012, fig. 1-1-26). In any case, what matters is that unemployment has increased, and unless we assume that those unemployed people are voluntarily unemployed, this issue needs to be addressed.

Some of the major characteristics of Japan's Great Stagnation have been the low inflation rate and, since the mid-1990s, deflation. Figure 1-3 shows the trend in the inflation rates in Japan in two measures, the changes in the consumer price index (CPI) and in the GDP deflator. Both show that the Japanese economy has been experiencing deflation since the mid- to later 1990s. It has been known that there is a 1 percent upper bias in the CPI

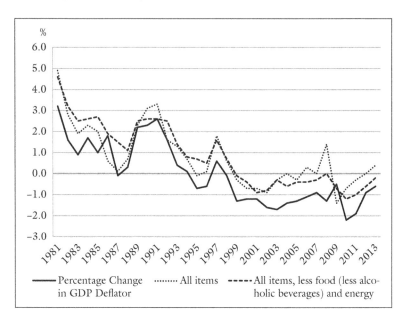

Figure 1-3 Japan's Inflation Rates from 1981 to 2014

Note/Source: The annual percentage change in CPI data are from the Ministry of Internal Affairs and Communications, Statistics Bureau. The percentage change in the GDP deflator in 1981–1994 is from the 1993 SNA settled in 2009 (with 2000 as base year). The percentage change in 1995–2012 is from the 1993 SNA settled in 2012 (with 2005 as base year). The 2013 data are from the Cabinet Office.

because the basket of goods and services that make the CPI are fixed, but Handbury, Watanabe, and Weinstein (2013) showed that this upward bias might be bigger than 2 percent. They argued that the information content would be lost when a change in the CPI goes below 2 percent.[7]

Another major characteristic of Japan's Great Stagnation has been its persistent asset price deflation after 1990. Figures 1-4 and 1-5 show the movement of stock prices and land prices, respectively. Carmen Reinhart and Kenneth Rogoff of Harvard University compiled long-term data on banking, currency, and economics crises (Reinhart and Rogoff 2009). These researchers designated five major crises occurring post–World War II and pre-2007 in advanced economies as the "Big Five." These crises include Japan after 1992. What is remarkable about Japan is its persistent asset price decrease in terms of land price: no other countries, whether they are in the "Big Five" or among other developing countries, ever experienced such a sustained decrease in asset prices. Figures 1-4 and 1-5 compare the movements of the stock land with the United States and United Kingdom.

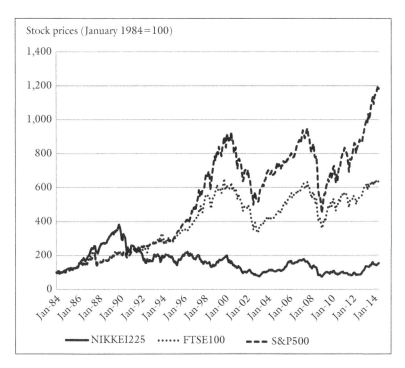

Figure 1-4 Stock Prices: United States, United Kingdom, and Japan
Source: Data from Yahoo Finance.

The exchange rate is quite important in understanding Japan's Great Stagnation because it started with the appreciation of the yen, which has coincided with lower inflation and deflation. Some wondered whether Japan's preoccupation with the exchange rate is an emergent market mentality. This is not correct in two respects. First, even the most advanced economies, such as the United States and Germany, are concerned with the exchange rates from time to time. The prime example is the Plaza Accord of 1985. As we see in Chapter 2, the American policymakers were worried about the appreciation of the U.S. dollar in the early 1980s, so they demanded that other advanced economies, including Japan and West Germany, "correct" their exchange rates. Second, as is clear from Figure 1-6, the real, effective exchange rate of Germany, from the time that East Germany and West Germany were separated, has been consistently stable throughout recent history. This is not a coincidence: Germany has been conducting its macroeconomic policy in a stable manner, so its exchange rate has been stable. Rather, in comparison, one could say that Japan has not been concerned enough about the exchange rate movement.

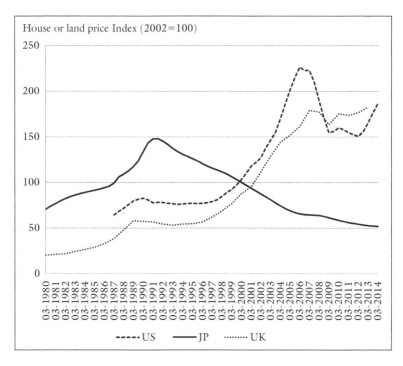

Figure 1-5 Land or House Price Comparisons: United States, United Kingdom, and Japan

Sources: Japanese (JP) data are from Chikakouji (2000 = 100); United States (US) data are from Case Shiller; United Kingdom (UK) data are from the House Price Index (2002 = 100).

The Great Stagnation has been damaging to the lives of the Japanese people, affecting their perceptions in an adverse way. The suicide rate (adjusted for number of people) increased from 1997 to 1998, remained constant for some time, and is now decreasing. The suicide rate and the unemployment rate in Japan have been shown to be strongly correlated (Chen et al. 2012), as is displayed in Figure 1-7. Surely people commit suicide for many reasons, but studies have shown there are economic reasons (Sawada, Ueda, and Matsubayashi 2013, chap. 2).

With the long stagnation, at least in nominal terms, Japanese households became poorer. According to the *Kokumin Seikatsu Kiso Chosa* (Comprehensive Survey of Living Conditions), compiled by Japan's Ministry of Health, Labor, and Welfare, the relative frequency distribution of households by income group shifted downward from 1994 to 2012 (Figure 1-8).[8] Also, the poverty rate for overall households has been increasing from 13.2 percent in

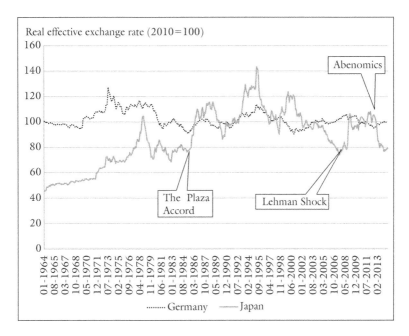

Figure 1-6   Real Effective Exchange Rate, Japan versus Germany

Source: Data from Bank of International Settlements.

1988 to 16.1 percent in 2012. For children (under 17), the poverty rate has been steadily increasing from 10.9 percent in 1988 to 16.3 percent in 2012.[9] By comparison, Japan's poverty rate ranks as the fifth worst among the Organisation for Economic Co-operation and Development (OECD) countries.[10]

With the stagnation of their nominal income, people's perceptions of their lives have soured. *Kokumin seikatsu kiso chosa* asked the Japanese people about the conditions of their lives: the percentage of those who responded "very hard" and "hard" combined has increased from 37.8 percent in 1990 to 59.8 percent in 2012.[11] Also, there is a growing sense of increased income inequality. Once Japan was considered to be one the most egalitarian societies, and it still is not as unequal as some other countries: among 24 OECD countries, Japan's Gini coefficient (at disposable income, posttax, and transfer) is above the average and below that of the United States and United Kingdom (OECD 2008, 25). A recent study showed inequality in Japan has increased during the 1990s but has either decreased from 2000 to 2005 (OECD 2008, 33) or stayed the same in the early 2000s,[12] although the perception of inequality has changed. Although Japanese people still see themselves as in

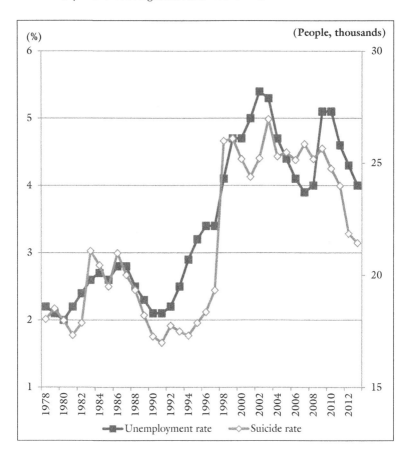

Figure 1-7   Unemployment and Suicide Rates in Japan from 1978 to 2013

Source: Data from Ministry of Internal Affairs and Communications Statistics Bureau; National Police Agency.

the middle range of income, they now are increasingly seeing the society as more unequal, with a pyramid-like structure (Hara 2010, 60).

III. Ideas, Policy, and Outcomes

Economics and History

Throughout the book, I emphasize tackling the problems with two tools: economics and history. Both are powerful and useful weapons when used with care. The reputations of economics and economists have been tarnished

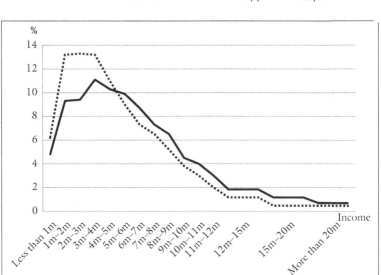

Figure 1-8   Relative Frequency Distribution of Households by Income Group

Note/Source: ¥12million–15million, ¥15million–20million, and more than ¥20million are averaged. Data from Ministry of Health, Labor, and Welfare.

by the recent experiences of Japan's Great Stagnation and the current financial and economic crises, dubbed as the Great Recession: there is more than enough evidence to be skeptical about the usefulness of *some* parts of economics.[13] However, we should be also careful about being too pessimistic about *everything* about economics. In fact, as I argue in this book, economics has many faces, and although the Great Recession has revealed vulnerable aspects of economics and the economics profession, there is still a lot to learn from economics if its principles are used in a productive manner. But how could we tell the useful part of economics from not so useful part of economics? This is the role of history. Economists can come up with many models that are logically consistent but that are not useful in explaining empirical facts: the internal consistency of a model does not necessarily guarantee its external consistency. After all, a social science like economics cannot engage in well-specified, controlled experiments over an extended period; therefore, any data or records of the facts are historical by nature. Thus, history is and should be our laboratory or the testing ground for economics. On the other hand, history is not be meant to be a mere collection of facts: history should be used for explorations of past events informed by logical reasoning. Therefore, there has to be an interaction between economics and history, and that interaction could be a potentially fruitful one: history would help us to distinguish the useful parts of economics from those that are not useful, while economics can shed light on history as a coherent story.

What Determines Policy

When I emphasize the role of history, I do so not only in terms of the history of events but also in terms of the history of ideas. There has been a great debate about what determines economic policy, or any policy for that matter. One side emphasizes the role of interests among other possible explanations. It has been the mainstream position on the issue as the flourishing subfield of public choice and new political economy testifies. Economics starts from the rationality of individuals, and the idea that political outcomes are determined by game-theoretic interactions between purposive behaviors of rational individuals rings true to many economists (Stigler 1971; Acemoglu and Robinson 2013). On the other hand, there is a view that emphasizes the role of ideas in shaping economic policy. This line of research is gaining some reception among social scientists. Dani Rodrik at the Institute for Advanced Studies at Princeton University argued that three elements of the optimization problems—preferences, constraints, and choice variables—depend on "an implicit set of ideas" (Rodrik 2014, 191). Even though, or especially when, we assume that a person is making a rational calculation, ideas and perceptions matter.

Knowledge as a Problem

When it comes to ideas and perception, there are further complications. As Adam Smith emphasizes, a society is made by the division of labor among many individuals, and in a modern society, the division of labor is complicated and complex. Part of the complexity comes from the division of knowledge among individuals: everyone knows something about something, but no one knows everything about everything. Moreover, knowledge has particular characteristics, distinct from other goods. First, it is very difficult for the knowledge producer to exclude those who do not pay the price (nonexcludability), and knowledge has externalities in that it diffuses in many forms. Second, knowledge can be used by the same person at many times or by others simultaneously (nonrivalrous). These two characteristics make knowledge a "public good." Third, knowledge is often asymmetrical.

These characteristics have similarities with a policy in a democratic society. A "good" policy is like a public good, and the knowledge to generate it is also like a public good. Under democracy, citizens must eventually choose a policy through voting: in other words, one individual's action would influence others' actions through voting. But the outcome of a policy choice may not be a "good" one. As a public good, the knowledge to generate a "good" policy may be undersupplied.

Knowledge can be diverse. Economists tend to assume the case in which professional economics knowledge is shared by all agents as a standard benchmark, as rational expectations theory assumes. But this may not account for the reality of the diversity of economic knowledge among agents. Knowledge is asymmetrical, and there are costs to acquiring it; therefore, it is reasonable to suppose that different agents have different sets of knowledge. There are several empirical studies on what ordinary citizens think about the economy (Blinder and Krueger 2004). Some have also studied the differences in economic knowledge between ordinary people and economists. With interviews in the United States, Germany, and Brazil, Shiller (1997) showed that ordinary citizens have a stronger aversion to inflation than do economists. Using the Survey of Americans and Economists on the Economy, compiled by *The Washington Post*, the Kaiser Family Foundation, and Harvard University in 1996, Caplan found "systematically biased beliefs" among ordinary people (Caplan 2002, 2007). These beliefs are the following:

1. Antimarket bias: ordinary citizen tend not to understand the market mechanism. When asked about the mechanism through which a gasoline price goes up, 86 percent of economists say that the increase is the result of supply and demand, while 26 percent of ordinary citizens answer that way. Instead, ordinary citizens associate a rise in gasoline prices with the "greediness" of corporations. Shiller (1997) also reported that many people attribute the cause of inflation to the "greediness" of corporations.

2. Antiforeign bias: ordinary citizens tend to underappreciate benefits, such as trade and immigration, from interactions with foreign countries and people. This has been confirmed by other studies. For example, Scheve and Slaughter (2001) showed that in some cases, more than a half of American voters support some forms of trade restrictions and protectionism. Hiscox (2006) also showed that when asked about whether they favor trade with other countries, respondents are more likely to be influenced by an antitrade introduction disfavoring trade than by a protrade introduction favoring trade.

3. Make work bias: ordinary citizens tend to favor toil and labor and overemphasize the effects of other economic factors on employment. For example, people tend to put too much emphasis on the effects of technological unemployment.

4. Pessimistic bias: economists tend to be more optimistic than are ordinary citizens about the future prospects of the economy; therefore, economists

worry less about downsizing, technological unemployment, and the future of economic growth.

Because of these empirical studies on the differences of opinions between ordinary people and economists, we may differentiate economic agents in terms of three categories of economic knowledge (Klamer and Meehan 1999).[14]

A. The professional economists: they are not necessarily the same as the academic economists; they can be business economists, and the professional economists are the producers and consumers of professional knowledge. What matters most is whether they follow the standard procedure of professional economics. This does not mean that they believe in one theory or approach or that they do not differ on major aspects of the economy. The professional economists do differ on many important issues, but their differences are usually—not always—expected to be based on the basic knowledge of economics. For example, one may dispute the merits of free trade, but any critic of free trade who is trained in the profession is expected to know David Ricardo's principle of comparative advantage.

B. The ordinary citizens: they comprise the majority of the population, including politicians, bureaucrats, and business people whose thinking is not informed by professional knowledge. What matters most is the fact that there are differences in their economic knowledge. Even though ordinary citizens are not trained in economics, they do hold some economic views: these views are not as systematic or as based on facts as professional knowledge, but ordinary citizens may exert a great deal of influence on policymaking.

C. The policy entrepreneur or mediator: they usually possess a certain professional knowledge and engage in policy entrepreneurship. This involves arbitrage behavior on the part of entrepreneurs. As an entrepreneur in the economic sphere exploits differences in markets, for example, buying low and selling high or selling higher quality products, an entrepreneur in the policy sphere exploits differences in economic knowledge.[15] In this sense, the policy entrepreneur can "bridge" between item A and item B with certain potential returns and risks. These returns include a mutually beneficial trade of knowledge for all parties in which the quality of a policy would be improved. However, there may also be risks: the mediator may not be recognized for this kind of activity by professional economists, and an asymmetry problem is still existent: traded knowledge may be a "lemon" in the sense of Akerlof (1970).

This categorization offers only a benchmark. However, there are three issues. First, as behavioral economics shows, human beings have cognitive biases, and so may economists. Second, professional knowledge is not always correct. On the contrary, as we shall see throughout the book, professional knowledge has often been wrong. Third, during the crisis time, the differences and diversity of economic opinions tend to widen. For instance, the recent growing concern with technological unemployment, increased income and wealth inequality, and secular stagnation may cast some doubt on the supposed consensus among economists (Brynjolfsson and McAfee 2014; Piketty 2014; Teulings and Baldwin 2014). To address the first issue, it should be emphasized that a benchmark helps us find precisely what "biases" professional economists may have. For the second issue, even though professional knowledge may not be always right, they are not always wrong. The third issue requires a dynamics of knowledge in times of crisis, which I discuss later.

Idea Trap and Economic Knowledge in Crisis

Knowledge and perception change over time. How could one theorize a dynamics of knowledge and perception? Bryan Caplan of George Mason University has advanced a concept of the "idea trap" (Caplan 2003): he assumed three-way feedbacks among idea, policy, and outcomes arguing that one variable affects the other two variables, and vice versa. Under this setting, an idea can influence policy, policy can influence outcomes, and outcomes can further influence an idea. It should also be noted that ideas could be endogenized. Suppose outcomes are measured in real GDP growth rate G, the quality of policy P, and policy ideas I, and further suppose that G depends on P and I both at the previous period, and P depends on G and I both at the previous period, and I depends of G and P both at the previous period. Caplan showed that there could emerge three different stationary equilibria, depending on the feedback mechanism from G to I, "good," "ordinary," and "bad" equilibria, where the "good" equilibrium is defined as a set of high G, good P, and good I. If the feedback from G to I is negative, for example, if policymakers learn from their failures, then all equilibria would converge to "ordinary" ones. If, however, this feedback is positive, for example, if cognitive bias exists, three stationary equilibria would emerge. Thus there exists a "bad" equilibrium in which all "bad" ideas, policies, and outcomes could happen. This is called an "idea trap."

What about the role of knowledge in crises? In political science, Mark Blyth, a political scientist at Johns Hopkins University, has been emphasizing the role of ideas in the policymaking process, especially during a crisis. His 2002 book offered a theory of institutional change, postulating five hypotheses:

> First . . . given an initial position of institutional disequilibrium and uncertainty, economic ideas allow agents to reduce uncertainty by interpreting the

nature of the crisis around them as a first step to constructing new institutions. Second . . . economic ideas serve as a collective action and coalition-building resources . . . third . . . agents use ideas as weapons that allow them to attack and delegitimate existing institutions. Fourth, ideas are seen as institutional blueprints that agents use after a period of contestation to construct new institutions. Finally, once a new set of ideas has become embedded within these new institutions, such institutions serve to coordinate expectations, thereby making institutional stability, and a particular distributional politics, possible over time. (Blyth 2002, 34–35)

This perspective is important in laying out its emphasis on the key roles that ideas can play in the crisis, which is marked by uncertainty. Also, this perspective is important in its recognition of the interrelationship between institutions and ideas: an institution is a set of rules, which implies that rules require people's understanding. Since then, Blyth has expanded his analysis to the contemporary issue. Blyth's study, in which he attributed the historical misapplication of austerity during the crises throughout the ages to the persistent incorrect ideas about austerity, has received considerable attention in the wake of the sovereign debt crisis and the Euro crisis (Blyth 2013).

In economics, there are not many studies on the political economy of economic crises, but Roger Congleton of George Mason University has done some seminal studies on the mechanism of crisis involving ideas (Congleton 2004, 2009). According to him, a crisis entails three elements: it is unpleasant, a surprise, and uncertain, so in that sense, a crisis poses a threat to the existing policy and knowledge, which offers an space for others to enter into the policy arena with their own pet ideas so that an idea competition emerges during the crisis. However, there is also a danger to this competition in the sense that a "bad," that is, noneffective, idea might win out in the heat of the crisis.

Applications to Japan's Great Stagnation

The applications of this "ideas matter" approach have grown in numbers and in an interdisciplinary way. As Japan's Great Stagnation became more prolonged than many expected it to be, several economists with a macroeconomic bent turned their attention to explanations for why Japanese macroeconomic policy continued to fail. Ronald McKinnon of Stanford University and Kenichi Ohno of the Graduate Research Institute for Policy Research have done pioneering work, proposing the concept of a "policy trap" (McKinnon and Ohno 1997) in which "wrong" theory induces "wrong" policy, which in turn leads to "unintended" outcome, which *reinforces* "wrong" theory (McKinnon and Ohno 1997, 156). This is more or less equivalent to the concept of an "idea trap." Their example was the Japan-U.S. trade disputes.

Many policymakers who were worried about the trade deficit in the United States believed in a particular theory, such as the "elasticities approach to balance of payment," which led to the policy of a deliberate depreciation of the dollar.[16] The problem was that it did not work, and the U.S. trade deficit persisted. Nevertheless, the failure of that policy further strengthened the effort to depreciate the dollar.

Adam Posen (2003) and Harrigan and Kuttner (2005) tackled the question, with the former examining fiscal and monetary policy and the latter examining monetary policy in particular: the "rigid adherence to certain economic doctrines" is among the three hypotheses that they pointed (Harrigan and Kuttner 2005, 103). I return to this issue in Chapter 6. Koichi Hamada of Yale University and Asahi Noguchi of Sensyu University compared two deflationary episodes in Japanese economic history, the 1930s Great Depression era and the 1990s Great Stagnation era, pointing out the prevalence of bad ideas, such as the "good deflation" idea, the monetary policy ineffectiveness doctrine, and creative destruction idea (Hamada and Noguchi 2005). They emphasize the role of preconceived ideas, as opposed to vested interests, as a crucial determinant of economic policy. Notably, they broaden their analysis from academic to media discourse, examining the editorial opinions of major newspapers in Japan. They concluded:

> We do not deny that group interests in policy making are important, particularly in areas like trade policy or deregulation, where the consequences of particular policies for group interests are more or less obvious. What we contend is that in an area like macroeconomic policy where the consequences of policies are either uncertain or unclear to the public, the role of misguided ideas can be substantial, and the consequences of policies based on mistaken ideas can be rather serious. (Hamada and Noguchi 2005, 104)

Another notable study is von Staden (2012). That study was based on Douglas North's theory of institutional change, with its emphasis on a "mental model" (North 2005) in which ideology "informs the actor of how, for example, a market should operate and shapes how decision makers respond to the need for change" (von Staden 2012, 190). The von Staden (2012) study explored how Japanese policymakers could not form a coherent ideology to push through reforms. Analyzing the Japanese records of one *shingikai* (council of deliberation) in 1999, which discussed the proposed changes in government structure, von Staden showed that "despite a decade of debate about reform measures, fundamental ideological conflict continued among key stakeholders about the very nature of Japan's future political economy" (von Staden 2012, 188). He further argued that "the reason why reform was less efficacious than one would expect is because the full implementation of market reform cut across the beliefs held by political decision makers and the Japanese people" (von Staden 2012, 188). Richard S. Grossman at Wesleyan University (Grossman 2013) analyzed nine economic policy failures, including the Irish Great Famine, Britain's return to the gold standard in 1925, the Great Depression, Japan's failure to deal with the bad loans problem, and the recent Great Recession, tracing their causes to "wrong" economic ideologies and theories. The present book belongs to this line of research.[17]

In the following chapters, it is argued that beliefs, ideas, ideologies, and perceptions matter in the policymaking process. But it is also argued that pace von Staden (2012), it is not beliefs, ideas, and ideologies about market-oriented reforms that matter but macroeconomic thinking or rather the lack thereof. Indeed, it is argued in the following chapters that there has been a preoccupation with the "structural factors" of the Japanese economy, whereas macroeconomic thinking has been systematically downplayed or neglected in the discussions of Japan's Great Stagnation.

IV. A Guided Tour of the Book

The rest of the book proceeds as follows: Chapter 2, "Thirty Years' Economic Crisis," chronicles Japan's Great Stagnation from 1985 to 2012, just before the launching of Abenomics. That chapter presents the book's basic perspective on the 30 years of crisis. The Great Stagnation started with a mistake in macroeconomic policy in 1985. Japan agreed with the United States to appreciate the yen, and within a short period, the policy and its aftermath generated the financial bubbles. The responses of the Japanese government and the BOJ were "too late, too little," exacerbating the situation: the Japanese policymakers deliberately dampened the stock and real estate prices after the bursting of the bubble. This shows that Japan seems to be the country where basic principles of standard, intermediate macroeconomics apply the best.

Chapter 3, "Thirty Years' Intellectual Crisis," turns to intellectual side of the crisis, analyzing economic controversies during the Great Stagnation period. With stagnation being prolonged, policymakers, economists, commentators, and journalists debated the causes and remedies of the stagnation for a long time and discussed almost everything that their American counterparts are debating right now, from the effectiveness of fiscal and monetary policy to the structural causes of the stagnation. There emerged a division between the structural view and the macroeconomic view of the economy: the former attributes the long stagnation to "structural factors" or the "system," to the point of neglecting macroeconomic policy failures, while the latter takes a series of macroeconomic failures seriously. It is argued that this division has shown up throughout the period, with different emphases, but the dominant view has been the structural view, the most famous variant of which is the *Kozo Kaikaku* ideology. The economic discourse in Japan is likely to be affected by popular biases, yet even among the professional economists there are biases. This is the age of globalized economic ideas: macroeconomists, mainly from the United States, became interested in Japan's deflation. The Krugman proposal was the most innovative, advancing the economic analysis and policy discussions, yet generating more controversies. The division of ideas remains visible.

Chapter 4, "The Shadow of History: Lessons from Japan's Great Depression in the 1930s," goes further into history, to the Great Depression, another deflationary recession episode. It chronicles the Japanese economy from 1918 to 1936, when Japanese policymakers and economists alike were preoccupied with and debated the return to the gold standard, which was finally decided and implemented by the Hamaguchi cabinet. The 1920s was Japan's Great Stagnation of the past. During that period, the gold standard mentality and liquidationism were the two dominant ideas. Proponents of these ideas pushed policymakers to return to the gold standard at prewar parity and to implement deflationary policies. On the other hand, a minority opposed the return to prewar parity and deflationary policies. Japan went back to the gold standard in 1930, and it was hit by the Great Depression. Confusion ensued, and the military challenged the party politicians. Finally, Japan escaped from the Great Depression with the so-called *Takahashi Zaisei*: Finance Minister Takahashi went off the gold standard, ending the deflationary regime. Then he engaged in expansionary monetary and fiscal policies, the so-called reflation policies. He succeeded in reflating and recovering the economy, but after his tragic assassination, Japan took another path. There was a competition among three regimes and ideas, the Washington-Genoa regime, the Takahashi reflation regime, and the *Dai Ajia Syugi* regime. The Washington-Genoa regime collapsed due to its adherence to the gold standard mentality and liquidations, and the Takahashi reflation regime was toppled by the military and the bureaucracy.

Chapter 5, "The Future Again? The Assessment of Abenomics," turns to the latest developments of the Japanese economy and economic policy, Abenomics. Abenomics has three pillars, or "arrows": a bold monetary initiative, a flexible fiscal policy, and the growth strategy. The initial phase has worked well, but there is uncertainty in the future. Abenomics has two faces: politics and economics. Abenomics is a product of political compromise among powerful LDP politicians, but it also makes sense as an economic policy for tackling deflation. Chapter 5 argues possible risks and the prospects of Abenomics. Here again, the course of action depends on economic policy ideas, and success depends on whether Shinzo Abe and his successors avoid the policy idea trap and bad economic policy ideas.

The last chapter of the book, Chapter 6, "Concluding Remarks: Beware of Japanization," summarizes what went wrong in Japan, why Japan went wrong, and what the lessons are for the world. Japan went wrong because of four macroeconomic and other mistakes that occurred from 1985 to 2012. Japan's macroeconomic policy toward the exchange rate control was derailed when the Plaza Accord was agreed on in 1985. Then the Japanese policymakers allowed a violent fluctuation in asset prices, generating the so-called bubble. Bursting the bubble was also problematic; they did too little to counter the subsequent asset deflation and general deflation. Japan's policymakers made mistakes in other areas, such as the resolution of the bad loans problem. The reasons that Japan made mistakes were multifold. There were surely institutional and even "structural" problems in the policymaking process. But it is most important that bad economic ideas became pervasive. The biggest lesson of all is that everyone can make mistakes and can learn from them. Nevertheless, the controversy tends to be prolonged: old ideas never die out, and they may gain influence in the time of a crisis.

CHAPTER 2

Thirty Years' Economic Crisis

I. Introduction

This chapter chronicles Japan's Great Stagnation during 1985–2012, from the Plaza Accord to just before the launching of Abenomics, and analyzes the economic thought of the Japanese policymakers. As see in the following chapters, economists and policymakers are divided on the true causes of Japan's Great Stagnation, and the debate continues in the present. Broadly speaking, there are two strands of thought, one emphasizing structural factors and the other emphasizing policy failures. The narrative in this chapter emphasizes Japan's macroeconomic policy failures, since this perspective clarifies the fact that Japan experienced not only exogenous shocks but also a series of mistakes in macroeconomic policy, although other problems, such as the bad loans problem and policy failures in other spheres, are not neglected.[1] This perspective could also help us point out more specific problems and draw more specific lessons from Japan's experiences than another perspective would allow.

Although the Japanese economy's years of stagnation since the 1990s has been known as the Lost Decade or Lost Two Decades of Japan,[2] it is more appropriate to consider the whole episode as the "Thirty Years' Crisis." Admittedly, there were years when Japan performed relatively better within these 30 years; nevertheless, I believe this perspective highlights the important aspect of Japan's Great Stagnation. It started in 1985, at the turning point of Japanese macroeconomic policy, when the Japanese government agreed with the United States and other Western governments to appreciate the yen. The appreciation of the yen was followed by the collapse of the bubble, and the slow recovery that occurred from 1990 to 1996. The period from 1997 to 2001 was the critical moment for the Japanese economy, as illustrated by the consumption tax hike, the banking crisis, and the onset of full-fledged deflation. With the emergence of Junichiro Koizumi and his close economic advisor Heizo Takenaka, the economy began recovering from 2002 to 2007. However, the policy was reversed in 2006 when the Bank of Japan (BOJ) terminated its quantitative easing (QE) policy. The following years saw the deepening of the crisis: even though Japan was not the center of the banking and financial crisis from 2007 to 2008 and its financial sector was largely unaffected, Japan was hit hardest among the developed economies by the crisis. In the wake of the crisis, the Democratic Party of Japan (DPJ) succeeded in ousting the governing Liberal Democratic Party (LDP) in September 2009, but the DPJ failed to deal with deflation and stagnation. Then, in November 2012, came the new economic policy package known as Abenomics. It is still uncertain that Abenomics can deliver robust and sustainable growth: early signs were promising, but the economy may plunge back to a recession with the consumption tax hike that is effective as of April 2014.

These 30 years have been one of the most changeable periods in politics. The ever-powerful LDP, which had dominated Japanese politics from 1955 onward, lost its power in August 1993, when a number of its own members abandoned it to form a new party and a coalition government with other parties. The LDP returned to power with the help of the Japan Socialist Party (JSP) in 1994. Electoral reform was implemented in the same year. The LDP remained in power until 2009, yet it was not alone: this was and still is a period of coalition governments. In August 2009, the DPJ finally won the general election, but it lost in December 2012. I do not delve into the dynamics of political economy during the period, yet suffice it to say that given the public expectations for a revival of the economy, the popularity and survival of the government depends on economic performance.

The chapter is organized as follows. Section II describes the 1985 Plaza Accord and its immediate aftermath. This set in motion the vicious spiral of the policy idea trap, with one mistake leading to another. Section III turns to the years after the bursting of the bubble. The government's responses were slow, with policymakers doing "too late, too little," especially in addressing asset price deflation and the resolving the bad loans problem. Section IV discusses the years from 1996 to 2001, the worst years of the Great Stagnation. The government contracted fiscal policy, the full-scale financial crisis broke out, and deflation rooted in. The crisis brought in new people, Junnichiro Koizumi and Heizo Takenaka, who are the topic of Section V. The Koizumi-Takenaka economic policy was controversial, but it finally solved the bad loans problem, and the economy recovered. However, the crisis was not over. Section VI deals with the period from 2006 to 2012, when a series of shocks and macroeconomic policy mistakes were repeated. Section VII concludes with a summary assessment of the economic ideas of the policymakers.

II. It All Began at the Plaza

The Plaza Accord

On September 22, 1985, the policymakers of five advanced economies gathered at the Plaza Hotel in New York to reach an agreement on the possible movement of currencies. The agreement, later known as the Plaza Accord, prompted the Japanese and West German governments to appreciate their currencies against the U.S. dollar.[3] The U.S. dollar had been appreciated since the economic policy under the Reagan administration implemented a tight monetary policy combined with an expansionary fiscal policy. After the accord, the Japanese yen appreciated rapidly from $1 = ¥240 to $1 = ¥200 in 1985. Fearing the depressive effect of the yen appreciation on the economy, however, Japanese policymakers changed their policy stance, engaging in expansionary macroeconomic policy by lowering the official discount rate and increasing government spending.

Japanese policymakers agreed with the Plaza Accord since at that time, the trade dispute with the United States was the major political and economic issue. The trade dispute became a domestically hot issue in the United States, with the image of American autoworkers smashing Japanese cars in front of the U.S. Capitol building being circulated. But it takes two to tango: Japanese policymakers also felt proud at being asked by the Americans to cooperate with them on monetary issues. Japan was not an original member of the Bretton Woods agreement, for an obvious reason. Noboru Takeshita, the then finance minister, was reported to have said that "The U.S. has been 'high above the sky' since the defeat of Japan, but now its government and Treasury Secretary Baker vowed to me deeply saying 'please, Minister Takeshita, help the U.S.' We are indebted to them a great deal. If they beg us for help, we have no choice but to help them" (Takita and Kajima Heiwa Kenkyujyo 2006, 219). These were days of increasing confidence among the Japanese policymakers and public alike: the academe, at home and abroad, began portraying Japan as a first-rate political and economic system, with the pioneering work of Ezra Vogel's *Japan as Number One* (Vogel 1979). Moreover, the idea of macroeconomic coordination was an intellectual fad in economic policy. The decision itself was a mistake in three respects, however. First, targeting the exchange rate distorted the internal balance, which went against the basic principle of the conduct of macroeconomic policy under the flexible exchange rate. Second, the subsequent responses by the government and the BOJ led to the asset price boom, known as the "bubble." Third, the decision did not help resolve the trade disputes with the United States: on the contrary, the trade issue became more aggravated and political, setting the "policy trap" (McKinnon and Ohno 1997) of a push for a futile policy option.

Endaka Fukyo *and* **Naiju Kakudai Ron**

The appreciation of the yen hit the Japanese economy severely, with the recession quickly being named "*endaka fukyo* (Yen Appreciation Recession)." The real gross domestic product (GDP) growth rate plunged to 1.9 percent in 1986 from 6.3 percent in 1985, and the unemployment rate increased from 2.7 percent in September 1985 to 3.1 percent in May 1987, the highest figure since the unemployment statistics were collected in 1953. In February 1987, the Plaza Accord was partially reversed by the Louvre Accord, to correct the appreciation.[4] The BOJ lowered the official discount rate until February 1987, keeping it at 2.5 percent until May 1989. Fiscal consolidation was also suspended. The government pushed for expansionary fiscal policy based on "*naiju kakudai ron* (Increased Domestic Demand Argument)," arguing that Japan, along with the United States and West Germany, was responsible for expanding their domestic demand to correct an international imbalance. The landmark policy paper popularly known as the Maekawa report advocated the expansion of domestic demand within Japan as the solution to the trade surplus problem. That government report was produced by a committee headed by Haruo Maekawa, a former BOJ governor. As we see in Chapter 3, the paper advocated the expansion of domestic demand through market-oriented reforms such as deregulation and privatization. But the LDP politicians used this opportunity to push for expansionary fiscal policy. Subsequently, the real GDP growth rate hit as high as 6.1 percent in 1987; asset prices, including land and stock prices, went up considerably. Despite expansionary fiscal policy, the booming economy brought a large amount of revenue, and the government almost succeeded in achieving "*Zozei Naki Zaisei Saiken* (fiscal consolidation without tax increase)." Japan's gross debt–GDP ratio peaked at 74.95 percent in 1987 and then continued declining to 68.7 percent in 1991; its primary balance–GDP ratio turned into a surplus, 0.43 percent in 1988, and continued to be a surplus until 1992.

With the prime minister changing from Nakasone to Noboru Takeshita, the government put more emphasis on countryside development projects than on investment in Tokyo and other urban regions. The supplementary budget of 1988 and, thereafter, the main budget of 1989 were to give ¥10 million to each and every municipality under a program named "*Furusato Sosei* (creating homeland)."[5] It was the heyday of old, LDP-style pork barrel politics. It became quite apparent that stock prices and land prices were rising rapidly. There were concerns voiced among members of the government and the BOJ about this asset price increase, but their concerns had to do more with public perceptions of wrongdoing related to the heated economy than with macroeconomic control. The bubble became a social and political problem. For example, art purchases made by major corporations were criticized as speculation.[6] The increase in land prices particularly outraged the public.[7] In the meantime, several political scandals broke out, and many powerful politicians were implicated.[8]

The BOJ under Governor Mieno and Baburu Tsubushi

As for the BOJ, on December 16, 1989, Yasushi Mieno succeeded Satoshi Sumita as governor of the BOJ. Mieno was under intense media and public pressure to bring down the increased land prices. The government and the BOJ shifted to *Baburu Tsubushi* (pricking the "bubble") by raising the official discount rate from 2.5 percent in May 1989 to 6 percent in August 1990, where it remained until July 1991. On the other hand, a 3 percent consumption tax was introduced in April 1989. Asset prices plunged, aggravating the balance sheet of the banks and firms and setting the deleveraging of the private, nonfinancial corporate sector. This marked the beginning of the *"Furyo Saiken Mondai* (bad loans, or nonperforming loans problem)."

Baburu no Hansei *(Lamenting on the Bubble)*

The bursting of the bubble has had intellectual ramifications. The word bubble has acquired negative connotations, since any recovery has been dubbed as "an X bubble" (X can be housing, government bonds, or exchange rates), or "a petit bubble." The government's *Annual Economic Report* in 1993 (Keizai Kikakucho 1993) showed the typical attitude toward the bubble. The net balance of a bubble is decidedly negative:

> Once a bubble happens, it incurs a large amount of economic costs in bringing forth disparities in wealth distribution and distorting resource allocations. A bubble would increase the value of assets held by the people and firms, enrich some portion of the people, and increase the domestic demand, thereby increasing the growth rate. On the other hand, these positive effects are only temporary, and must be followed by the subsequent deflationary effects. Considering the process from the emergence to collapse of a bubble as a whole, there is no economic merit to a bubble, but only demerits. This is what the current experience tells us. (Keizai Kikakucho 1993 [quoted in Naikakufu 2011, 1, 388–389])[9]

The fact that the report set out the future policy action is noteworthy. Examining three ways of improving the living standard of the people—an increase in productivity, an improvement in the terms of trade, and an increase in asset prices through a bubble—the government concluded that an increase in productivity is the only sustainable and plus-sum economic activity. What Japan needed was a "macroeconomic increase in productivity and microeconomic restructuring." What is lacking here is any discussion of the appropriate macroeconomic management, not only before but also after the bursting of a bubble. This diagnosis led to Japan's later policy that was characterized by its emphasis on structural reforms and its lack of reference to macroeconomic policies.

III. After the Bubble: 1990–1995

The Rise of Kisei Kaikaku *(Regulatory Reform)*

Kiichi Miyazawa, who became a prime minister in November 1991, was a clever politician with more insights into the working of the economy than any other politician had. The *Financial Times* carried an article on Japan's bad loans problem on May 17, 1992: the newspaper estimated that the bad loans exceeded $5 billion, far more than the amount announced by the government. Miyazawa was one of the rare Japanese politicians who read foreign magazines and newspapers on regular basis.[10] He foresaw the coming crisis in August 1992 when the Nikkei index plunged into ¥15,000. He toyed with the idea of shutting down the Tokyo Stock Exchange for one day, telling the public about the critical situation of the financial sector, and using public funds to clear the bad loans. But Ministry of Finance (MOF) officials dissuaded him from pursuing the plan (Mikuriya and Nakamura 2005, 283–285; Nihon Keizai Shinbunsha 2001; Nishino 2003, 28–46). Later, the injection of public funds into the financial sector became highly politicized and was delayed until the last minute. However, Miyazawa's other policy initiatives were questionable. Echoing the Maekawa report, his cabinet promoted Japan as "*seikatsu taikoku* (great livable country)": to increase domestic demand, the Reduction of Working Hours Promotion Law was enacted in 1992. This law aimed to reduce working hours to eighteen hundred per year.[11] The government also initiated a deregulation policy, starting with the financial sector.

This was a turbulent period in Japanese politics also: with the defection, led by Ichiro Ozawa (1942–), of a number of LDP members over the necessity of electoral reform, the LDP lost its dominant position in the election of July 1993. Ozawa demanded the reform, but Prime Minister Miyazawa did not persist in reforms. In August, the coalition government was formed without the LDP and the Communist Party of Japan, which marked the end of the post-World War II political regime. Political reform became the focus of the national discussion, culminating in the introduction of electoral reform in 1994. Economic issues like the bad loans problem did not attract the attention of politicians.

From Kisei Keikaku to Kozo Kaikaku

Despite governmental change, or because of it, the new government pushed for further economic reforms. Ichiro Ozawa's *Nihon kaizo keikaku* (Blueprint for a new Japan), published in June 1993, became an instant bestseller. The book emphasized Japan's need to reform and transform into a "normal country." The original title of the book literally means *plan for transforming Japan*. The book starts with an impressive anecdote: there is no fence in the Grand Canyon Park, but no Americans complain about it. This anecdote illustrates the suggestion that Japan's new vision should be modeled on the United States and that the Japanese people should change their life philosophy from dependence to self-responsibility (*jiko sekinin*). The economic part of the book proposes market-oriented reforms such as deregulation, decentralization, and trade liberalization. Conspicuously lacking in that book, however, is a discussion about macroeconomic policy.[12]

A similar vision was infused into the government's reports. Prime Minister Hosokawa set up the *Keizai Kaikaku Kenkyukai* (Research Taskforce on Economic Reforms) and commissioned a report on the future vision of Japan. Its interim and final reports are known as the Hiraiwa report, named after the chairman of the taskforce, Gaishi Hiraiwa, then the President of *Keidanren* (Federation of Economic Organizations). The final report, submitted in December 1993,[13] used the expression *keizai kozo kaikaku* (Economic Structural Reforms). The report is in line with Ozawa (1993), emphasizing self-responsibility and a freer and more creative economic society (Keizai Kaikaku Kenkyukai 1993). The primary purpose of the Hiraiwa report was different from that of the Maekawa report since the former did not emphasize the reduction of current account surplus, yet the basic logic was the same in that the report advocated achieving the goal by structural measures. Again, a specific discussion about countercyclical macroeconomic policy was lacking.[14]

At the same time, the government warned about the overselling of deregulation. In its *Annual Economic Report*, the government rightly pointed out that deregulation had very little to do with getting out of a recession: "It takes time for deregulations to increase productivity and business opportunities; such effects happen gradually and in the long term." Thus, deregulation should not be confused with countercyclical measures. The report also pointed out that deregulation has demand-expanding effects as well as shrinking effects, so the net effect would be ambiguous (Keizai Kikakucho 1994;

Naikakufu Keizaishakai Sogo Kenkyusho 2011, 526–527). The fact that the government's official economic report had to remind the public not to expect too much from deregulation shows that deregulation was indeed sold to the public as a panacea for overcoming recession and stagnation.

In the meantime, the appreciation of the yen accelerated. The recession in Japan *increased* the trade surplus against the United States, which President Bill Clinton, who took office in 1993, vehemently criticized: he demanded the appreciation of the yen, setting the "policy trap" in motion once again. The Federal Reserve under Alan Greenspan engaged in an expansionary monetary policy from 1993 to 1994, which dampened the U.S. dollar. The appreciation at this juncture coincided with the onset of deflation in Japan. The GDP deflator recorded negative numbers. On April 19, 1995, the yen was exchanged at $1 = ¥79.75, the highest value at that time, a record that would be superseded in October 31, 2011, at $1 = ¥75.32. Haruhiko Kuroda, then at the International Finance Bureau of the MOF, later recalled that "there were no more serious macroeconomic issues than the appreciation of yen and deflation" (Kuroda 2005, 156).

In June 1994, the LDP came back to power with the JSP and another party. The leader of the JSP, Tomiichi Murayama (1924–), became prime minister. The bad loans problem emerged first in the resolution of two small credit unions in Tokyo in December 1994: the government and the BOJ offered ¥20 billion each to resolve the problem, but this measure was very unpopular among the public and was potentially harmful to the standing of the politicians involved (Kume 2002, 114–115). Then, the problem became bigger from August 1995 to December 1995 over *Jusen* (*Jutaku Senmon Kinyu Kaisya*, nonbank financial institutions for housing loans). Faced with stern public disapproval and political opposition,[15] the government injected public funds worth ¥68.5 billion into the *Jusen* to resolve the bad loans problem, but Finance Minister Masayoshi Takemura had promised not to use public funds to rescue financial institutions. This would have unfortunate repercussions, delaying the discussion of further solutions for the bad loans problem.[16]

In the midst of the bad loans problem, the drive to *Kozo Kaikaku* did not wane: rather, it accelerated. On November 29, 1995, the *Kozo Kaikakaku no Tame no Keizai Shakai Keikaku* (Economic and Social Plan for Structural Reforms) was set up. Its "basic direction" stated that the "process of structural reforms would inevitably entail certain pains associated with change, but without structural reforms, we cannot clear up the sense of uncertainty about our future, and create the mid- to long-term development." As long as deregulation and *Kozo Kaikaku* were considered, the continuity and consistency of the government policy was striking. This also had unfortunate repercussions: to stress the benefits of deregulation, the government began referring to the correction of *Ko Kosuto Kozo* (the high cost structure) of the Japanese economy. Attacking high costs was innocuous and necessary with regard to regulated relative prices, but this was soon conflated with a decline in the general price level, a deflation. This fed the "good deflation" argument that deflation benefits people by lowering prices.

IV: The Dark Moments: 1996–2001

The Consumption Tax Hike of 1997

In January 1996, Ryutaro Hashimoto (1937–2006) of the LDP became the prime minister of Japan. Among the many prime ministers who served during the Great Stagnation period, he was one of the most tragic. The "*Kozo Kaikaku* (structural reforms)" of the Japanese political and economic system are remembered as the hallmark of Prime Minister Koizumi, but it was Hashimoto who first advocated these reforms on a large scale. As Figure 2-1 shows, the first peak of attention to structural reforms happened in the time of the Hashimoto cabinet. Hashimoto's plan was impressively comprehensive and ambitious enough to implement major reforms in six spheres; the public administration, the fiscal structure, the economic structure, the financial system, the social security system, and the education system. The economy had somehow recovered with the increase in government expenditures in 1996, yet Hashimoto implemented a drastic fiscal consolidation as a part of the "*Kozo Kaikaku*." The Fiscal Structural Reform Act was enacted in November 1997, the consumption tax was raised from 3 percent to 5 percent in April 1997, and cuts were made in medical insurance and other transfer payments: the cuts amounted to ¥9 trillion, about 2 percent of the nominal GDP. It was later revealed that Prime Minister Hashimoto was informed of the exact amount of austerity just before the implementation (Karube and Nishino 1999, 137).

The crisis of the Japanese economy worsened in 1997: along with the Asian currency crisis in July, the financial crisis erupted in November, and several small banks and major stockbrokerages went bankrupt, including Yamaichi Securities, which was once rescued in 1965. Deflation took hold in 1998, the so-called balance sheet recession deepened, and the unemployment rate increased drastically from 3.5 percent to 5 percent within a year. Any obstacle to the injection of public funds into the financial sector disappeared, and Keizo Obuchi the next prime minister and successor to Hashimoto, who resigned due to an election loss, pursued a more expansionary fiscal policy to revamp the economy. Without any contingent clause, the Fiscal Structural Reform Act was suspended and later abolished.

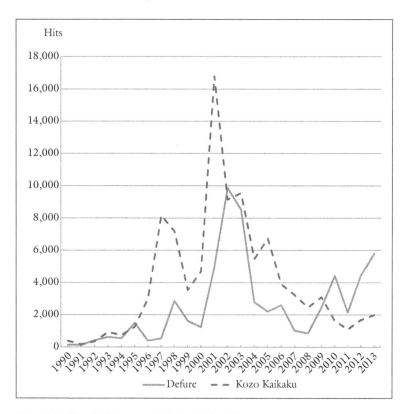

Figure 2-1   Kozo Kaikaku versus Deflation in Major Newspapers

Note: Hits per year of the term "Kozo kaikaku (Structual reforms)" and "Defure (Deflation)" in the five biggest Japanese newspapers: Asahi, Mainichi, Yomiuri, Sankei, and Nihon Keizai Shimbun.

The BOJ after the New Law

The BOJ gained formal independence in April 1998. It was not fought for gain by the BOJ; it was by accident. In the early 1998, the corruption of MOF officials was reported and became a scandal. Due to the public outcry, the MOF was divided, and its power became curtailed: the Banking Bureau and Securities Bureau of the MOF were transferred to the newly set up Financial Service Agency, and the old BOJ Law of 1942 was revised. Unlike the Bank of England, whose independence was articulated as an instrumental one rather than as a goal one and further specified in the inflation-targeting framework set by the UK government, the exact nature of the BOJ's independence was not specified (Mabuchi 1997).[17] Although Article I of the new act specified that the purpose of the BOJ is to achieve and maintain "price stability," there was no explicit discussion about the definition of price stability. Also, even though Article IV of the new act required cooperation between the government and the BOJ, it did not specify the exact mechanism through which that cooperation was to be ensured. Furthermore, the position of the BOJ governor was more firmly protected under the new law than under the old: the government cannot replace the governor except for special reasons, which include personal bankruptcy or mental unfitness.

The first governor under the new BOJ law was Masaru Hayami (1925–2009), an ex-BOJ veteran; he was already in his 70s when he took the position. His economic ideas were influenced by his personal experiences: he entered the BOJ in 1947, in the midst of the post-World War II high inflation, and worked mainly in the International Department, which deals with currency matters. Therefore, he detested any hint of inflation and depreciation of the yen. Instead, he took pride in the appreciation of yen and viewed that as a good sign for the Japanese economy, referring very fondly to *The Strong Yen, The Strong Economy* (Hayami 2005). The exact meaning of the "strong yen" seemed somewhat elusive, but it was meant to be "higher yen," so he tended to downplay or neglect the detrimental effects of the appreciation of the yen on the Japanese economy, and he even welcomed deflation.[18] On the other hand, he liked to express a Schumpeterian belief that only innovation-induced structural reforms could help boost the economy during recessions. In a sense, he was an antimacroeconomics central banker.

During the 1990s, the policy interest rate changed from the official discount rate to the overnight call rate. The overnight call rate was already below 1 percent by 1995, and the BOJ lowered the rate to zero in February 1999. This was the beginning of the "*Zero Kinri Seisaku* (zero interest rate policy; ZIRP)." The BOJ had an uneasy time with the ZIRP. The so-called Internet technology boom from 1999 to 2000 brought some recovery to the economy. Having judged that the economy was already turning the corner, in August 2000, the BOJ decided to raise the call rate: the government exercised its right within the new law to protest the BOJ's decision, requesting that the BOJ postpone the decision.[19] The BOJ rejected the request and raised the call rate. The economy subsequently went into a downturn in late 2000, and as a result, the BOJ had to resume the ZIRP soon after. It was against this context that the BOJ introduced the "*Ryoteki Kanwa Seisaku* (QE)" on March 19, 2001. The BOJ's target was changed from the overnight call rate to the size of the demand deposits of the BOJ; it conducted open market operations of longer-term government bonds, with the announcement that the policy should be continued until the changes in the consumer price index (CPI) become stabilized above 0 percent. However, upon the introduction of QE, the BOJ revealed its "internal rule" that the BOJ prohibits itself from purchasing long-term government bonds above the amount of the amount of BOJ notes. The BOJ argued that the rule was necessary to defend itself from political pressure to finance fiscal deficits and debt, echoing the "lesson from history" that the direct purchase of government bonds in the prewar era led to high inflation.[20]

The BOJ has had close contact with eminent domestic and foreign scholars, appointing some as consultants and frequently inviting them to conferences:[21] the informational flow became precise and rapid so that criticisms by eminent foreign scholars had been known to the BOJ. The BOJ defended its policy adamantly. Seiji Adachi, business economist and director of economic research at Marusan Securites, extensively examined the official statements and speeches of the BOJ Monetary Policy Board members during the Hayami era (Adachi 2013). In the period from 2000 to the end of the ZIRP, the board members used three arguments: (1) "good deflation," (2) "trickle down-like transmission," and (3) "impediments to structural reforms." (1) The board members argued that the sources of deflation were information technology progress and the increased inexpensive imports from China; therefore, deflation would improve the real welfare of the population. (2) They emphasized that current monetary policy would work slowly but steadily: first, through increased corporate profits and second, through increased household income. (3) They warned that a prolonged ZIRP would lead to a "moral hazard" for firms because an extremely low cost of financing would impede the firms' real structural reforms.

After the debacle of the premature termination of the ZIRP and the subsequent launch of the QE policy, the board members had to change their arguments. They justified this change in policy by treating the new policy as if it were the continuation of the old policy with an emphasis on the effect on the longer-term interest rate: the BOJ had stuck to its traditional understanding of monetary policy. Coinciding with the rise of Koizumi and the start of the recovery from early 2002, supported by the QE, the attention of the economists and the media turned to structural reforms and the bad loans problem, in particular. The BOJ insisted that the money supply would not increase without the revival of the bank loans.[22]

As for inflation targeting, the BOJ board members' opposition was persistent and vigorous. First, they argued that inflation targeting had been used to suppress inflation, but there was no precedent of ending deflation. Second, it is usually supposed that inflation targeting works through inflationary expectations, but the BOJ board members claimed that working on expectations was extremely difficult. Third, once inflation was set into motion, it would spiral out of control to high or hyperinflation. Fourth, the technical difficulties associated with determining which price index to choose was pointed out.[23]

However, there was an ideological or a moralistic dimension to the discussions: Governor Hayami emphatically refused to use inflation targeting because he believed that using inflation as a solution was not the route that developed countries should take. Vice Governor Masaya Fujiwara said relying on inflation was dangerous. The historical example they frequently invoked was Korekiyo Takahashi's "failure" in the 1930s (see Chapter 5).

The only exception among the Monetary Policy Board members was Nobuyuki Nakahara (1934–).[24] Using his vast network of academic and business economists,[25] he presented his own diagnosis and policy remedies without any support from the other BOJ board members. He proposed the ZIRP on November 27, 1998, proposed monetary base targeting with an inflation target on February 25, 1999, and proposed targeting the demand deposits of the BOJ on February 24, 2000. His policy proposals were always ahead of other members; therefore, his were always rejected when they were first proposed, but they eventually had to be adopted, except for the explicit inflation targeting. He was perceptive since his forecast of the economy was cautious. Consulting many economists outside the BOJ, he was also free from a conventional *"Nichigin-ryu Riron* (BOJ doctrine)" with its emphasis on interest rates and the passivity of the BOJ.[26]

V. The Koizumi-Takenaka Recovery: 2001–2006

In April 2001, maverick LDP politician Junichiro Koizumi became the prime minister of Japan. Heizo Takenaka, a professor of economics at Keio University and a self-conscious policy promoter, was appointed as his minister for economic and fiscal policy.[27] The Koizumi-Takenaka team used the word *Kozo Kaikaku* as its main economic policy slogan. Although the precise meaning was unclear, the term became immensely popular among the economists and the general public alike (see Chapter 3). More important, Takenaka was tactful and purposeful: during Japan's Great Stagnation period, he was determined to coordinate, for the first time, the fragmented governmental economic policymaking structure. First, he utilized the *Keizai Zaisei Shimon Kaigi* (Council of Economic and Fiscal Policy) to fullest extent.[28] Second, he constantly announced several plans and schedules and opened up discussions to the public. Third, he insisted on setting the numerical target by which the progress of a particular policy would be measured. These measures were based on his belief that transparency of the policymaking process should empower him within the government bureaucracy. His popularity as an economist contributed a great deal to deal with the bureaucracy: he appeared on television while he was minister.

As an economist, Takenaka is a chimera-like personality. His first set of specific policy proposals reflected his supply-side thinking: he argued that the long period of low growth of the Japanese economy should be attributed not to the temporary shortage of demand but to supply-side problems. Thus, he advocated deregulation, privatization, and cuts in public spending (Takanaka 2006, 15–16, 251). His primary focus, however, was on the bad loans problem. He constantly criticized Hakuo Yanagisawa, the minister in charge of financial affairs, for not dealing with the bad loans problem, and Takenaka succeeded Yanagisawa in September 2002.[29] He assembled experts on the bad loans issue, forming a task force dubbed the "Takenaka Project Team." Upon this news, stock prices plummeted, in further anticipation of a tougher approach to the problem. His initial proclaimed approach was to be tougher toward the financial sector, to allow the bankruptcy of bank, yet when the Resona Bank, one of Japan's major banks, went bankrupt in May 2003, he promptly injected public money into it, thereby shifting the policy objective.

On the other hand, Takenaka was one of the first major politicians to recognize the importance of deflation: from the beginning, Takenaka had been aware of the danger of deflation. While his first approach to tackling deflation was to link the bad loans problem with deflation and to subscribe occasionally to a "supply-side" explanation of deflation, he began to recognize the crucial role of monetary policy and to advocate inflation targeting in particular. As early as August 2001, at the Monetary Policy Board Meeting of the BOJ, Takenaka asked the members to consider the adoption of inflation targeting as a way to communicate the resolve of the BOJ as a "deflation fighter" (Nihon Ginko Seisaku Iinnkai 2001a,110).[30] In September, he suggested that the government and the BOJ might need a joint goal to overcome deflation, even though he admitted that central bank independence was a "touchy" subject for the BOJ (Nihon Ginko Seisaku Iinnkai 2001b, 64–65). He was also instrumental in introducing 10-year inflation-indexed bonds to Japan in March 2004, to estimate the break-even inflation rate, a proxy for the expected rate of inflation.[31]

As deflation deepened, the media coverage of deflation increased as well, even surpassing that of "*Kozo Kaikaku*" (Figure 2-1).[32] The economy started to recover slowly in early 2002, which led to the gradual appreciation of the yen. The International Bureau of the MOF, headed by Zembei Mizoguchi (1948–), then vice minister for international affairs, asked the U.S. Treasury to approve an intervention in the exchange market. His American counterpart, John B. Taylor, then undersecretary of the treasury, had been concerned with deflation in Japan and allowed massive intervention by the MOF (Taylor 2007, 286–287). The MOF intervened in the foreign exchange market from January 2003 to March 2004, selling ¥35.177 trillion in currency. Thanks to this intervention, Mizoguchi was called "Mr. Dollar" by *Business Week* (Bremmer 2004). Also, unlike Hayami, Governor Toshihiko Fukui, newly appointed in March 2003, was more cooperative with the government than Hayami was.[33] Emphasizing the significance of QE, Fukui successively raised the target amount of the demand deposits of the BOJ, continuing QE: along with the foreign exchange intervention, this halted the appreciation of yen and stabilized the yen around U.S.$1 = ¥110.[34] In its February 14, 2004 issue, *The Economist* named Governor Fukui as the world's best central banker, above Alan Greenspan and Jean-Claude Trichet, for his continuation of QE: in the same article, Hayami was called "possibly the world's worst central banker" (*Economist* 2004).

With the economic recovery, the so-called structural problems began to disappear or became easier to tackle. The persistent bad loans problem was finally solved. Omura and Mizumura (2009) argued that two factors contributed to the reduction of bad loans: the recovering economy and Takenaka's policy focused on resolving the bad loans problem. There was also progress in other areas. Contrary to popular perception, the Koizumi administration did not do much on the deregulation front, except that it did deregulate the labor market and introduce the *Keizai Tokku* (special economic zone).[35] Despite the slogan of "*Kozo Kaikaku*," what the administration did could be summarized in three items: the resolution of the bad loans problem, the reform of the Japan Post Office, and the reform of government-sponsored financial institutions. The reform of the Japan Post Office was a lifetime ambition for politician Koizumi. It was not clear why this was so important to him, but it makes sense for three reasons. First, the office's sheer size mattered: this was the privatization of the country's largest public corporation, which included the world's largest financial institution within it. Second, the savings account of the Japan Post Office had been financially subsidized by the *Zaisei Toyushi* (Fiscal Investment and Loan Program), but the support was terminated in a wholesale reform of Fiscal Investment and Loan Program during the mid-1990s (Takahashi 2007). Third, the privatization of the largest financial institution stimulated further reforms of government-sponsored financial institutions.

In the later years of the Koizumi administration, the controversy regarding the proper way to handle fiscal consolidation erupted within the administration. After the landslide victory at the 2005 general election, Koizumi reshuffled his cabinet, appointing Takenaka as the minister of internal affairs and communication who was in charge of the postal reform and appointing Kaoru Yosano as Takenaka's replacement as minister of state for economic and fiscal policy. Takenaka and Yosano clashed over the best way to achieve fiscal consolidation. Takenaka, together with Hidenao Nakagawa, then of LDP, maintained that the priority should be on achieving a nominal GDP growth rate of 4 percent, while Yosano insisted on fiscal consolidation through increases in taxes (Shimizu 2007). Their controversy was dubbed the clash between the "Rising Tide" and the "Fiscal Hawks" factions. One of their main contentions involved the relationship between the nominal long-term interest rate and the nominal growth rate, known as the Domar condition. Given that the primary balance is neither in surplus nor in deficit, the long-term dynamics of debt relative to the GDP ratio depends on the relationship between the nominal long-term interest rate (r) and the nominal growth rate (g); if r exceeds g, the debt-GDP ratio would spiral out, and if g exceeds r, the debt-GDP ratio would decrease. Takenaka and Nakagawa argued that the government should aim for higher g, while Yoshino and Hiroshi Yoshikawa argued that r should be higher than g, so the government should aim for tax increases, especially in the consumption tax. Koizumi eventually decided not to raise the tax.[36] As a matter of fact, this "growth first" policy made some progress in fiscal consolidation. The primary balance-GDP ratio declined from its deficit peak of 7.19 percent in 2003 to a deficit of 2.7 percent in 2007. The net (gross) debt–GDP ratio declined from its peak of 82.4 percent (186) in 2004 (2005) to 80.4 percent (183) in 2007.

On the monetary policy front, however, there was a backlash. The BOJ decided to put an end to QE in March 2006, against unofficial protestations from the government and the powerful LDP politicians.[37] Nothing could stop the BOJ from ending the QE under the current law. The official reason for ending the QE was that the inflation rate measured by the headline CPI excluding food increased to around 2 percent, but it had been known that the statistics would be revised downward in June. However, on delivering the decision, the BOJ added a new twist: it released the "understanding of the policy board members of the price behavior" in which they "forecasted," on average, 0 to 2 percent inflation in the near future. The BOJ typically avoided any explicit language of "targeting" or concrete numbers. Some argued that this was a political maneuver: "The BOJ's March 2006 announcement to focus on an inflation rate between 0 and 2 percent might be interpreted as a move to fend off any institutional redesign by the government unfavorable to the BOJ, especially in the form of an explicit inflation target" (Cargill and Sakamoto 2008, 137). The BOJ's noncommitment became clear, as later episodes showed.[38]

VI. Continuing Crises: 2006–2012

LDP Governments in Disarray

The first administration of Shinzo Abe started with great hope yet ended as an utter failure. He was enthusiastic about "big issues," such as reforming Japan's post-WWII constitutional framework ("ending the post-War regime," Abe's speech, September 2007) and the public administration system, about which he wrote extensively in his book (Abe 2007). His initial economic plan was ambitious enough to aim for a 4 percent nominal GDP growth rate, which accorded with the economic vision of the "Rising Tide" people. It was at this time that the word "Abenomics" was first used in media discourse, promoted by Nakagawa (Nakagawa 2007). However, Abe began to lose his popularity when he allowed the reentrance of former LDP politicians who opposed the Japan Postal Reform to the LDP, and he lost more popularity when a series of political scandals erupted. The LDP lost the majority in the Upper House election in August 2007. Abe tried to cling to his post for about a month, but he gave up in September 2007.

The subsequent LDP governments of Yasushi Fukuda and Taro Aso had difficulty dealing with the divided governments since the LDP and its coalition partner, Komeito Party, did not hold a majority in the House of Councillors, in the Upper House of the National Diet. Fukuda did not show any enthusiasm for economic reform or economic policy, resigning after just one year in his post.[39] On the other hand, as a former president of his company, Taro Aso took pride in his knowledge about the economy and was quite willing to engage in policy discussions. However, his economic view is heavily influenced by the old way of economic thinking, with a strong emphasis on fiscal policy of the public works variety and on downplaying the role of monetary policy. On one occasion, he said that "to tackle deflation, monetary policy only is not effective. Fiscal policy and industrial policy should accompany it (Aso 2013)"

The BOJ under Governor Shirakawa

Deflation did not end. Masaaki Shirakawa (1949–) was chosen as the governor of Japan in March 2008. The decision was accidental: he was not the first choice for the governorship by the government. He was first appointed as deputy governor, but the opposition Democratic Party, seizing the majority of the Upper House, blocked a series of proposals by the government: in the end, the government succumbed to the DPJ, and Shirakawa was reappointed as the governor. He has been known as the man behind major policy decisions by the BOJ such as the ZIRP and the QE; however, he has been quite reluctant to engage in expansionary monetary policy. He also has an academic bent: his 450-page tome on monetary policy, which was published just before his appointment as the governor, is the latest version of the BOJ view (Shirakawa 2008). As a University of Chicago graduate with a master of arts degree, he did not say that inflation is not always and everywhere a monetary phenomenon: yet, he said that deflation might not be a monetary phenomenon, in light of the recent Japanese experience (Shirakawa 2008, 275).

Then came the world financial crisis of 2007 to 2008. The Japanese economy had already began contracting by the time the financial crisis started, sometime around the summer of 2007. Furthermore, Japan was hit by the crisis most severely, even though Japan's financial sector was little affected by the crisis: this is evidence that Japan's financial institutions have lagged behind in terms of globalization. One way to solve this mystery lies in the BOJ's timid responses to the crisis. The output gap widened to around ¥45 trillion in 2008. The government's fiscal policy put ¥10 trillion in the economy, but the BOJ did not cooperate with the government.

The Japanese economy has been hit by crisis after crisis: first, the global financial and economic crisis of 2007 to 2008 and then, the Great East Japan Earthquake of March 2011. After the collapse of the Lehman Brothers in September 2008, central banks all over the world reacted vigorously by increasing their balance sheets (Figure 2-2). The increase in their balance sheets led to the depreciation of currencies (Figure 2-3), which further prevented production and employment from plunging (Figure 2-4). There was a major exception: the BOJ. The BOJ was reluctant to increase its balance sheet, allowing the yen to appreciate and production to plunge. In consequence, Japan was hit most severely by the downturn even though it was not the center of the financial crisis.

The BOJ justified this action, or lack thereof, on three grounds. First, they pointed out that the *level* of money supply relative to nominal GDP was much higher in Japan than in other advanced countries, so monetary policy had already been eased at the maximum level.[40] Second, they argued that the real exchange rate was not as high as it used to be, so there was no appreciation about which to be concerned. Third, they argued that Japan's overreliance on the manufacturing sector exposed the economy to the outside shock (Umeda 2011). The BOJ also began pointing out that the economic performance of the Japanese economy was not as bad as many have presumed: "Even in 1998, the worst year in the postbubble period, Japan's growth rate was minus 1.5 percent, apparently less dismal than the sharp slowdown we are facing now. Also, even during the financial crisis, Japan's real GDP did not fall below the level registered at the peak of the bubble days (1989)" (Shirakawa 2009). Later Shirakawa would emphasize the shrinking population as a reason for Japan's better performance (Shirakawa 2012; see Chapter 1).

The Coming of the Democratic Party Government

The LDP lost its general election in 2009, and the DPJ took power in a landslide victory. Yukio Hatoyama (1947–), the newly appointed prime minister, had a different economic philosophy. His article is worth quoting at length:

> The recent economic crisis resulted from a way of thinking based on the idea that American-style free-market economics represents a universal and ideal economic

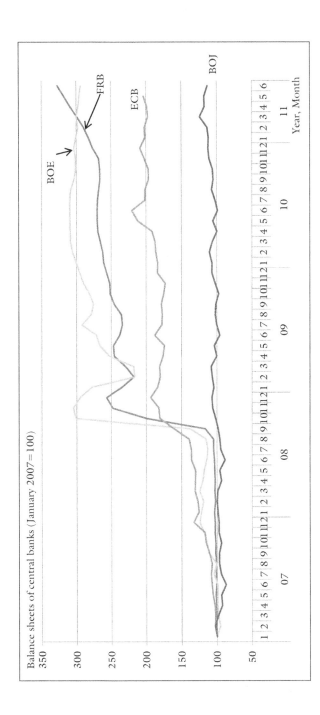

Figure 2-2 Changes in Balance Sheets of Central Banks

Note/Source: BOE = Bank of England, FRB = Federal Reserve Board, ECB = European Central Bank, BOJ = Bank of Japan. Data from homepages of BOE, BOJ, ECB, FRB.

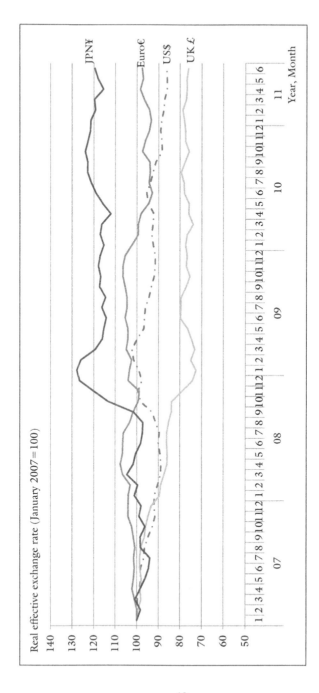

Figure 2-3 Changes in Real Effective Exchange Rate

Note/Source. JPN = Japan, US = the United States, UK = the United Kingdom. Data from Bank of International Settlement Statistics.

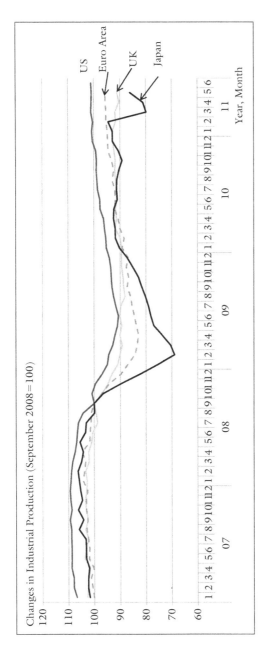

Figure 2-4   Changes in Industrial Production

Sources: Data from Ministry of Economy, Trade and Industry, Federal Reserve Board, Eurostat, and ONB.

order, and that all countries should modify the traditions and regulations governing their economies in line with global (or rather American) standards.

In Japan, opinion was divided on how far the trend toward globalization should go. Some advocated the active embrace of globalism and leaving everything up to the dictates of the market. Others favored a more reticent approach, believing that efforts should be made to expand the social safety net and protect our traditional economic activities. Since the administration of Prime Minister Junichiro Koizumi (2001–2006), the LDP has stressed the former, while we in the DPJ have tended toward the latter position . . . If we look back on the changes in Japanese society since the end of the Cold War, I believe it is no exaggeration to say that the global economy has damaged traditional economic activities and destroyed local communities. (Hatoyama 2009)

As Ohtake (2010) points out, this contains anticompetition ideology, although it was toned down in his speeches when he became prime minister (Ohtake 2010, 14–15). This also reflects his view on two episodes in recent economic events, the Koizumi-Takenaka recovery and the global economic crisis, with both being grouped together under the name of globalism. In other areas, the DPJ deliberately broke with the Koizumi-Takenaka policy-making style: they suspended the Council of Economic and Fiscal Policy and did not pursue deregulation further.[41]

The DPJ comprises of a wide variety of politicians whose political and economic thought is never homogenous.[42] Yet, they had a unifying emphasis on redistribution. For after 2006, there had been a growing sense of Japan becoming more unequal in its income and wealth distribution. It also made sense politically to focus on redistribution since that could undermine the power base of the LDP by changing the redistribution system. Therefore, the DPJ promised free tuition for public high schools, *Kodomo Teate* (transfer payments for households with children), and pension reform. It is true that Japan desperately needs a proper redistribution policy, yet redistribution without stabilization and growth eventually prove to be futile. It was a golden opportunity for the DPJ to learn from the past policy mistakes, the macroeconomic ones in particular, and to make a fresh start. And the DPJ could have adopted a proper macroeconomic policy since the DPJ and its coalition partners had majorities in both Houses of the National Diet. But despite a few promising policy initiatives, the DPJ government failed to take this opportunity. The DPJ could not deliver what it promised in the manifesto since the DPJ could not find enough revenue sources.

Transformation of Kansian Economics

Naoto Kan (1946–), the next prime minister, showed a few good signs on the macroeconomic policy front before he became prime minister. On

November 20, 2009, as minister of state for national policy, he declared that the Japanese economy was indeed in deflation. When he became finance minister in January 2010, he suggested that the depreciation of the yen was desirable, which moved the market about ¥2 against the dollar. Clearly he hoped to inject fresh thinking into economic policy. On January 7, 2010, the *Financial Times* carried an editorial on Kan's economic policy titled "Kansian Economics." It articulated the challenges that Kan faced: "But he cannot achieve this alone. For this, he will need to relax the country's excessively tight monetary policy: the BOJ has been too scared of inflation to fight the country's deflation with much vigour." Nevertheless, the article concluded with this hope: "One must hope that Mr. Kan, a deficit dove and deflation hawk, follows his instincts—and does so bravely. The country simply cannot afford to lose another decade."

It turned out that Kan became a fiscal hawk. In June 2010, the Group of Eight summit meeting was held at Huntsville, Canada. This was when the euro and sovereign debt crises erupted, and the Greek situation was heavily discussed. Having attended the meeting as finance minister, Kan returned home determined to pursue fiscal consolidation, but with a twist. He toyed with the idea of increasing taxes to spend more on welfare to grow the economy: to him it seemed the perfect solution to the trade-offs between growth, stabilization, and redistribution. Now Kansian economics was transformed to taxing and spending economics.[43] He went to the election of the House of Councillors on June 2010, arguing for the necessity of fiscal consolidation with the consumption tax hike. The DPJ and coalition partners lost the election, and the divided government returned.

Another Crisis: The Great East Japan Earthquake

On March 11, 2011, a magnitude nine earthquake hit the northeastern part of Japan. The death toll rose to more than ten thousand people, mostly caused by the tsunami afterward. The economic costs were estimated around ¥16 trillion to ¥25 trillion by the World Bank and the Cabinet Office. However, the nuclear disaster caused by the tsunami has had a long-lasting effect. This was not a natural disaster; it was a man-made one. David Pilling of the *Financial Times* writes that the "performance of Japan's leaders after the tsunami only soured the public further on a political system in which it had already lost faith"(Pilling 2014, 279). One such example is the drive to fiscal consolidation, the tax hike in particular, right after the earthquake hit. A tax increase was contemplated on the first day of the meeting of *Higashi Nihon Daishinsai Fukko Koso Kaigi* (the Reconstruction Design Council), on April 14, 2011.[44]

Yoshihiko Noda (1957–) became the prime minister after being the finance minister in September 2011. While he was finance minister, the appreciation continued, yet Noda claimed that he was paying strict attention to developments. Although he did intervene in the market on September 15, 2010, when $1 became equal to ¥82, he did nothing further. As was shown later in his attack on Abenomics, he was not interested in monetary policy. What concerned him most was fiscal consolidation.

Mounting Pressure on the BOJ

Against the background of persistent deflation and the ever-rising yen, the popular frustration against deflation surged, turning into a minor movement.[45] The pressure on the BOJ mounted. Especially after the great earthquake, acute politicians discerned the inaction of the BOJ and demanded more policy action.[46] Some politicians began to talk about the direct purchase of government bonds by the BOJ. Under Article V of the Fiscal Law of Japan, direct purchase is prohibited on principle but can be allowed under special circumstances, provided that the National Diet votes for it; in fact, direct purchase has recently been implemented in every year. The BOJ vigorously denied the validity of such a policy. Governor Shirakawa repeatedly denied even a hint of such a policy. On August 31, 2011, in his lecture at *Nihon Shoken Keizai Kenkyusho*, a private research institute, Shirakawa categorically denied the direct purchase of government bonds by the BOJ: he argued that a direct purchase would be contrary to the fundamental rule of the country and would thwart "what constitutes this country." He also insisted that the BOJ had increased the base money more than other central banks had; therefore, one could not blame the BOJ for the stagnation of the Japanese economy: one should look for other ways to increase the growth, namely, structural reforms.[47]

Even though they downplayed the monetary factors, the BOJ began to lend money to "possible growth sectors." The BOJ's actions were based on the assumption that the stagnation of nominal growth in Japan was mainly attributable to the stagnation of the real growth rate; therefore, the BOJ should help the real side achieve a higher nominal growth rate. The BOJ's loan scheme was suited to the government's "growth strategy," which has an affinity with developmentalism, an old economic idea that emphasizes the government targeting industries: the BOJ preferred industrial policy rather than reflation policy.

The biggest pressure came from the Federal Reserve Board (FRB). On January 25, 2012, the FRB formally adopted an inflation target in the name of the "price stability goal." The BOJ's reaction was one of defense: Governor Shirakawa explained that "as I understand, both the FRB and the BOJ have been conducting monetary policy with the same purpose." He further explained that "the current framework of the BOJ took all advantages of inflation targeting and deleted all shortcomings."[48] This did not stop politicians from questioning the current BOJ policy stance. The politicians and the general public began to understand what was lacking at the BOJ.

On February 14, 2012, the BOJ announced the "*Chu Choki tekina Bukka Anteika no Mede*" (Price Stability Goal for Medium to Long Term) with 1 percent inflation rate for a while. It was called the "Valentine" easing. The yen depreciated from $1 = ¥79 to $1 = ¥83 within a month, but it was short-lived. The BOJ translated this "*medo*" as the "goal," but the Japanese word *medo* has multiple meaning: it could mean a goal, but it could also mean an aim or just a prospect or outlook. In short, this was not full-fledged inflation targeting, which requires commitment and transparency. Compared with the FRB, the BOJ did not provide a clear and logical explanation for engaging in monetary easing. The FRB said that the "inflation rate over the longer run is primarily determined by monetary policy, and hence the committee has the ability to specify a longer-run goal for inflation," and the FRB has been influencing inflation expectations (FRB 2012). On the other hand, the BOJ attributed the "low price level" in Japan to a low expected growth rate caused by depopulation and aging and to people's perception of a low price level. The contrast was quite clear: the BOJ is very passive on monetary policy.

With the pressure from politicians mounting, Governor Shirakawa gradually and grudgingly increased base money. However, even with this less than half-hearted price stability goal and an increase in base money, the market reacted.[49] The action only strengthened the demand for the BOJ to do more.

The Road to the Consumption Tax Increase

In the year 2012, Japan's foreign relationship deteriorated. On July 3, 2012, Russian President Dmitri Medvedev visited the Kurile Islands, a northern island territory whose control is disputed by Japan and Russia: no Russian or former Soviet leaders ever visited the islands before this. On August 10, 2012, South Korean president Lee Myung-Bak visited the Takeshima Islands, another disputed territory in Japan: again, no South Korean president had ever done this. On September 11, 2012, Japan nationalized the Senkaku Islands, a territory disputed with China. Immediately after, anti-Japanese mass protests broke out across China, further straining the relationship between two countries. The DPJ's reputation deteriorated on the diplomatic front.

At this juncture, small parties sprung up and gained popularity as an alternative to the existing two major parties. One notable example was *Minna no To* (Your Party), headed by maverick ex-LDP politician Yoshimi Wanatabe. *Osaka Ishin no Kai* (Osaka Restoration Association), headed by lawyer turned television personality turned politician Toru Hashitomo, is a local party based in the stagnating Kansai area. It absorbed other members to become *Nihon Ishin no Kai* (Japan Restoration Party). The party reflected the popular discontent with and frustration toward the establishment and the central government. Both have *Chiho Bunken* (decentralization) in their platforms, and *Minna no To* is openly advocating inflation targeting and the revision of the BOJ law.

On the economic front, the DPJ leaders pushed for fiscal consolidation in earnest, although their party manifesto specifically denied that they would increase taxes.[50] In negotiations with two major opposition parties, the LDP and Komeito, the DPJ agreed on the Plan for Comprehensive Reform of Social Security and Taxation Systems: the gist of the plan was to make the consumption tax the revenue source of social security and raise the tax from 5 to 10 percent until October 2015. The two-step consumption tax hike was approved; the first increase was from 5 to 8 percent in April 2014, and the second increase was from 8 to 10 percent in October 2015. Only 1 percent of the 5 percent goes to the improvement of social security, and the rest offsets the fiscal balance deficit; therefore, this would have purely contractionary effects on the economy. The DPJ was hugely divided on the issue, and eventually a group of more than 70 members of the National Diet led by Ichiro Ozawa left the party. As a compromise with the opposing group, an additional clause on the state of the economy was added: the government should carefully watch the economic circumstances and must not raise the consumption tax when the real growth rate does not exceed 2 percent and the nominal growth rate does not exceed 3 percent. But this clause is not binding at all. On March 30, 2012, the cabinet decided to legislate the laws, and they became legislated on August 8.

Toward Abenomics

Given the minority position of reflationist ideas within academic and policy circles, it is puzzling why Abe came to embrace them. Yet, several factors may have contributed to this. First, he personally experienced a series of backlashes from the monetary policy: he was deputy cabinet secretary when the BOJ raised its policy rate in August 2000, and he was cabinet secretary when the BOJ terminated the QE in March 2006. Second, his close advisors and associates, including Hidenao Nakagawa, Nobuyuki Nakahara, Heizo Takenaka, and Yoichi Takahashi, had all been advising reflation policies. Third, an increasingly tumultuous relationship with China and the 3/11 earthquake-tsunami incident might have strengthened his sense of urgency. Abe was asked by Kozo Yamamoto (1948–), a lone yet ardent advocate of reflation policy in the LDP,[51] to become the chairman of a group which consisted of members of the National Diet and to consider ways, other than tax increases, to raise revenue for the Great East Japan Earthquake recovery. Abe accepted the offer. At this time, 211 members of the National Diet signed a petition to ask the government and the BOJ to engage in reflation policy. Through this activity, Abe became exposed to reflation ideas.[52]

The final act of the resurgence of the LDP, the comeback of Abe as prime minister, and the onset of Abenomics owed a great deal to the coincidence of many contingencies. The term of Sadakazu Tanigaki, former LDP leader, expired on September 2012, and despite his intention to keep the job, other LDP politicians saw a golden opportunity to become the next prime minister. Abe was not the LDP's favorite choice, but he ran for the leadership against the advice of his closest allies, and he prevailed. As a leader of the LDP, Abe began circulating reflation policy ideas, putting pressure on Noda to hold the general election. Noda decided to go to the general election on November 14, 2012.

VII. Conclusion

Once Japan used to be among the best performers of the world, and now it has become the showcase for all sorts of problems. What characterizes Japan's Great Stagnation, however, is its series of macroeconomic mistakes. The logic behind this policy dynamic can be summarized as follows. Japan's Great Stagnation started with one policy mistake, but that mistake was followed by a series of mistakes. The Plaza Accord brought the precipitous appreciation of the yen, which had negative consequences for the economy. To counter these negative impacts, the government and the BOJ changed their policy stances, which generated asset price booms. To "correct" this mistake, they completely reversed their policy stances once again, this time to prick the bubble. Then came the lesson of the recent experience: the government and the BOJ should have responded to asset price deflation with expansionary policy, but they chose not to repeat the same mistake. Instead, they tried another solution, deregulation and liberalization, which eventually evolved into a policy slogan, "structural reforms."

However, those structural reforms could not deliver the recovery without macroeconomic policy: the Koizumi-Takenaka recovery succeeded, albeit short-lived and half-hearted, precisely because it was supported by an expansionary monetary policy. Lamentably, macroeconomic failures such as doing "too little, too late" and an uncoordinated policy mix created the perception among the public that macroeconomic policy did not work. The Japanese policymakers should have corrected macroeconomic mistakes with proper macroeconomic policy.

Behind this failure lies policymakers' economic thought. First, they were concerned with international pressures at the cost of the domestic economy. Admittedly, some of these pressures, mainly from the United States, were not based on sound economic logic. But the Japanese policymakers were concerned not as much with the lack of logic as with the demands from foreign countries. More specifically, the policymakers could not see the connection between the exchange rate policy and the domestic economy. For example, Toyoo Gyohten, who was the director of the International Finance Bureau of the MOF when the Plaza Accord was agreed on, did not seem to be concerned with the deleterious effects of the appreciation. As he later revealed, he believed that it was natural for the yen to appreciate (Naikakufu Keizaishakai Kenkyusho 2001, 3, 514).[53]

Second, policymakers did not seem to understand basic macroeconomics. Koichi Kato, a powerful LDP politician who was once considered a candidate for prime minister, candidly recalled that he believed that bureaucrats always came up with an idea to deal with macroeconomic issues:

> At that time I believed that politicians should not be involved with matters of financial sector . . . After the War up to the present time, we thought that macroeconomic management was left to someone else to contemplate. We used to have a vague trust in the bureaucrats. Perhaps, apart from us politicians, someone like administrative vice minister of the MOF, governor of the BOJ, or administrative vice minister of the Ministry of Trade and Industry, got together, in the night somewhere like the BOJ's Hikawa guesthouse at Akasaka, to come up with a brilliant plan, and informed us later. We were to modify a little bit and implement it. That kind of trust began to collapse after the burst of the bubble. And there was an outcry that politicians should exercise leadership, but we were not prepared for it. (Naikakufu Keizaishakai Kenkyusho 2001, 3, 432)

The former prime ministers Noboru Takeshita, the finance minister at the time of the Plaza Accord, represented this old style politics of small adjustment and compromise. He was willing to accommodate the United States' demands for the appreciation of the yen, and he identified macroeconomic policy with public works.[54]

The only exception was probably Kiichi Miyazawa, who did understand some aspect of macroeconomics:[55] as finance minister in 1987, concerned with the rapid appreciation of the yen, he expressed his anger toward Takashita on the Plaza Accord,[56] and Miyazawa tried to reverse the appreciation at the Louvre Accord. Miyazawa also promoted fiscal expansion. As prime minister in 1992, he foresaw the danger posed by the bad loans problem. As finance minister again, in the Obuchi administration, Miyazawa engaged in expansionary fiscal policy. But even he could not understand the logic of reflation: in 2003, when a reflation policy using inflation targeting was hotly discussed, he visited the then Prime Minister Koizumi to advise that inflation targeting should not be adopted (Nishino 2003).[57] If a government official has any understanding of macroeconomics, this understanding is a caricaturized version of Keynesian economics that is heavily reliant on public works.

Ichiro Ozawa, arguably the most influential power broker during the period, was willing to exercise political leadership. But he did not have any interest in macroeconomics, as his words (Ozawa 1994) and deeds showed. Instead, what captured most of the imaginations of politicians was Kozo Kaiakaku (structural reforms), which was hugely popular among the general public during the Koizumi-Takenaka period. According to the public opinion survey conducted by *Asahi Shumbun* (Asahi Newspaper, the second largest circulating newspaper in Japan), the support for the Koizumi administration fluctuated during his term, while the support for his structural reform was most often more than 50 percent, and that support remained high (Kume 2010).[58] In the next chapter, we explore the background and evolution of structural reform ideology in relation to other economic thought.

CHAPTER 3

Thirty Years' Intellectual Crisis

I. Introduction

Economic controversies during the Great Stagnation were fiercely fought, and these controversies involved a wide variety of people, from policymakers to academic and business economists, the media, and the general public. As I argue in Chapter 1, any crisis involves that in the existing knowledge and policies, and in the time of an economic crisis, competition emerges among economic ideas. The focus of the controversies changed considerably over time, yet one can discern the recurrence of several dominant ideas. According to Asahi Noguchi of Sensyu University, who meticulously surveyed economic controversies from the late 1980s to the early 1990s, "Upon reviewing the policy discussions during the Great Stagnation, what strikes me is the fact that the same pattern of disagreements has emerged over and over again in a different context" (Noguchi 2005–2006, first installment, 35; Noguchi 2014). That same pattern is the conflict between two contending views of the economy, the structural view versus the macroeconomic view. The structural view seeks out the "deeper" causes of the Great Stagnation, whereas the macroeconomic view considers macroeconomic policy failures as the causes of the Great Stagnation. The structural view further identifies these "deeper" causes with the economic and legal structure of the Japanese economic system, although the precise meaning of the system tends to be elusive.

A background in Japanese media discourse is helpful. From early on, Japan has had a very rich tradition of economic media discourse. In this time of Great Stagnation, Japan has five major national newspapers, one being the economic newspaper, the *Nikkei*, founded in 1876, with circulation of two to three million copies during aforementioned period. Japan also has three major weekly economic magazines, *Shukan Toyo Keizai*, *Shukan Diamond*, and *Shukan Economist*,[1] which constantly carry articles on economic affairs. General magazines occasionally carry articles on economic affairs; therefore, economists in Japan have plenty of opportunities to write for the general public. Especially noteworthy are the article formats called *taidan* (dialogue between two people), or *zadan* (roundtable discussion with more than three discussants). Economists in Japan frequently appear in these economic media and discuss the economic issues of the day. This means that there are more interactions between economic discourse and the general public, potentially facilitating the economic understanding of the public yet also potentially making the discussions diffused.

The time of crisis is a time of engagement for economists. An increasing number of Japanese economists became personally involved in the government and the Bank of Japan (BOJ).[2] The *Keizai Zaisei Shimon Kaigi* (Council on Economic and Fiscal Policy), established in January 2001, routinely includes two economists among the four members from the private sector. On the Monetary Policy Board of the BOJ, under the new Bank Law of 1998, two out of six board member positions (excluding the governor and two deputy governors) are allocated to economists. The most famous, and undoubtedly the most controversial, was Heizo Takenaka, who became the minister of state for economic and fiscal policy in April 2001 and the minister of state for financial services in September 2002. His direct policy involvement attracted a great deal of attention to the role of economists during the time of the crisis.[3]

In accordance with the perspective of the "Thirty Years' Economic Crisis," this chapter starts with the 1980s, chronicling economic controversies during that period up to the present time. Section II deals with the controversy surrounding the Maekawa report in 1986. This marks the emergence of the pattern in which the structural view competes against the macroeconomic view. As Section III describes, after the bubble burst, a pattern evolved under asset deflation whereby those who adhered to the structural view considered the recession necessary, while those who adhered to the macroeconomic view tried to counter the recession. Section IV turns to the rise of "*Kozo kaikaku ron* (structural reforms argument)," the most dominant economic ideology, and the structural view during the period. Origins of the structural view can be traced back to the 1970s. Section V deals with the onset of deflation and the globalized debate, which is the most fiercely debated part of these long controversies. Deflation makes the Japanese episode the concern of economists worldwide. Section VI traces the development after the Koizumi-Takenaka recovery. Even though deflation is recognized as a problem, there is no consensus about the cause and remedy. Why the structural view took hold is the topic of Section VII. Section VIII concludes with a discussion of major strands in economic thought during Japan's Great Stagnation.

II. The Emergence of the Pattern:
The Maekawa Report and Its Critics

In the early 1980s, during the period leading up to and following the Plaza Accord, the focus of the economic discourse was on the international coordination of macroeconomic policies. The dominant preoccupation at that time was increasing "domestic demand," and the "transformation from export-led to domestic demand-led, livable power" became the slogan. The most representative document was the report by the prime minister's Commissioned Study Group on Adjustment of the Economic Structure for International Cooperation, the so-called Maekawa report, published in 1986. Its influence was long lasting and far-reaching.

The report starts with a declaration: "It is imperative that we recognize that large current balance accounts create a critical situation not only for the management of the Japanese economy, but for the harmonious development of the world economy" (Okimoto and Rohlen 1988, 252). Taking into account this new responsibility, it argued: "The time has thus come for Japan to make a historical transformation in its traditional policies on economic management and the nation's lifestyle." More specifically, it proposed (1) the expansion of domestic demand, (2) a shift to an international, harmonious industrial structure, (3) the improvement of market access and the encouragement of imports, and (4) the stabilization of the international currency value and the liberalization and internationalization of the financial sector. Even for expanding domestic demand, there was no explicit discussion of fiscal and monetary policy except to say that in "the implementation of these recommendations, fiscal and monetary policy have a significant role to play" (Okimoto and Rohlen 1988, 256). Instead, the report recommended the continuation of fiscal consolidation and the use of *Kisei Kanwa* (deregulation) and *Minkan Katsuryoku no Katsuyo* (utilization of vitality of the private sector) as the measures to tackle the current account imbalance problem: these two words became policy buzzwords in the following decades. The report is significant since it laid out the basic threads of the "structural" view. First, as a diagnosis, the analysis was based on the premise that Japan's "economic structure" as an export-led economy was responsible for macroeconomic problems such as the large current account imbalance; second, as a remedy, it was argued that the "structure" should be changed or reformed to solve the problem; and third, the measures were defined as everything but macroeconomic policy.

The report was hailed as the vision for Japan in the years to come. But there were a few who severely criticized it: Ryutaro Komiya, then professor of economics at the University of Tokyo, pointed out the report was based on an utter misunderstanding of basic economics: (1) the current account surplus of Japan and the current account deficit of the United States reflected the saving over investment balances in both countries, so that international cooperation on macroeconomic policies was unnecessary and futile; (2) the current account surplus or deficit should not be the concern of the nation; and (3) there was an inconsistency in the specific policy proposals, since the report recommended increased foreign aid as a tool to decrease the current account surplus (Komiya 1986). The majority of economists, however, embraced this report, and those who questioned it remained a minority. There were other critics of the report, but they were either merely expressing their anti-American sentiments or using outdated economic tools to attack the U.S. position (Noguchi 2005–2006, third installment, 37–38). The defenders of the report, all of them members of the Maekawa committee, argued in a wide variety of ways. Hiroshi Kato at Keio University and Yutaka Kosai at the Tokyo Institute of Technology both admitted that open markets and deregulation would not contribute to the reduction of the current account surplus; rather, they both considered the report a political document to accommodate demands from the United States. On the other hand, Isamu Miyazaki at the Economic Planning Agency advocated expansionary fiscal policy to increase domestic demand, thereby decreasing the current account surplus. This made economic sense, but there was no consensus at this point regarding the use of expansionary fiscal policy; rather, fiscal consolidation was the consensus (Noguchi 2005–2006, third installment, 38–39). Miyazaki would later push for expansionary fiscal policy during the Murayama administration (1995–1996), in which he served as the minister of the Economic Planning Agency.

As is reflected in the Maekawa report, another preoccupation at this time was the uniqueness of Japan: this was the heyday of books on Japan, including such titles as *Japan as Number One* (Vogel 1979), *MITI and the Japanese Miracle* (Johnson 1982), and *Trading Places: How We Are Giving Our Future to Japan and How to Reclaim It* (Prestowitz 1993). They all recognized the good economic performance of the Japanese economy, yet they attributed it to various aspects of the Japanese system; curiously, there was no reference to macroeconomic policy.[4] In psychology, there is a cognitive bias concept called the halo effect (Thorndike 1920; Rozenzweig 2007): when people see an attractive person, they tend to attribute good traits to the person, no matter what the person's real traits are. This intellectual bias feeds into the structural view.

III. Evolution of the Pattern under Asset Price Deflation

In the early 1990s, Japan's recession became obvious to most economists, and the first controversy erupted over the appropriateness of macroeconomic stabilization policy. Three issues were discussed during this phase. The first issue was the desirability of policymakers' responses to the bursting of the bubble. With the accelerating deleveraging induced by the decrease in asset prices, people began discussing the "balance sheet recession." However, some economists did not want the government and BOJ to engage in macroeconomic policy to counter deleveraging. Yukio Noguchi, then professor of economics at the University of Tokyo, opposed countercyclical macroeconomic policy, advocating a continuation of monetary contraction even in 1991. His 1992 book titled *Baburu no keizaigaku* (The economics of bubbles), an instant bestseller, was written on the premise that bubbles were not only detrimental to the economy but also moralistically evil:

> A society which does not reward industrious labor properly is a wrong one. The bubble brought us a wide variety of evils, but the most serious one was that people's values went mad because of an extraordinary rise in asset prices. Many corporations became too much absorbed in financial transactions, going astray from their proper corporate mission to real estate investment. The assets of those who happened to have land and stocks from the past ballooned to several thousand million yen without effort, while workers in general were put into a situation where they could hardly afford to buy a house to live even though they work hard. All of these denigrate the integrity of work. (Noguchi 1992, 2)

The moralistic tone of his writing is striking. Although he analyzed the economic forces leading up to the bubble from macro- and microeconomic perspectives, including distorted financial liberalization, the BOJ's low interest rate policy, and an overemphasized fiscal consolidation, and he admitted that a bubble could not be eradicated in a market economy, he nonetheless demanded that authorities to pursue a contractionary macroeconomic policy and never repeat the same mistake of engendering a bubble. Noguchi became the foremost proponent of the structural reforms argument and the staunchest critic of macroeconomic policy.

Second, there emerged another type of argument against countercyclical macroeconomic policy. Masaru Yoshitomi,[5] then director of economic coordination at the Economic Planning Agency, defended the government's initial policy in 1991: Yoshitomi was instrumental in devising the plan. His defense revealed a common view of what is known as "liquidationism" (De Long 1990): he not only defended the government policy from the criticism of doing "too little, too late" but also argued for the necessity of a recession after the boom. Instead, what he envisioned was a self-sustaining recovery led by the private sector's Schumpeterian technological and managerial innovations (Yoshitomi 1991). His view was not surprising since he studied Marxian economics, writing his thesis on the Great Depression in the United States from a Marxian point of view (Yoshitomi 1965). He was also typical among Japanese economists in his favorable reference to Joseph A. Schumpeter, an Austrian-born American economist. As we shall see later, Schumpeter has frequently been cited by Japanese economists during the Great Stagnation period. Takahiro Miyao, then at Tsukuba University, debated with both Noguchi and Yoshitomi.[6] He was worried about the massive deleveraging induced by a sharp fall in asset prices. Naming the ongoing recession as the "asset price deflationary recession," or the "balance sheet recession" he criticized the government's slow reaction to the recession. He further criticized the government and the BOJ's deliberate "*baburu tsubushi* (bubble crashing)" as they initiated a sharp asset price deflation (Miyao 1992).

Third, during this period, the money supply fluctuated dramatically, with its growth rate plunging to the lower rate (Figure 3-1), and from late 1992 to early 1993, the controversy over the behavior of the money supply and its economic significance erupted. This would be later be called the "Iwata versus Okina" controversy, or the money supply controversy, which marks the beginning of a long series of debates regarding monetary policy and the

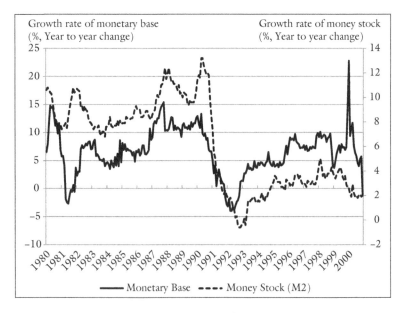

Figure 3-1   Changes in Money Growth Rates, Japan from 1980 to 2000

Note/Source: M2 = Currency in circulation + deposits. Data from the Bank of Japan.

BOJ. It was initiated by Kikuo Iwata, a well-known economist and a former student of Komiya's. Iwata attacked the BOJ for its inappropriate monetary policy conduct. First, the BOJ emphasized the stability of the policy interest rate, allowing unnecessary fluctuations of the money supply, which led to the violent fall of stock and land prices and the subsequent downturn. Second, the policy rate was determined inappropriately, with the BOJ aiming at the wrong targets, including the exchange rate and the asset prices. Third, the BOJ should have changed the policy target from the policy rate to the monetary base (Iwata 1992a, 1992b; cf. Adachi 2013; Noguchi 2005–2006, 2012). Kunio Okina is a graduate of the University of Tokyo, with a PhD from the University of Chicago, and a prominent BOJ economist. Okina, who would become the director of the Institute for Monetary and Economic Studies of the BOJ, defended the BOJ policy by explicating the "BOJ doctrine." This entailed the BOJ controlling the reserve at the short-term money market, first controlling the short-term interest rate by announcing an implicit target rate to the market and thereby controlling the money supply. He further argued that abandoning the "BOJ doctrine" would lead to great disturbances in the short-term financial market and, thus, to the confusion of the Japanese economy itself. He also argued that there was no empirically stable relationship between base money and money supply; therefore, money supply could not be controlled by base money (Okina 1992a, 1992b).

IV. *The Rise of* Kozo Kaikaku Ron *(Structural Reforms)*

From the mid-1990s to the late 1990s, the focus of the debate shifted to "structural reforms," but the precise meaning varied from commentator to commentator.[7] It largely refers to the bad loans problem, the heavy regulation, the public corporations, and the rigid Japanese economic "system." The exact origin of structural reforms in Japan is hard to trace. One source in economics was "structural adjustment" advocated mainly by economists associated with development economics and international organizations.[8] Its emphasis on macroeconomic stabilization, usually austerity measures, and a structural policy package including deregulation, liberalization, and privatization has a strong affinity with structural reforms, but Japan was not among the developing countries that needed the International Monetary Fund (IMF)–prescribed cure and remedy. Japan was considered *the* success until the 1990s. Another important source was the market-oriented reforms of the Reagan and Thatcher administrations from the late 1970s to the 1980s. Clearly, this experience later became a focal point and model for advocates of structural reforms, but I argue that the origins are rooted more in Japanese economists' perception of the Japanese economy. As for the timing, some economists advocated the wholesale change of the system before the Reagan-Thatcher reforms.

Theory Innovations and the Japanese Economy

There was a series of innovations in economic theory during the 1970s. Game theory in the noncooperative setting and the economics of information revolutionized applied microeconomic theory, including industrial organization and international trade. Along with the insights of the new institutional economics of Douglass North and the economics of the firm and organizations of Ronald H. Coase and Oliver Williamson, economists became more equipped with analytical tools to understand a wide variety of customs, habits, and institutions that had once been considered "unique" or "peculiar." This has enabled Japanese and other economists to analyze, explain, and even justify the "unique" or "peculiar" Japanese economic institutions or system in terms of mainstream economics. One example is the reconsideration of industrial policy in Japan. Although the general tone of the conference volume that was devoted to the topic was highly critical toward the efficacy of industrial policy (Komiya, Okuno, and Suzumura 1984), the theorists who presented their papers viewed industrial policy in a more positive manner than did the previous literature (Ito et al. 1988).

Masahiko Aoki (1938–) represents this trend in Japanese and international academia. He used to be a radical student activist,[9] but he turned to mathematical economics and received a PhD at the University of Minnesota. His interests have moved from the design of resource allocation mechanisms á la Leonid Hurwitz to a game-theoretic new approach to firms and organizations and, eventually, comparative institutional analysis. Although Aoki specifically denied that his was an uncritical justification of the Japanese economic system, saying that he "did not side with *Japan as Number One* thinking á la Ezra Vogel's bestseller" (Aoki 2008, 169–170), his analysis was welcomed since it was the time that the Japanese economic system received a considerable amount of attention. Aoki offered an attractive explanation based on the analytical tools of mainstream economics. According to him, the Japanese economic system is a coherent one with rank-hierarchical personnel and a decision-making structure; it can perform well under certain conditions, yet it may not be easy to change since components of institutions have strong complementarity. However, he did not really specify what went wrong with the Japanese economic system after the bursting of the bubble in the late 1980s, except to say that global competition intensified. His analysis also lacked any discussion of macroeconomic factors despite his casual remarks about the bubble and the bursting of the bubble: conspicuously absent was any discussion about deflation, which has been hotly debated subject.

A System Understanding of the Japanese Economy

The most influential argument for structural reform directed toward the general public came earlier from Noguchi and Sakakibara (1977). The authors, Yukio Noguchi and Eisuke Sakakibara (1941–), both came from the Ministry of Finance (MOF), received PhDs in economics from American graduate schools, and later became influential economists and media pundits. They argued that the postwar economic system was forged during the war and remained intact despite postwar reforms by American occupation forces. Against this background, the postwar economic system was a highly controlled one, with the MOF and the BOJ playing the role of the arbiter. But this system, they argued, could not survive in a new and changing environment: Japan needed a wholesale, systemic reform. It is true that as economists, Noguchi and Sakakibara introduced the concept of rational expectations into Japan, and they were highly critical about of Keynesian economics, but their arguments were framed for the Japanese context. Later, Noguchi would write in a similar vein, popularizing the concept "1940-nen Taisei" (the 1940 system) (Noguchi 1995, 1998) as a focal point for structural reforms.

Aoki's comparative institutional analysis and Noguchi and Sakakibara's perspective inspired other economists. Group of economists led by University of Tokyo professors conducted an economic and a historical analysis of the origins of the Japanese economic system (Okuno-Fujiwara and Okazaki 1993). For the financial sector reform, Kazuhito Ikeo (1953–) played an important role. He is an expert on banking who is known for applying the economics of information (Ikeo 1985) to banking and advocating the "Big-Ban" approach to financial sector reform. He attacked the inefficiency of Japan's financial sector as a remnant of developmentalism: once it was successful, yet now it was outdated (Ikeo 2006). His diagnosis and remedy are also heavily influenced by an "institutional" or a "system" approach. The outmoded Japanese economic system should be replaced by a newer economic system altogether; thus, he endorsed the wholesale reform of the financial sector. But unlike Heizo Takenaka, in the course of Japan's Great Stagnation, he became more pessimistic about the possibility of reform and the curability of the Japanese system (Ikeo 2003).[10]

There was a powerful dissenting voice. Yasusuke Murakami (1931–1991) wrote his magnum opus in 1992 (Murakami 1992). Extending the "developmental state" concept of Chalmers Johnson (Johnson 1982), Murakami defended developmentalism as an economic and thought system that was as coherent and justifiable as a Western one. Developmentalism relied on dynamic, increasing returns, and the system's implication led to some form of industrial policy, protectionism, and regulation. But he was keenly aware of the important role of efficient bureaucracy. In this sense, his analytical framework was similar to that of Aoki's and those of the analysts of industrial policy. His favorable evaluation of developmentalism was different from others, yet it is noteworthy that both the advocates and critics of developmentalism shared the same concept and framework.

Nakatani and Kisei Kanwa Ron

These academic discussions were to feed into domestic and foreign commentators' popular account of what went wrong with Japan. Nakatani, who was a corroborator on Aoki's academic work, became one of the most famous proponents. He became a member of the Hiraiwa committee, and he wrote a popular account of the influential Hiraiwa report for the general public (Nakatani and Ohta 1994). His 1996 book represented the arguments in favor of reforms. Being inspired by the surge of new growth theory literature in the 1980s to 1990s, his book diagnosed the current stagnation as rooted in a decline in the potential growth rate of the Japanese economy. Compared with the United States, Japan was lagging behind in terms of the information technology and the restructuring of corporate organizations. Therefore, "even though fiscal and monetary policy and resolution of bad loans were taken to the fullest extent, the stagnation of the Japanese economy would continue." On the contrary, "if bold fiscal and monetary policy were taken without dealing with structural problems, it would be likely that we can not only cure the disease but also worsen it" (Nakatani 1996, 71). He argued that Japan desperately needed to break with the old political and economic model and embrace the new one.

A good example by a foreign observer is Richard Katz's *Japan: The System That Soured* (Katz 1998), which argued that the nature of Japan's economic malaise lies in Japan's failed transformation from a "developmental state": "The root of the problem is that Japan is still mired in the structures, policies and mental habits that prevailed from the 1950s to the 1960s. What we have come to think of as the 'Japanese economic system' was a marvelous system to help a backward Japan catch up to the West. But it turned into a terrible system once Japan had in fact caught up" (Katz 1998, 4).[11]

Those authors who argued for the once efficient and effective developmental economic system did not provide systematic empirical evidence for it: for instance, the success of Japan's industrial policy was taken for granted rather than examined.[12] Other possible contributing factors to Japan's high economic growth, including the macroeconomic policy, the trade liberalization, the highly educated and growing working population, or the fixed exchange rate favorable to the past, were not taken into account.

It should be noted that *Kisei Kanwa Ron* (arguments for deregulation) encountered several oppositions in media discourse. For example, journalist Katsuto Uchihashi and other journalists criticized deregulation (Group 2001, 1994a, 1994b; Uchihashi and Group 2001, 1995). Their main target was the Hiraiwa paper, and they reported that deregulation in the United States did not produce the supposed benefits that the Hiraiwa paper promised for Japan. Deregulation did not produce more jobs, and even though new industries emerged, unemployed workers could not get jobs. Nakatani responded to this criticism by writing a rebuttal with Takatoshi Ito, a then colleague at Hitotsubashi University (Nakatani and Ito 1994). Nevertheless, those who opposed deregulation did not really attack flaws in the logic of deregulation: the supposed claim that deregulation brought more jobs was examined, but not in a systematic way.[13] The negative reactions against economics and economists in the criticisms of deregulation are also noteworthy. The more economists engaged in policy and policy discussion, the more hostility they could generate. Anyway, the government embraced the idea of deregulation, and this set the general tone of the discussion in the media as well in the following decades (Chapter 2).

The Rise of Heizo Takenaka

Heizo Takenaka (1951–) is an outsider to Japanese academic circle. He did not graduate from a graduate school, but he managed to learn and teach economics.[14] Indeed economics is his main weapon, and his understanding of economics was formed during his stay at the United States in the 1980s. His American experience showed him three "models" for his later career. One is a mainstream economic model. The 1980s was the heyday of the rational expectation revolution and supply-side economics: this would later become the backbone of his policy thinking.[15] The second model is the American economy and society itself: he would use the United States as reference point for reforms in Japan. The third model is that of economic policymaking: he was mesmerized by the "revolving door" style engagements of policy-oriented professional economists in the United States, and he later consciously tried to import the United States' economic policymaking style by promoting think-tank activities and becoming a policy entrepreneur himself. He also appeared on media, TV in particular, to propagate his ideas. He is a public intellectual in the age of markets for ideas (Mata and Medema 2014).

As for his economics, Takenaka showed some sympathy toward the "shock therapy" advocated by the IMF and others in the late 1980s to the early 1990s. Referring to Jeffrey Sachs's program for the former communist countries, he said that "in general, the shock therapy has not been popular in Japan . . . Even though Japan is a country of gradualism, it is greatly doubtful that gradualism has been successful . . . On the other hand, it could be argued that Japan has adopted a shock therapy at critical junctures" (Takenaka 1993, 80–81). As the stagnation of the Japanese economy became apparent, Takenaka became more and more convinced that the root cause of the problem was structural, in the sense that Japan lost its ability to adjust to the changing, more global environment: "More important is the basic point that the Japanese economy has lost an enough adaptability, while the market economy around the world has significantly transformed" (Takenaka 1999, 16). As we see in Chapter 2, he would apply some of this thinking but would also change to adjust the situation.

V. The Onset of Deflation and the Globalized Debate

Initial Reactions to Deflation

As financial and economic crisis deepened after 1997, economists began discussing deflation, first as "asset and financial" deflation, then as a "true" deflation, since it took for a while for them to recognize what was happening in the Japanese economy. The wholesale price index began falling around 1994 and the consumer price index began falling around 1997, while the gross domestic product (GDP) deflator began falling in the third quarter of 1994. Against this backdrop, both Japanese economists and economists around the world started to discuss the causes and remedies of deflation. However, a negative image of inflationary policy was circulating in the economic media: any proposal for inflationary policy or reflation policy tended to be associated with the "*Chosei Infure Ron* (adjustment inflation argument)." This goes back to the early 1970s when Yasuhiro Nakasone, then minister for trade and industry, proposed to use inflation to ease the pains of the appreciation of the yen during the transition from the Bretton Woods system to the flexible exchange system.[16] Since then, inflationary policy has acquired a bad reputation.[17] For example, the *Asahi Shimbun* carried an editorial on June 25, 1995, titled "Choki Tenbo wo Hiraku Keiki Taisaku wo (stimulus with long-term perspective is needed)," in which expansionary macroeconomic policy was criticized as a variation of "*Chosei Infure Ron*," and a structural reform such as deregulation was recommended. As is clear from this editorial, *Kozo Kaikaku Ron*, the most dominant economic ideology, exerted a great influence on economic discussions. So great was the influence that many economists, in business and academia, felt obliged to add deregulation and other structural reform measures when they dealt with deflation.[18]

Takahiro Miyao was one of the earliest of those who warned against asset and general price deflation after 1990. As early as 1995, he analyzed three hypotheses about the stagnation: these hypotheses were that the stagnation was caused by (1) the aftermath of the bursting of the bubble, (2) structural factors, and (3) deflation (Miyao 1995). He dismissed the first two and presented the third one as his own. But if the stagnation was due to deflation, it must have been caused by a series of macroeconomic failures; he had to explain the reason for this. In a sense, this was a "structural recession"; although the Japanese economy as a system did not have problems, the policymaking process had a problem: the rigid bureaucracy, especially in the MOF. To correct it, he proposed deregulating the land market to counter asset deflation and breaking up and reorganizing the MOF.

The Debate Globalized

The economic debate about Japan's Great Stagnation was the first globalized economic debate for Japan. Unlike other episodes of Japanese macroeconomic management, this one attracted a considerable amount of attention from abroad. As Gillian Tett of the *Financial Times* observed in 2004, "Indeed in recent years, the country's problems have become akin to a bizarre laboratory test tube for Western economists" (Tett 2004, 321). It should be noted that foreign commentators were also divided on the causes and remedies of the Great Stagnation. For example, Richard Katz and Edward Lincoln argued that it was a system-wide failure to adapt to the new economic environment (Katz 1998, Lincoln 2001). Edward Kane of Boston College was one of the first to take note of Japan's delayed responses to the bad loans problem, drawing lessons from the U.S. savings and loan crisis (Kane 1993). Later, Anil Kashyap of the University of Chicago, together with Takeo Hoshi, then at the University of California, San Diego, and currently at Stanford University, emphasized the problem in the banking sector, connecting bank loans to zombie firms with bad loans problem (Hoshi and Kashyap 1999).[19]

However, the long-lasting contribution came from macroeconomic analyses by foreign commentators. Jeffrey Sachs, then at Harvard University and currently at Columbia University, took notice of the malfunctioning of the Japanese economy and wrote an article published November 27, 1995, in *Nihon Keizai Shimbun*, advocating a more vigorous expansionary macroeconomic policy, including the purchasing of the foreign government bonds to boost the economy.[20] Adam S. Posen, then senior fellow at the Institute for

International Economy, and currently at the Peterson Institute of International Economics advocated an expansionary macroeconomic policy (Posen 1998; Kuttner and Posen 2001). His diagnosis was straightforward: the slowing down of Japan's growth rate was not a "structural stagnation" but a result of "macroeconomic mistakes." Although he focused more on the efficacy of fiscal policy, an opinion very unpopular at that time in Japan, he nonetheless did not fail to endorse a more expansionary monetary policy as well; after all, Posen was one of the first to recognize the importance of inflation targeting (Bernanke et al. 1999), and he recommended that the BOJ adopt a 3 percent inflation target.

The Krugman Proposal

The most powerful argument for reflation came from Paul Krugman. The pretext was a debate about the desirability of zero inflation around the early to mid-1990s, when central banks around the world succeed in subduing the high inflation of the 1970s and contemplated aiming at zero inflation. Krugman argued against aiming for zero inflation. Citing an influential study by George Akerlof et al. (1996), he argued that nominal rigidities would make a zero inflation rate policy unwise; instead, he recommended that central banks "adopt as a long-run target fairly low but not zero inflation, say 3–4%. This is high enough to accommodate most of the real wages cuts that markets impose, while the costs of the inflation itself will still be very small" (Krugman 1996, 21).

Krugman's (1998a) model became extremely influential since it was based on standard, modern macroeconomic theorizing with microeconomic foundation. The model demonstrates the following: It is assumed that the real equilibrium interest rate required to generate enough demand to achieve full-employment level output was negative due to the aging and decreasing working population and the dysfunctional financial sector. The nominal interest rate cannot be negative. The "liquidity trap" can be redefined as the situation in which the nominal interest rate was lowered to zero, but the real interest rate remains high due to the deflationary expectation; therefore, the BOJ should announce the "long-term commitment to inflation" and should work on generating an inflationary expectation. Last, the BOJ purchase of long-term government bonds would be a good tool of its commitment to 4 percent inflation targeting for 15 years (Krugman 1998a; Adachi 2013, 113–116).[21] Critics questioned Krugman's assumption of a negative real equilibrium rate, although this is not necessarily the required condition. What is needed is the persistent discrepancy between nominal and real interest rates due to the zero lower bound of nominal interest rate. Krugman's assumption should be interpreted as a preemptive rebuttal of the proponents of "structural reforms": a negative equilibrium rate was assumed not necessarily because Krugman believed that was the case but because he wanted to show that a reflationary monetary and fiscal policy was effective even under the assumptions that the structural reform proponents often made. He later rephrased his insights in a more familiar IS-LM framework (Krugman 1998b): Japan's problem was a macroeconomic demand shortage, so the necessary remedy was expansionary macroeconomic policy. It is not surprising that he described Takenaka's policy of "*Kozo Kaikaku*" as a "leap in the dark" (Krugman 2001).[22]

Other Reflation Proposals

Another plan was proposed by Lars Svensson, then at Princeton University: the BOJ, together with the government, should set the target yen/dollar exchange rate temporarily at the depreciated level of the yen, which corresponded to the desirable price level, using purchase of foreign government bonds. Once the target level is achieved, the BOJ could switch to the ordinary inflation target (Svensson 2003). More monetarist or quantity theoretical lines were taken by Robert Hetzel, an economist at the Federal Reserve Bank of Richmond (Hetzel 1999, 2004) and Benett T. McCullum of Carnegie Mellon University (McCullum 2001a, 2001b): using the so-called McCullum rule, McCullum calculated the necessary base money growth rate to achieve a desirable nominal GDP growth rate, showing that the current monetary growth rate was far smaller than the desirable one.

Yet another proposal was made by Ben S. Bernanke, who was a Princeton University professor then. Although he admitted that the Japanese economy had several structural weaknesses, including the rigidity of the banking sector and other sectors, he argued that the BOJ could cooperate with the government more productively. His specific proposals included the BOJ's commitment to the zero interest rate policy with explicit inflation targeting, the depreciation of yen, which is similar to the Svensson plan, and a money-financed transfer. He also offered the clearest explanation of why monetary policy would eventually change the price level. Bernanke's *reductio ad absurdum* argument (as it is commonly called in Japan) countered the view that the BOJ's monetary policy is impotent: "To rebut this view, one can apply a reductio ad absurdum argument, based on my earlier observation that money issuance must affect prices, else printing money will create infinite purchasing power. Suppose the Bank of Japan prints yen and uses them to acquire foreign assets. If the yen did not depreciate as a result, and if there were no reciprocal demand for Japanese goods or assets (which would drive up domestic prices), what in principle would prevent the BOJ from acquiring infinite quantities of foreign assets, leaving foreigners nothing to hold but idle yen balances? Obviously this will not happen in equilibrium" (Bernanke 2000, 162). He concluded, "To this outsider, at least, Japanese monetary policy seems to be suffering from a self-induced paralysis. Most striking is the apparent unwillingness of the monetary authorities to experiment, to try anything that isn't absolutely guaranteed to work. Perhaps it's time for some Rooseveltian resolve in Japan" (Bernanke 2000, 165).[23] When Bernanke became the governor of the Federal Reserve Bank (FRB) in 2002, he articulated the basic strategy of the FRB, which was to not repeat the mistakes of the BOJ and the FRB of the Great Depression years (Bernanke 2002; Ahearn et al. 2002; Wessel 2009).

The proposals by Krugman, Svensson, and Bernake are based on the development of modern macroeconomics, and have furthered the development of modern macroeconomics in four respects. First, the proposals are based on modern macroeconomics of the new Keynesian variety, which consists of new IS-LM analysis coupled with a new Keynesian Phillips curve. Second, with Japan's policy rate reaching zero during the 1990s, economists have turned to the question of optimal monetary policy under the zero interest rate lower bound: in the process, Krugman resurrected the notion of the "liquidity trap" in modern macroeconomics. Third, inflation targeting, which had become adopted by the central banks during the 1990s as the standard policy framework, came to be spotlighted: for those who emphasized deflation and deflationary expectations, the most urgent issue was how to generate inflationary expectations; therefore, inflation targeting was seen as one of the most powerful tools to overcome deflation and deflationary expectation. Fourth, some economists have been developing the role of the financial sector in a model. The model is known as the financial accelerator: it supposes an informational asymmetry between a lender and a borrower in the sense that a borrower knows the quality of his or her project, while a lender does not. There emerges a necessary role of information production by financial institutions and that of collateral: a borrower uses collateral submitted by a lender as a proxy for the quality of the project, and the amount of borrowing thereby increases as the value of collateral increases. As the value of collateral is affected by asset prices, the amount of loans will increase when asset prices increase, while the amount of loans will decrease when a financial crisis hits the economy by decreasing asset prices and thereby decreasing the value of collateral. The economists developing this model include Ben S. Bernanke.[24]

Joseph E. Stiglitz, a Nobel laureate in economics, came up with more radical proposal. In his lecture titled "Deflation, Globalization, and the New Paradigm of Monetary Economics," which was given to Council on Customs, Tariff, Foreign Exchange, and Other Transactions of the MOF on April

16, 2003, he argued for government money.[25] On the basis of his work with Bruce Greenwald (Greenwald and Stiglitz 2003), Stiglitz emphasized the role of credit as opposed to currency in its effect on the macroeconomy. His perspective, which he called the "new paradigm in monetary economics," is an attack on the current consensus of "equilibrium macroeconomics," which was formed during the 1970s and 1980s under the influence of monetarism and a rational expectation revolution. Turning to the Japanese situation, Stiglitz suggested that the main problem of the Japanese economy was the lack of aggregate demand due to the balance-sheet problem: after the bursting of asset bubbles, the balance sheets of the firms had deteriorated. Like many others, he did not ignore structural issues such as low productivity in the service sector, but he insisted that the structural issues could be tackled only after one solved the aggregate demand deficiency. Unlike Richard Koo, however, Stiglitz proposed to inflate the economy to counter the increased real burden of debt caused by balance sheet recession. Although he was skeptical about the effect of the real interest rate on investment demand, he expected that reversing deflation to inflation would decrease the real interest rate.

As for the diagnosis for the Japanese economy, Stiglitz urged policymakers to generate inflation by using the depreciation of the Japanese yen and by other means. Yet, unlike Krugman and Bernanke, Stiglitz did not trust inflation targeting to generate a sufficient level of inflationary expectations; hence, he proposed using government money, which was considered as an absolute evil in the economics profession.[26] Having ensured that this would not lead to hyperinflation since there is no empirical evidence to support the sudden burst of hyperinflation, he pointed out two advantages of his proposal: first, unlike the new issue of public debt, the government did not have to repay anything; second, the money could be directed to useful purposes without damaging the debt situation. This recommendation of government money would resurface during the later period of Japan's Great Stagnation and the darkest moments of the Great Recession. Compared with others, Joseph E. Stiglitz's recommendations seemed to stand against the current consensus. But despite the many criticisms hurled against contemporary economics and economic policymaking, particularly by the IMF, Stiglitz was on the side that attributed the main cause of Japan's long stagnation to the lack of aggregate demand, and he emphasized the critical role of nonconventional monetary policy.

Reactions to the Krugman Proposal

These discussions had a tremendous effect on the controversy in Japan. Japanese economists who had already argued for expansionary monetary policy came to embrace the Krugman proposal, some with and some without initial hesitation. From 1998 to the early 2000s, those economists were called the "reflationists": they emphasized deflation and deflationary expectations as one of the most important causes of the Great Stagnation, advocating a reflation policy of reversing deflation and restoring the modest inflationary path using inflation targeting. These economists included Takatoshi Ito and Motoshige Ito, both at the University of Tokyo; Takeo Hoshi currenly at Stanford University; Kikuo Iwata at Gakushuin University; Koichi Hamada at Yale University; and Mitsuhiro Fukao at Keio University.[27] There were initial hesitations among them. Hoshi and Motoshige Ito quickly endorsed the Krugman proposal. Hoshi (1998) proposed the adoption of inflation targeting to fight against deflationary expectations, but he did not specify a number. When Motoshige Ito and Takatoshi Ito gathered to discuss the inflationary policy as an option, Motoshige Ito was willing to accept the Krugman proposal of a 3 to 4 percent inflation target. Takatoshi Ito was skeptical and hesitant since he thought the Krugman proposal was one variation of the *Chosei Infure* and since he believed the resultant depreciation of the yen associated with the adoption of the inflation target would be detrimental to the Japanese economy (Ito and Ito 1998). However, Takatoshi Ito overcame his initial hesitation when he attended the conference in 1999 to discuss the Krugman proposal.[28]

It turned out that the Krugman proposal sparked more controversies and more heated controversies than ever before, and the differences and divisions among the economists still remained. In December 1999, the Research Institute attached to the Ministry of Trade and Industry organized a conference on "Restoring the Japanese Economy and Issues of Macroeconomic Policy" (Yoshikawa et al. 2000). It centered on the main guest, Krugman, whose presentation was followed by comments from six participants. Two of them, Takatoshi Ito, then deputy vice minister of finance for international affairs at the MOF, and Nobuhiro Kiyotaki, then at London School of Economics, supported Krugman: Ito concurred with Krugman and proposed 1 to 3 percent inflation targeting. Kiyotaki, of the Kiyotaki and Moore (1997) model fame, emphasized that inflationary expectations have the redistribution effects of assets, which could introduce some problems but might nonetheless be worth pursuing. But reactions from other participants varied. Masaru Yoshitomi argued that the transmission mechanism was unclear; therefore, he preferred the exchange rate target. Mikio Wakatsuki, an ex-BOJ official, was extremely skeptical: he thought Krugman's assumption of a negative real interest rate was too pessimistic, and he also inquired about the transmission mechanism, the available policy tools, and the legal framework. The most negative reaction came from Hirokazu Hayashi, who was then a MITI official. He flatly rejected inflation targeting based on a "value judgment" that it should not be pursued as a policy. He also believed that the current deflation was good because he associated deflation with the correction of high costs. Also, he believed that any change in asset distribution would make people unhappy. Furthermore, he believed the government should pursue structural reforms. At the end of his remarks, Krugman stressed that the Japanese economy needed to experiment with every conceivable plan, yet he was convinced that the Bank of Japan would never be willing to implement any policy unless the BOJ was absolutely certain that the plan would work.

Keynesian Reactions to the Krugman Proposal

There are some Keynesian-leaning economists who vigorously oppose reflation policy.[29] The most representative member of these economists is Hiroshi Yoshikawa, a professor of economics at the University of Tokyo and a member of *Keizai Zaisei Shimon Kaigi* (the Economic and Fiscal Policy Council), which was set up in 2001. Yoshikawa attended the meeting with Krugman and developed his own theory to explain Japan's Great Stagnation, arguing that it was caused by demand saturation (Yoshikawa 1999). Yoshikawa's theoretical vision was ambitious enough: he tried to integrate the economic ideas of John Maynard Keynes and Joseph A. Schumpeter to argue that the Great Stagnation was a result of an effective demand shortage and that the fiscal and monetary policy cannot be used to recover the economy since the demand shortage was due to demand saturation. Instead, Yoshikawa conceived his remedy in the emergence of new industries through the "demand-generating structural reform": explicitly referring to Schumpeter, he asserted that the introduction of new goods and the development of new markets would generate more effective demand: "technical advances still contribute to economic growth via the creation of new high demand growth goods . . . under the demand-side model, innovation contributes to economic growth through the creation of high demand growth goods" (Yoshikawa 1999, 210).[30] Moreover, Yoshikawa was highly critical about the Krugman proposal, since he believed that it was based on modern macroeconomics and the quantity theory of money, both of which Yoshikawa firmly denied. In 1999, he supported the combination of more fiscal policy with the current low interest rate. Even so, when deflation received the most attention in 2003, Yoshikawa signed a joint appeal with others to promote inflation targeting.[31]

Another economist is Yoshiyasu Ono, professor of economics at Osaka University. He also developed his own theory of the Great Stagnation. In contrast to Yoshikawa's, his theory is based on the standard assumptions of utility maximizing rational agents. However, there is one specific assumption in his model: the utility of holding money could be infinite, and the "love of money" becomes too powerful to be overcome by monetary policy. Under such an assumption, the agents would like to demand an infinite amount of money, which leads to a general oversupply of goods and services. In essence, Ono constructed a Keynesian world within a neoclassical framework. His policy prescription varied from time to time: on one occasion, he emphasized expansionary fiscal policy, while on another occasion, he hoped the emergence of a new generation with different preferences would push the economy out of the recession. But Ono remained a staunch opponent of inflation targeting since he thought that the demand for money became infinite and that monetary policy would be ineffective (Ono 1994, 2001, 2007).[32]

Reflationists and Their Critics

As is shown in Figure 2-1, there was a surge in interest in deflation and inflation targeting from 2000 to 2003. The typical arguments directed against inflation targeting are summarized as follows.

> I. Inflation targeting is not effective.
>> A. Import deflation argument: Current deflation is caused by inexpensive imports from China; therefore, monetary policy cannot overcome it.
>> B. Transmission mechanism: Under a zero nominal interest rate, it is unclear how monetary policy can influence the real economy.
>> C. Precedent: There is no historical precedent for using inflation targeting under deflation.
>
> II. Inflation targeting has demerits.
>> D. Hyperinflation: If inflation targeting is introduced, there will be hyperinflation.
>> E. Sharp increase in interest rate: Inflation expectations would increase the nominal interest rate, which would damage the balance sheets of banks and the BOJ.
>> F. Compromise fiscal discipline: If inflation targeting is adopted, it would weaken fiscal discipline, and Japan would default fiscally.
>> G. Hinder reforms: If inflation targeting is adopted and the economy recovers, then reforms would not progress.

Japanese reflationists countered these arguments one by one (Iwata 2001, 2003, 2004). Criticism A can be easily refuted since other countries, such as the United States, import more goods from China, but the United States is not in deflation. Related to criticism B, some argued that the prices would not rise unless the bank loans also rose. Also, when the bad loans problem was the center of the discussion, stagnating bank loans were connected to deflation. Furthermore, those who were skeptical about the transmission mechanism tended to accept the old understanding of the liquidity trap, and they supported fiscal policy. As Chapter 4 discusses, reflationists examined history during the Great Depression to show that bank loans did not go up with a rising inflation rate; rather, loans lagged behind inflation. As for fiscal policy, reflationists relied on either the Krugman model or the Mundell-Fleming model: in either model, monetary policy with inflation targeting was the key to recovery, although reflationists did not deny that fiscal policy could be a subsidiary measure. Criticism C revealed the conservatism or timidity of critics. When it comes to a historical example, during the Great Depression, Sweden allegedly engaged in price level targeting (Berg 1999). More important, no nations other than Japan experienced deflation in the post-World War II world, yet critics did not seem to take deflation seriously enough.[33]

Criticism D is a typical antireflationary argument. Reflationists again counter this with history and empirical research: hyper- or high inflation occurred in defeated countries after the war or in countries undergoing revolution. Criticisms E and F have become popular as Japan's fiscal condition deteriorates. Reflationists have countered that the nominal interest rate would not rise during the reflation process since the economy has excess capacity, again citing a historical example during the Great Depression period. They also emphasized that reflation policies would be the necessary prerequisite for fiscal consolidation; fiscal consolidation is not possible under a deflation where nominal GDP stagnates. The last criticism echoes a liquidationism sentiment. Reflationists have countered this argument with several observations: the primary purpose of economic policy is not reform itself but the improvement of the welfare of the nation, and there is no convincing evidence that a liquidationist policy has worked. Some of these criticisms are extremely persistent and are still being raised even in the present (see Chapter 5).

The Impact of Hayashi and Prescott

Although Yoshikawa and Ono have been influential in policy circles, Yoshikawa in particular, they are somewhat outsiders among the mainstream Japanese economics profession since they have been developing their own models and theories: Yoshikawa believed that the developments since the rational expectations revolution of the 1970s are a "retrogress" rather than progress (Yoshikawa 1999, 245). But the analysis by Fumio Hayashi, then professor of economics at the University of Tokyo, was quite different. With Nobel laureate Edward Prescott of the University of Arizona, they offered an explanation of the Great Stagnation based on the real business cycle model, according to which the shortening of the working hours in 1992 and the stagnation of the growth of total factor productivity due to heavy regulation were the two main culprits. There are criticisms against this model: the model is a basic real business cycle variant with no role for money in it. However, being firmly embedded into the mainstream, Hayashi and Prescott (2002) had a great impact on the research direction: Japanese economists turned to the analysis of productivity and its implications for macroeconomics.

By 2004, Japanese economists had held several conferences to argue their cases against each other, hoping to resolve their differences: two conference volumes emerged (Iwata and Miyagawa 2004; Hamada and Horiuchi 2004). However, it was quite clear that the deep differences and divisions of opinions had not been easily resolved: in the case of Hamada and Horichi (2004), even two distinguished scholar-editors could not agree on the content of the editors' introduction, so they had to write two separate introductions.

In the same year that the two conference volumes were published, the Japanese Economic Association held its fall meeting. One panel session discussed "What Lessons Macroeconomics Has Learned from the 'Lost Decade'" (Horioka et al. 2007). Etsuro Shioji at Hitotsubashi University delivered a keynote speech that listed the following six lessons for macroeconomics: (1) macro effects of sectoral resource allocations matter, (2) dynamic general equilibrium matters, (3) the central bank's policy to affect economic agents' expectations about the future matters, (4) expectations about the future also matter for fiscal policy, (5) macroeconomic impacts of demography or the composition of population matter, and (6) the accumulated empirical studies matter. As the recovery began taking hold around 2004, the controversy waned, but it was just suspended for a time being.

VI. The "Recovery without Any Felt Benefit" and After

Shifts in Interest

As the economy recovered, deflation and the fear of it receded, although deflation never stopped. In the beginning of 2006, the media started calling the recovery the "*Jikkan naki keiki kaifuku* (recovery without any felt benefit)" and talking about *Kakusa Shakai* (disparity society). The discussions about Japan's growing inequality had already begun in the late 1990s (Tachibanaki 1998; Sato 2000; Ohtake 2005),[34] and there was a growing perception that Koizumi and Tekenaka brought *Kakusa Shakai*.[35] Also discussed was the status of employment, especially that of the youth: they became increasingly employed on a nonregular basis. The term "NEET" was used to describe the youth who were "not in education, employment, or training." The slogan of the first administration of Prime Minister Abe "*Sai Chosen* (Rechallenge)" was in part an attempt to address this concern with *Kakusa Shakai.*

After the Lehman Shock

After the Lehman crisis, some economists went through a change of heart. One notable example was the conversion of Iwao Nakatani, one of the most vocal proponents of deregulation and the Koizumi structural reform: Nakatani wrote a book titled *Why Capitalism Self-Destructed* (Nakatani 2008) that became an instant bestseller, selling more than one hundred thousand copies. The book's blurb advertised it as the "'book of repentance' written by leading advocate of structural reform" and "the Lehman shock, unequal society, indiscriminate killing, the collapse of medicine, and a cover-up in the food industry were all caused by the 'Market Principle.'" Calling global capital a "monster," Nakatani denounced "American-style economics" and the market economy principle as the sources of such problems as the financial crisis, an increased income disparity, and a deteriorated environment. He confessed that he was "totally taken over" by the American-style economics and way of life until now, tracing its origin to his days as a PhD. student at Harvard. His real target was the Koizumi-Takenaka structural reform. Once an ally of Takenaka, Nakatani now implicitly criticized him.

Curiously, even though Nakatani keeps his popular macroeconomics textbook updated and available on the market, there is no discussion of deflation, the appreciation of the yen, or macroeconomic policy in Nakatani (2008). Instead, he proposed a tax reform, the overhaul of the pension system with a consumption tax as the revenue source for the basic pension, and the introduction of the basic income scheme. In a sense, his thinking is still in the "structural reforms" mode, although he denounces structural reforms as a policy package.

Even after the Lehman shock, when central banks began engaging in unconventional monetary policy on a larger scale, there was no strong consensus on the efficacy of reflation policies as a way to end deflation in Japan. In 2009, to mark the 75th anniversary of the founding of the Japanese Economic Association, the association sent out questionnaire to its own members (Shibata and Hanabuchi 2010). Among the 560 respondents, 87.5 percent said agreed with the statement that "Japan's experience during the 1990s could teach some lessons about the responses to the current crisis." However, in response to the question "What do you think about the BOJ policy?" 34.8 percent said the current policy was fine; only 17.7 percent said the BOJ should do more, while 38.2 percent said the BOJ should consider the exit strategy from the current policy.

Economists are still divided on the cause of deflation. Reflecting the preference for structural factors, one recent favorite is demographics: the former Governor Shirakawa identified Japan's shrinking population as a cause of declining potential growth rate. The depopulation deflation argument became so popular that even the government's *Keizai Zaisei Hakusyo* (Annual report on the Japanese economy and public finance, 2011) examined it. The report reached the conclusions that there was no statistical relationship between the population growth rate and inflation or deflation but that there was a relationship between the expected growth rate and the inflation rate, and between the population growth rate and the expected growth rate. The report ended with a caution: it suggest there might be a relationship between the population growth rate and deflation, but there are other factors to influence the expected growth rate.

Another popular account of deflation is wage deflation. Its main proponent, Yoshikawa (2013), argued that deflation is the result of the declining nominal wages that occurred under the Japanese employment relationship. Japan has maintained a relatively lower unemployment rate and declining nominal wages during the deflationary period. This was the result of the choice that Japanese firms and workers made: they accepted a wage decrease to maintain employment. However, Japan experienced inflation under the Japanese employment relationship before the 1990s; therefore, the root cause must be the stagnation. What explains stagnation after all? Yoshikawa (2013) takes a multiple causes approach in pointing out the importance of the financial crisis of 1997–1998 and the bad loans problem in 2001–2003, but he denies the importance of monetary factors. Rather, he restates Yoshikawa's (1999) claim that the lack of "product" as opposed to "process" innovation caused the long stagnation: "The deficiency of demand-generating product innovation has caused the long stagnation with resultant deflation, and deflation in turn has atrophied product innovation" (Yoshikawa 2013, 211–212). However, he does not offer empirical evidence for the paucity of product innovation in Japan.

Questioning the Demand versus Supply Distinction

With Hayashi-Prescott (2002), there emerged a new trend among Japanese economists of relating supply explanations to demand explanations. The key variable here is productivity: the slowdown in productivity would induce demand failure. Referring to Miyao (2006), Etsuro Shioji summarized the productivity view as follows: "if a current productivity slowdown induces households to revise their estimates of permanent income downward, or if it lowers a firm's expected future marginal product of capital, it could reduce demand as well as supply. Whether it could reduce demand more than supply, for a sustained period of time, needs further investigation" (Shioji 2013, 326). Fukao (2012) is by far the state-of-the-art explanation based on the productivity induced demand failure explanation. The policy implications of this approach are different from those of reflationists. He countered Meltzer (1999) and Hamada and Okada (2009), who called for more monetary easing to depreciate the yen. He is also pessimistic about the effectiveness of monetary policy when the nominal interest rate reaches the zero: "Considering the facts that the effect of intervention into the foreign exchange market without lowering the interest rate is limited and that deflation and the liquidity trap prevented the depreciation policy through lowering the real interest rate, it is doubtful that a large scale depreciation of the yen was possible" (Fukao 2012, 8). Also, he thought that the United States would not have allowed a large-scale depreciation of the yen.

VII. Why the Structural View Took Hold

Every idea has its own history. This section explores the historical roots of ideas expressed in the Great Stagnation. There are several characteristics of the economic ideas that have persisted and repeated during this period. First, macroeconomic arguments were dominated by other ideas: the most dominant idea was a wide variety of the structural view, which resonated with various proposals of structural reforms. Although the foci and exact topics at issue shifted throughout the period, almost everything was made to relate to a "fundamental" cause of the stagnation. Against this background, structural reforms took many forms, from the resolution of the bad loans problem, a change in corporate governance, and deregulation to the political electoral reform.

Second, economic arguments were dominated by noneconomic arguments: moralistic arguments against bubbles, arguments against macroeconomic policy as relief, and liquidationism were influential from the beginning to the rise of structural reforms. As we have already seen, Noguchi (1992) was representative in his not only economic but also moral indignation about bubbles as evil. Third, monetary policy arguments were dominated by other arguments: whenever a macroeconomic case for stimulus was made, fiscal policy received the most attention; especially after the BOJ's policy rate reached zero, the proponents of monetary policy had to confront critics.

Why did the structural view take hold? First, in the early phase of the Great Stagnation, the failure of macroeconomic policies to boost the economy reinforced the impression among the economists and the public that macroeconomic policies would not work. Heizo Takenaka's policy philosophy echoed this sentiment:

> During the 1990s, economic policy involved mainly demand-stimulus policy, which should have been adopted when the economy suffers from a temporary demand shortage. This is the so-called Keynesian policy. Keynes' theory is not wrong. But Japan since the 90s has been stagnating not due to a temporary demand shortage, but due to the serious supply-side problems such as bad loans. This was my analysis. Without solving these problems, the economy could no way recover to a proper growth path, no matter what amount of fiscal policy was engaged. (Takenaka 2006, 251)

In the process, the name of Keynes and Keynesian economics received negative connotations. It was in part because Keynes's name has been strongly associated with not only Keynesian economics but also macroeconomics in Japan. On the other hand, the demise of Keynesian economics was in part engineered by policymakers and economists. As two journalists reported, the MOF resisted expansionary fiscal policy in the early phase of the recession, deliberately promoting the message that "the age of Keynesianism was over." In the years leading up to the consumption tax hike in 1997, the MOF recruited several prominent academic economists to endorse the idea of "non-Keynesian effects" (Karube and Nishino 1999, 39–42).

As the reputation of Keynes went down, other economists became highlighted. The favorite great economist in Japan was Joseph A. Schumpeter: unlike in the American economic discourse, F. A. Hayek has not been referred to as often as Schumpeter.[36] He has been popular in Japanese academic and media discussions throughout the post-World War II era. Personal connections mattered: Tsuru and other Japanese economists knew Schumpeter personally, and almost all of Schumpeter's works have been translated into Japanese. Schumpeter appealed to a wide variety of people; those who emphasized the necessity of innovation for a Japanese recovery loved to refer to him, and the BOJ's Governor Masaru Hayami favorably referred to "creative destruction." Also, Schumpeter's theory has been conveniently associated with a sort of economics that emphasizes the "real" rather than the monetary factors. Hiroshi Yoshikawa's work is a case in point. As we have seen in Section III, he envisioned the integration of Schumpeter and Keynes.[37]

Second, modern macroeconomics tends to strengthen the perception that macroeconomics would not work. The standard workhorse model of modern macroeconomics tends to assume away a long-lasting stagnation as a long-run phenomenon. Even though the "long-run" in economics is an abstraction in which full employment of resources prevails, economists tend to confuse the abstract concept with the real time concept. Hayashi and Prescott's (2002) article is a prime example, and this confusion also explains Takenaka's thinking since he started his career as a "supply-sider" economist after the rational expectations revolution in the late 1970s. Although Takenaka did not argue against monetary policy, and did indeed advocate a more expansionary monetary policy when it came to deflation (see Chapter 2), many others argued against monetary policy with the presumption that monetary forces could not explain the "long" stagnation of the economy.

Third, the structural view is consistent with the economics culture and history of Japan.[38] Historically, economic thinking in Japan has been dominated by two ideas, Marxism and developmentalism. Until the 1980s, the majority of academic economists were neither Keynesians nor neoclassical economists: they were Marxians. Keynesian and/or neoclassical economics were called *Kindai Keizaigaku* (modern economics) and treated as a different type of economics.[39] Marxian economists dominated the economics departments of Japanese universities for a long time, including the University of Tokyo, arguably the most prestigious and well-funded national university in Japan.[40] The situation gradually changed throughout the 1970s and 1980s, but the influence had been felt in the media discourse throughout the period. As for the influence of developmentalism, there was a strong tendency among the Japanese economists to regard promoting economic development positively as the role of the state. Some modern economists were proponents of the idea of Japan as a developmental state or, as it was later called, developmentalism (Gao 1997; Noguchi 2000; Garside 2012, chap. 3). Many academic economists took for granted the success of Japanese economic development as state-driven, the so-called industrial policy of the MITI being a prime successful example of state-driven characteristics.[41] Furthermore, we must note the diversity of Keynesianism in Japan in the post-World War II period. Here, the strong presence of Marxian economics and the prevalence of developmentalism in the Japanese academic and media discourse played an important role: Keynes was accepted as someone who endorsed the role of government in the economy, and Keynesianism in Japan had more affinity with the structural view. The early generation of Keynesian economists in Japan felt sympathy toward Marxian, institutionalist, and even Schumpeterian economics; they were concerned with the structural problems of the Japanese economy such as the "dual structure of the economy," which refers to inter- and intraindustrial disparities regarding wages and salaries. Naturally, they were inclined to endorse British-type Keynesians who considered money to be endogenously determined. To be fair, there was a different type of Keynesianism in Japan: American Keynesianism-like economists who eventually grew in number. But monetarism did not gain support in Japanese economics academia.

This history has had several implications and influences. First, economists in Japan tend to focus more on "structural" or "real" factors than on effective demand shortage and expansionary policy as remedies. Therefore, these economists see "structural reforms" in a decisively favorable light; even self-proclaimed Keynesians such as Yoshikawa, emphasized the "real" cause of the shortage of effective demand: the saturation of demand. Second, when it comes to macroeconomic policy, fiscal policy has been preferred to monetary policy. The British-type Keynesians' emphasis on endogenous money and its antagonism toward monetarism, coupled with an old-fashioned understanding of the liquidity trap, tilted the balance against monetary policy. Monetary policy ineffectiveness has resonated with the "*Nichigin-ryu Riron* (the BOJ theory)," the modern successor of the real bills doctrine. Yoshikawa is a staunch opponent of the quantity theory of money and monetarism: he criticized Krugman's 1998 paper since it was considered to be based on the quantity theory of money. Instead, Yoshikawa adopted the accounting theory of inflation/deflation, a cost-push theory in which prices are determined by costs.

VIII. Conclusion

The major arguments advanced during Japan's Great Stagnation can be summarized as follows:

1. Liquidationism, or policy nihilism: A boom needs the subsequent recession to "cleanse" the economy of bad projects, firms, and industries through natural selection; therefore, countercyclical policy is not desirable.
2. Macroeconomic ineffectiveness doctrine or structural reforms ideology: Japan's stagnation is structural in nature and could not be solved with macroeconomic policy; therefore, the restoration of the economy requires measures other than macroeconomic policy—that is, structural reforms.
3. "Only fiscal policy works" doctrine: When macroeconomic policy works, the main tool must be fiscal policy, and public works are preferable to tax cuts. This is likely to be combined with the old understanding of the liquidity trap and the argument in item eight.
4. Austerity doctrine—modern treasury view: Fiscal consolidation should be the first and foremost goal of economic policy. In its extreme version, this entails fiscal policy ineffectiveness, and monetary policy would not solve the consolidation problem.
5. Good deflation doctrine: Deflation is good since the prices are decreasing.

6. Structural explanations for deflation: The causes of deflation are globalization, economic integration with China in particular; decreased population or working population; or stagnant bank loans due to the bad loans problem.

7. Monetary policy ineffectiveness doctrine—the BOJ doctrine: The money supply cannot be controlled, the price level cannot be controlled, the concept of real interest rate is useless, or the quantity theory of money cannot hold since there is an infinite demand for money under the zero interest rate environment (the money supply would be sucked into the hands of households and firms like a star would be sucked into a black hole).

8. Belief in industrial policy—modern MITI view: The government has to, and can, effectively target and support specific industries for economic growth.

9. Antigrowth sentiment—limits to growth doctrine: Economic growth is undesirable and impossible for the Japanese economy.

In other words, exactly when Japan needs a proper dose of macroeconomic remedies, antimacroeconomic arguments, the structural view in particular, have been dominant. It is no surprise that Japanese macroeconomic policy has been marred by a series of macroeconomic failures.[42]

Moreover, there is an intellectual dynamic between ideas, policies, and events: as macroeconomic policy seems to keep "failing," economists and commentators became disappointed with macroeconomic policy, turning away from the macroeconomic view and being drawn to the structural view. In reality, as we see in Chapter 2, there were a series of macroeconomic policy failures precisely because they were not carried out properly: there were execution problems. Also, macroeconomic failures were conceptual problems: many relied heavily on fiscal policy, thinking that monetary policy would be ineffective, especially after the policy interest rate hit the zero lower bound. New ideas such as inflation targeting did not gain much support among Japanese economists, commentators, and the media.

CHAPTER 4

The Shadow of History: Lessons from Japan's Great Depression in the 1930s

I. Introduction

The Great Recession has resurrected an interest in another major crisis, the Great Depression. For example, Alan Greenspan talked about the Great Recession as a "once in fifty years, or in a century" event, hinting that the Great Recession is the Second Great Depression (Greenspan 2007). Ben S. Bernake, chairman of the Federal Reserve Board from 2006–2014, and Christina D. Romer, chair of Council of Economic Advisors from 2009–2010, both foremost experts on the Great Depression, drew lessons from the Great Depression for today's Great Recession (Bernanke 2012; Romer 2009, 2013). Barry Eichengreen and Kevin O'Rourke explicitly compared the two crises, stating that the initial phase of the Great Recession was more severe than the Great Depression was in terms of declining stock prices and the volume of exports (Eichengreen and O'Rourke 2009). Academic economic historians gathered to discuss the "Lessons from the 1930s Great Depression for the Making of Economic Policy."[1] A similar comparison has already been made during Japan's Great Stagnation. This chapter goes back further, to the 1930s, showing disturbing similarities between the policy mistakes of the 1930s and those of the 1990s in Japan. The Great Depression is commonly known in Japan as the Showa Depression, named after the years of the reign of Emperor Hirohito. The Showa Depression has acted as a litmus test for Japanese economists, revealing an almost a similar range of diversity of opinions on how economists should deal with economic and financial crises. More noteworthy is the fact that the Showa Depression has been a major source of inspiration for Japanese reflationsists and the launch of Abenomics. Kikuo Iwata, who would become deputy governor of the Bank of Japan (BOJ) in 2013, wrote extensively on the experiences of the Great and Showa Depressions.[2]

The study of the Great Depression itself is the history of macroeconomics. As Ben Bernanke put it when speaking of the difficulties and significance of the study of the Great Depression, understanding the Great Depression is the "holy grail of macroeconomics" (Bernanke 2000, 5). Indeed the very emergence and evolution of macroeconomics is closely related with interpretations of the Great Depression. For macroeconomics right after World War II, the Great Depression was attributed to the unstable nature of the market economy, with fiscal policy being designated as the remedy. On the other hand, during the 1960, Milton Friedman and his associates challenged the Keynesian consensus, arguing that the inept monetary policy of the Federal Reserve Bank caused a recession to turn into the Great Depression (Friedman and Schwartz 1963). A fierce controversy among the Keynesians and the Monetarists ensued, yet the heavy reliance on U.S. data prevented researchers from reaching a consensus.[3] The breakthrough came when economists began comparing international data: in studies pioneered by the work of Choudhri and Kochin (1980), economists compared different paths of contraction and recovery, and discovered the key role of the gold standard in exacerbating and propagating the Great Depression. From these emerged the so-called international view of the Great Depression, which forms the current consensus.[4]

Also, the rational expectations revolution in the 1970s brought the concept of policy regime into the literature. Policy regime sets the rules of the game that guide agents' actions in economic transactions: when the rules of the game change, agents change their behavior accordingly.[5] The gold standard is a certain set of rules under which governments and central banks cannot pursue expansionary fiscal and monetary policy for an extended period. Therefore, once a deflationary depression hits the economy, under the gold standard, governments and central banks have no choice but to engage in a contractionary fiscal and monetary policy. Thus, the gold standard is often called the deflationary policy regime. Ending the Great Depression required ending this deflationary policy regime (Temin and Wigmore 1990; Eggertsson 2008).[6]

This chapter goes back in history, examining economic policy and economic ideas before and during Japan's Great Depression of the 1930s. I argue that the variety of economic ideas that one sees in the present were similarly prevalent and at play during Japan's Great Stagnation of the 1920s and during the Great Depression in the 1930s. Also, I argue that the crisis was a time of economic controversies, and the crisis was not only economic and political but also intellectual. Japan in the 1920s was caught in the "policy idea" trap. The chapter focuses mainly on two prevalent ideas: the gold standard mentality and liquidationism. The gold standard was one of the central themes among leading monetary economists during the interwar period. Gustav Cassel, Irving Fisher, Ralph G. Hawtrey, and John Maynard Keynes were all involved in the controversies surrounding the gold standard. As they were fully aware, the gold standard had its ideological connotations: it represented something "good, sound, prudent, and moral" (Eichengreen and Temin 2003). This gold standard mentality constrained policymakers and economists alike exactly when its abandonment was necessary to have a recovery. Liquidationism is the "crime and punishment" view of the business cycle, with reference to a set of beliefs that treats the liquidation of investments, projects, or enterprises as an inevitable, necessary, and even desirable process of the business cycle (De Long 1990): it entails policy nihilism as to the use of economic policy to mitigate a depression or stabilize production, employment, and prices (Laidler 1999).[7] Both ideas constrain the room for countercyclical policy and have moralistic overtones.

What could the Japanese story tell us? Liaquat Ahmed's *Lords of Finance: Bankers Who Broke the World* (Ahmed 2009), the best business book of the year as selected by the *Financial Times*, shows that behind the onset of the Great Depression lay concerted efforts to restore the gold standard system by central bankers Montagu Norman, Benjamin Strong, Emile Moreau, and Hjalmar Schacht. This interpretation broadly accords with the current consensus of the international view of the Great Depression, yet there is one missing piece in this story: Japan. The Japanese story could serve as a good illustration since Japan went back to the gold standard as late as November 1929, exactly when the Great Depression started; therefore, Japanese policymakers and economists were acutely aware of the linkage between the Great Depression and the gold standard. Also, Japan had experienced the Great Stagnation-like long-term stagnation before the Great Depression happened. The resemblance was uncanny: Japan experienced an asset price boom, an underperforming growth rate, a financial panic, a persistent mild deflation, and even a great earthquake during the 1920s. Furthermore, Japan's escape from the Great Depression—Japan's Great Escape—was exemplary, defeating deflation and recovering from the Great Depression rapidly. However, there was a tragic ending to the Great Escape in Japan: Korekiyo Takahashi, the architect of Japan's Great Escape was assassinated, and his reflation policy was taken over by the military to fund the war: this would cast a long shadow even to today.

The chapter is organized as follows. Section II chronicles the Japanese economy from 1918 to 1930. During this period, the Japanese policymakers and economists alike were preoccupied with and were debating the return to the gold standard, which was decided and finally implemented by the Hamaguchi cabinet. The decision coincided with the Great Depression, analysis of which is the topic of Section III. Controversy continued, with the gold standard as the focus of possible remedies. Section IV turns to the escape from the Great Depression by the so-called *Takahashi zaisei* and its tragic end. Takahashi went off the gold standard, ending the deflationary regime. He then engaged in expansionary monetary and fiscal policies, the so-called reflation policies. Section V concludes the chapter.

II. Japan's Great Stagnation in the 1920s: The Road to the *Showa Kyoko*

Another "Lost Decade"

The interwar period was a turbulent period for the Japanese economy. Table 4-1 summarizes the basic performance of the Japanese economy. It experienced a boom due to World War I but experienced long-term stagflation with mild deflation after the boom collapsed.

As is clear from the increase in stock and land prices, the boom was accompanied by asset price inflation, and the public saw it as the "bubble," without using the term. Some might argue that the performance of the Japanese economy was not as bad as the performance of other major economies, a claim reminiscent of the one directed at Japan's Great Stagnation from 1990 to 2012: for example, Japan's average annual growth rate from 1922 to 1929 was 2.9 percent, which was higher than Spain's was. Japan's growth rate became higher than the trend growth rate of the previous periods from 1885 to 1914 (Faini and Toniolo 1992, 123–124). However, this comparison can be misleading since Japan's potential output had become higher during World War I, which was utilized in later periods, especially after the Takahashi reflation. The nominal growth rate had also decreased: Japan experienced deflation, however mild that was, and asset prices were decreasing.

The period from 1918 to 1932, known as the *Taisho Democracy*, was a great "developing democracy" period in Japanese politics;[8] the franchise was

Table 4-1 Economic Performance after 1915 (%)

Year	Nominal Rate of Growth	Real Rate of Growth	Changes in Consumer Price Index	Changes in Stock Price	Changes in Land Price	Growth Rate of Money
1915–1919	27.3	7.3	14.7	67.6	178.0	31.6
1920–1929	0.6	1.9	–1.6	–63.5	–25.9	2.9
1930–1931	–9.6	0.7	–10.8	–29.4	–21.4	–4.2
1932–1935	8.3	7.2	2.0	70.3	1.0	5.6

Source: Iwata et al. (2008). Reproduced with the permission of Gaskuhuin Daigaku Keizai Gakkai.

expanded to the male population over 25 years old, increasing the coverage from 5.5 percent in 1920 to 20 percent in 1928; party politics eventually won over the Meiji oligarchs after political struggles, establishing a custom in which the leader of the party that won the general election would customarily become prime minister. By 1928, two political parties had emerged, *Seiyukai* and *Minseito*. In foreign relationships, this was a developmental phase for Japan: the country was fully recognized as one of the "Five Powers" in the 1919 Peace Conference and the subsequent establishment of the League of Nations in 1920, with Japan becoming one of four permanent member states of the council (Dickinson 2013). The foreign policy fluctuated depending on which political parties formed the government, but the dominant foreign policy philosophy was *Tai Eibei Kyocho* (Cooperation with the United Kingdom and the United States): Japan agreed to ratify a series of arms reduction in the Washington Naval Treaty of 1921 and the London Naval Treaty of 1930.

In contrast to the growing self-perception of the Japanese government and the public, the economy stagnated. As was pointed out before, it was relatively good by international standards, but there was a reason for its stagnation, namely, deflation. The key to understanding the economic malaise of the Japanese economy from 1920 to 1929 was the gold standard. As Faini and Toniolo (1992) argued, Japan's monetary and fiscal policy during this period was not consistently deflationary, even though the price index had continued falling. The burgeoning party politics brought a countercyclical macroeconomic policy to some extent, and a series of crises, the *Great Kanto Earthquake* of 1923 and the *Showa Kinyu Kyoko* (Showa Financial Crisis) of 1927, necessitated the government's action. If there was a "muddle" (Patrick 1971) in economic policy, it was the inconsistent, "stop and go" type of macroeconomic policy. The Japanese economy experienced the interwar version of the "ever-higher yen syndrome." At the Genoa Conference held in 1922, major powers agreed to adopt the gold exchange standard to ease the difficulties associated with the shortage of gold. Also, major powers confirmed their commitment to return to the gold standard system. Japan was one of them, and it would be widely assumed that Japan would keep this commitment. Furthermore, as we see later, the consensus was to return to the gold standard at the prewar parity, which meant the appreciation of the yen. With this consensus on the return to the gold standard, agents "were led to expect not only a regime switch from a mostly flexible system of exchange rates to a regime of fixed parities but also a significant appreciation of the yen. In turn, the expectation that the exchange rate would appreciate at a future, albeit uncertain, date was bound to have an immediate impact on agents' behavior and, most likely result . . . in an immediate decline of the exchange rate itself (in a flexible rate system) and on the price level (in a flexible and fixed exchange rate regime)" (Faini and Toniolo 1992, 132).

Kin Kaikin Ronso *(Controversies over the Return to Gold Standard)*[9]

Japan suspended the gold standard on September 12, 1917, when the United States joined World War I, and returned to it on January 11, 1930. However, in the meantime, there was a constant discussion about the desirability and timing and method of returning to the standard. The controversy erupted after the United States returned to it sooner than other countries, on June 9, 1919. The controversy continued with a shifting emphasis on and connections to the major issues of the Japanese economy. Finally, the Hamaguchi cabinet decided to return to the standard, and they implemented it, yet the controversy did not end; rather, it continued more fiercely with the arrival of the Great Depression, with the controversy coming to an end when Finance Minister Korekiyo Takahashi of the Inukai cabinet resuspended the gold standard on December 13, 1931, and engaged in a full-fledged reflation policy in November 1932.

To understand this controversy, it is necessary to understand the atmosphere of the age. Secular stagnation with mild deflation dominated the public perception of the performance of the Japanese economy: countercyclical measures taken during the period were considered to bring forth "*Zaisei no Homanka* (irresponsible fiscal spending)," with the BOJ becoming "*Kyusai Ginko* (the bank for bailouts)" and the economy becoming "*Ibi Shochin* (despondent)." As other great powers such as the United States, Germany, the United Kingdom, and France returned to the gold standard, people felt frustration. The controversy reflected the people's frustration. The development of media, newspapers, and magazines grew rapidly in this period, providing a lively arena for debate and potential power to influence policy through the public opinion.

Kin Kaikin Ronso was a part of the global controversy on the gold standard. This was the burgeoning period for the emergence of macroeconomics: the interwar experience of rapid changes in the price level and exchange rates brought insights into the theory of the price and exchange rate determination. The information set available to economists was changing constantly. The gold standard was a good example. As the gold standard was the pillar of the "age of globalization" (James 2001) from the 1880s to World War I, it was an integral part and parcel of the "orthodoxy." Yet, in light of the interwar and other experiences, several prominent economists such as John Maynard Keynes, Irving Fisher, and Gustav Cassel began to discuss serious defects in the gold standard. Indeed, what was to be called macroeconomics emerged out of these discussions. Therefore, even though the gold standard was still part of the "orthodoxy," it had been increasingly examined and questioned.

Britain received the most attention from the participants of *Kin Kaikin Ronso*. Although that country's status was shaken, it was still a center of international economic relationships and the model country for Japan to emulate. There was a debate in Britain when it went back to the gold standard. The context is similar to that of Japan: Britain suffered a sluggish economy after the war, and the government and the Bank of England decided to return to the gold standard. The major opponent to the return was John Maynard Keynes, who pointed out the problems in terms of price stability (Keynes 1923): The gold standard puts a priority on the exchange rate stability over the price stability; however, fluctuations in the price level cause a discrepancy between nominal and real values. Neither inflation nor deflation is desirable, yet deflation would raise the real interest rate and real wages, squeezing the profit rate, resulting in stagnant enterprise and increased unemployment. The return to the gold standard at the prewar parity required a deflationary policy, which would be problematic. If the return is necessary, the British government should choose devaluation over deflation.

When Britain returned to the gold standard in April 1925, Keynes wrote the *Economic Consequences of Mr. Churchill* in June (Keynes 1926): the subject of this pamphlet was the attack on liquidationism. He repudiated Churchill's argument that the return to the gold standard at the prewar parity would liquidate inefficient industries such as coal mining, arguing that liquidation of an individual industry would not solve the slump when the overall economy was in recession. The pamphlet was soon translated into Japanese (Matsukata 1926), Later, Keynes became more cautious about proposing the deliberate devaluation policy, trying to find the best solution within the gold standard constraint. However, Keynes's activities and works became well known to Japan, including his *Treatise on Money* (Keynes 1930) and *The Report on the Macmillan Committee*, released in July 1931.

Another important source of information was the United States: the United States returned to the gold standard in 1919 and experienced a prosperous time during the most of 1920s, despite a sharp, severe, albeit short, recession immediately after the return. Japan looked to Britain as their model for the return, but after the onset of the Great Depression, the United States received a great deal of attention, along with Irving Fisher's reflation policy. Fisher has been the foremost proponent of price stabilization; in *The Purchasing Power of Money*, he proposed the improvement of the gold standard (Fisher [1911] 1997, chap. 13). He supported Keynes's works, and he expressed doubts about the gold standard from a price stability perspective in his *Money Illusion* (Fisher 1928): Fisher argued that neither inflation nor deflation was desirable to manage the use of credit; however, under the gold standard, the quantity of money was limited by the amount of gold. To counter this problem, he contemplated a shift to the managed currency system through the abolition of the gold standard. Although at this point he was opposed to the abolition since he was not sure about the disciplinary mechanism to properly restrain the issue of money, he suggested suspending the standard during emergencies. He would later recommend the suspension of the gold standard in 1932 when the depression deepened. Fisher (1928) was translated to Japanese in 1929 by a BOJ official, with a preface by Eigo Fukai, then deputy governor of the BOJ.

The third eminent source of information was Swedish economist Gustav Cassel.[10] Internationally known as the proponent of the purchasing power parity theory of the exchange rate, he was the most active public intellectual and policy entrepreneur economist before the rise of Keynes; Cassel attended the 1920 Brussel conference and the 1922 Genoa conference. After World War I, he also emphasized the problems of both inflation and deflation in his works, with the aim of price stability (Cassel 1921, 1922). According to him, the main purpose of the 1922 Genoa conference was achieving price stability and allowing devaluation, not returning to the gold standard per se (Cassel 1924, 175). His interpretation was not necessarily shared by others. Nevertheless, it is important to note that there were alternatives to the return at the prewar parity. Ironically, Cassel endorsed the British return to the prewar parity based on his observation that the ongoing exchange rate was sufficiently approaching the prewar parity (Cassel 1924, 174). However, in 1926, when he advised Japan (Cassel 1926), he considered devaluation more meritorious than the return at the prewar parity with deflation, whose implementation would be painful. Cassel (1926) was translated into Japanese by the Research Division of the BOJ.[11]

Of course, there were proponents of the return at the prewar parity among economists such as Edwin Cannan and T. E. Gregory at the London School of Economics. There were also economists who were ambiguous. However, even Gregory had to admit that Keynes, Cassel, and Fisher were exerting a great deal of influence in the economics academia (Gregory 1924). The opinions on the gold standard were evolving, and the alternatives to the return at the prewar parity were available. It is against this background that the controversy in Japan happened.

Kyu Heika Kaikin-ha *(The Prewar Parity Group)*

The majority of the Japanese policymakers, business people, academic and business economists, and journalists were decidedly in favor of the return at the prewar parity. They were called *Kyu Heika Kaikin-ha* (the Prewar Parity Group). The most famous politician who promoted the prewar parity return was Junnosuke Inoue, who became the government spokesman for the prewar parity return, but he was not a strong proponent before his appointment. During the 1920s, most politicians favored the prewar parity return in varying degrees. Among the two major parties, the Minseito politicians were more favorable toward the return, while the Seiyukai were less so. Korekiyo Takahashi, who as finance minister subdued the financial panic of 1927, was reluctant to return to the prewar parity.

It was quite remarkable that two representative academic economists of the 1920s, Tokuzo Fukuda (Tokyo College of Commerce) and Hajime Kawakami (Imperial University of Kyoto) were in favor of the prewar parity return. Although Fukuda was cautious about the return in the beginning, he changed his mind around 1925, supporting the return at the old parity. The main reason, according to him, was the existence of huge "nonperforming loans," which he believed made the monetary policy of the BOJ ineffective. Promoting *Zaikai Seiri* (liquidation of the economy) was a necessary policy. On the other hand, he became very critical of the advocates of the return to the gold standard at a new parity. They "want to return to the standard, without having pains which the Japanese economy should feel in due course. These pains should be felt one way or another. To avoid such pains would only prolong the solution. The important task at hand is to ease, diffuse and lessen the pains within what we could bear upon. The contractionary policy [of the Hamaguchi cabinet] is the most appropriate way for that purpose" (Fukuda 1930, 242). He also criticized those advocates of the return at a new parity who learned much from Keynes and Cassel, probably having in mind people like Ishibashi: "The unemployment problem in Great Britain only applies to Great Britain, not to the rest of the world, and not to Japan at all" (Fukuda 1930, 242). The root cause of the stagnation of the Japanese economy was its *Strukturwandle* (structural change). But "in this country there are many of those who have a blind faith in Keynes and Cassel. As for the current problem of the return, there are those who advocate the return at the new parity, relying on Keynes' pamphlet or Professor Cassel's purchasing power parity over and over again, like the same old tune" (Fukuda 1930, 222–223).

Kawakami changed his mind more drastically than Fukuda. Before he became the most well-known Marxian economist, he was the one of the first to introduce I. Fisher's theory to Japan in 1913. However, after he converted to a full-fledge Marxian economics, he insisted that a depression was an inevitable and integral part of capitalism and that countercyclical measures were futile since a recession would cleanse inefficiency of the economy out. As for the gold standard, it was an indispensable part of capitalism; therefore, its abolition was impossible within capitalism. During this period before the state censorship began, there was a strong Marxian influence among the economic academia and in media discourse. Most Marxians subscribed to a perfect combination of the gold standard mentality and liquidationism.

Turning to business economists, Teiji Katsuta (1893–1955) is probably the best representative of the advocates of the return to the standard at the prewar parity. Katsuta was the director of economic research at the Nomura Securities and the director of the Business Cycle Research Institute at *Jiji Shimpo*. He wrote extensively, and his economic thought favored a typical combination of the gold standard mentality and liquidationism. For him, the nature of the return lay in its international aspect: it should be seen "externally as the first step to constitute the world economy," and its purpose was the "internationalization of the business community through the globalization of the value of the currency" (Katsuta 1929, 5–6). The return was inseparable from *Zaikai Seiri*, criticizing *Shin Heika Kaikin-ha* (new parity return group), those who advocated the return at the new parity: Katsuta rightly believed that they separated the gold standard and *Zaikai Seiri*.

What was *Zaikai Seiri* then? It comprised the "advancement, control, and globalization of the economy," where the advancement meant concentration, industrialization, and selection of small and medium size firms; control meant cartelization and monopolization; and globalization and meant adjustments to global prices, price levels, interest rates, wages, and world markets. The return to the gold standard would enable the Japanese economy to achieve them. Even though he emphasized that *Zaikai Seiri* was distinct from the "contraction of the economy," he thought the contraction was inevitable since the Japanese economy had been "pathologically bloated" by the postwar boom: this "bubble," or "vain wealth," was brought forth by exorbitantly increased land prices and loans from banks that lent out based on land collateral. It was, so went the argument, necessary to correct this "irrationality," and the "return is only way to burst this bubble and correct the economy" (Katsuta 1929, 167). In a nutshell, *Zaikai Seiri* was Katsuta's liquidationism.

Noteworthy was the fact that Katsuta was well aware of the deleterious effects of the return at the prewar parity: he knew nominal rigidities such as factor prices and debt would slow down the adjustment process. Nevertheless, he dismissed them as a matter of "time lag," hoping for the return to bring "*zaikai seiri*" effects, for "stabilization and opportunity for further growth would be gained after" sacrifices (Katsuta 1929, 66). He never doubted that a recession had an equilibrating effect. However, Japan was not ready for the return to the gold standard. Therefore, people "had to be ready for a crisis in a country like Japan, which has been marred by irrationality and bloating" (Katsuta 1929, 66). Thus, concluded he, an economic crisis was not an evil;

rather, it offered the best opportunity to promote "*zaikai seiri*." Later, he would say that he wanted to facilitate the crisis in the midst of the Great Depression.

Shin Heika Kaikin-ha (The New Parity Return Group)

Those who opposed to the prewar parity return were called *Shin Heika Kaikin-ha*. They were decidedly a minority group. They did include several powerful business people and academic economists, but the core members of *Shin Heika Kaikin-ha* were the group of economic journalists, the so-called "Toyo Keizai Shimpo Ippa (Toyo Kezai Shimpo group)." Their high reputation in history is now rightly secured precisely because of their activities against the return to the gold standard at the prewar parity, but at the time, their reputation was not high, as the main proponent Tanzan Ishibashi himself recalled (Ogura 1955, 402). One Ministry of Finance (MOF) bureaucrat, Kazuo Aoki, who was the secretary to Finance Minister Inoue, thought the new parity return group did not have any influence on the public opinion (Ando 1965, vol. I, 75). It should be noted that the media these journalists worked for were small in circulations.

The group consisted of four prominent economic journalists, Tanzan Ishibashi, Kamekichi Takahashi, Toshie Obama, and Seijun Yamazaki. The central figure of the group was Tanzan Ishibashi (1884–1973), who was the proprietor, president, and editor-in-chief of *Toyo Keizai Shimpo* from December 1926 to May 1946. As the editor in chief, he confronted both the gold standard mentality and liquidationism during the debate. First, he did not consider the gold standard as essentially desirable: it just happened to have worked well so far. The managed currency system was desirable. Although there might be a concern about the loss of discipline under the managed currency, the problem could be dealt with when the institution for the control of money was properly organized: as long as it was not dominated by the government, the value of the currency would be stabilized.

Second, he criticized liquidationism. Ishibashi detected in the economic policy of Hamaguchi and Inoue a notion that a boom was a "vain and wrong thing." They "misconstrue that sound economy and finance would be born out of a recession." But a recession meant not using labor, the true source of wealth; thus it must be considered the "worst evil in human society" (Ishibashi 1970–1972, vol. 7, 519). How, then, can "a human society . . . sustain a boom"? He answered that "one can sustain a boom, or eliminate a recession so much, only by minimizing the fluctuations in the value of a currency." His arguments revealed how deeply Ishibashi learned from economists like Fisher and Keynes: he endorsed the idea of economic stabilization through price stabilization.

Ishibashi used his status as a proprietor of a media company to its greatest advantage. Using his own media, he edited his weekly magazine *Toyo Keizai Shimpo* in his own line, although he welcomed and invited the opinions of the opponents. He also encouraged translations of articles from foreign sources, facilitating the dissemination of precise information. Furthermore, he organized many *Zadan kai* (roundtable discussions) in magazine and lecture tours all over the country with other three proponents to further promote his cause.

The second most important among the group was Kamekichi Takahashi (1891–1977), who was an ex-colleague of Ishibashi's. He became famous as a freelance economic commentator, energetically engaging in almost all problems of the Japanese economy during the period. This in part explains some of his inconsistencies: he toyed with the idea of "structural deflation" argument reminiscent of that of the 2000s in the sense that deflation was caused by the post-World War I reentrance of Europe, Russia, and China and was thus "permanent" by nature (Takahashi 1931a). He declared that Japan needed a reduction in real wages and even "Zaikai Seiri" for Japan to adapt itself to the new, changed world. Therefore, he partly subscribed to liquidationism. However, he was different from other commentators like Katsuta in his attention to macroeconomic stability: he was the one to persuade Ishibashi to convert to the new parity return side in 1924. When the Hamaguchi-Inoue deflation hit the economy, he would argue that "Zaikai Seiri" was necessary, but it would not proceed under a deflationary recession; therefore, the government had to change from contractionary policies to reflation policies by suspending the gold standard once again (Takahashi 1930b).

Two other journalists, Toshie Obama (1889–1972) and Seijun Yamazaki (1894–1966), came to the new parity return camp independent of Ishibashi and Takahashi, but their paths eventually converged. Obama was the director of the Economic Section of the *Chugai Shogyo Shimpo*, later to be *Nihon Keizai Shimbun*. Obama changed his mind around 1929 when he listened to Fukai Eigo's public lecture. Upon listening to the lecture, Obama became aware of the pains associated with the return to the gold standard at the pre-war parity and skeptical about it. Yamazaki, who became the director of Economic Section of *Yomiuri Shimbun* and who was Obama's friend, changed his mind around the same time as Obama did. He wrote an insightful and penetrating analysis of the debate.

Issues in the Controversy

The issues surrounding the gold standard controversy changed during the 1920s and 1930s. But there was a basic pattern: the return to the gold standard was considered as the "fundamental solution" to a wide variety of problems at the time, such as fluctuations of the exchange rate and inflation. After the financial panic of 1927, it was expected to be the solution to the long stagnation. There were also practical needs for it. With other major powers returning to the gold standard, there was a growing pressure exerted on Japan to do likewise. Furthermore, Japan's *Zaigai Seika*, species reserved abroad, rapidly declined due to the current account deficit.[12] The overall majority felt compelled to return to the gold standard. The remaining questions were the timing and the parity.

Why was the prewar parity desirable? During the long controversy, the reasons shifted, but there were four of them. First was the stability of the exchange rate. Almost no one contested its desirability. Before the major powers returned to the gold standard, some economists such as Keynes considered managed currency desirable, yet even he stopped proposing it after the *Tract on Monetary Reform* (Keynes 1923). Second was deflation. The prewar parity return meant the appreciation of the yen; therefore, it would require deflation and reduction of domestic production costs by contractionary fiscal and monetary policies. There was a perception that Japan's price level was a lot higher than the "international price level," thus deflation by means of the return to the gold standard was considered as an "adjustment to the international price level" (Tokyo Shogyo Kaigisho 1927, 7–8). Against the background was a further concern that Japan's international competitiveness had declined since the current account deficit widened. It was argued that deliberate deflation would induce the reduction in production costs, which would in turn restore Japan's international competitiveness. It should also be recalled that people remembered high domestic inflation and hyperinflation in mid-European countries vividly: these experiences strengthened people's aversion to inflation. Third was "sentiment and face." When Eigo Fukai gave a speech at Osaka in 1928, he said the following, having in mind the argument by the new parity return: "if we devalue the currency when we return to the gold standard, we can avoid its [deleterious] effects. But the benefits and costs of devaluation are very complicated. Also there is a sentiment and face other than cool benefit and cost calculation. Therefore, one cannot conclude hastily that devaluation is meritorious especially under the condition now that the current exchange rate does not diverge from the legal parity" (Fukai 1928, 121). The return to the gold standard was perceived as the "global trend" (Tokyo Shogyo Kaigisyo 1927, 1). After the United States returned to the gold standard in 1919, the United Kingdom and the pound sterling area returned to the gold standard at the prewar parity in 1925, and France decided to return to the standard in 1926, implementing it in 1928. These international actions combined with the gold standard mentality created an economic environment in which Japan had no choice but to return to the gold standard at the prewar parity.

Fourth, the recessionary effects of the prewar parity return to the gold standard were well understood among the proponents. Junnosuke Inoue warned against the new parity group: "If we could return to the gold standard without feeling any pains and damages, Japan would not have suffered for the past 12 years" (Inoue 1929, 104). And here one can detect the influence of liquidationism. On the basis of this perception, some argued for the countermeasure for unemployment. Seibi Hijikata, professor of economics at the Tokyo Imperial University, argued that even though we required liquidation, we should attend to the "pains" associated with the return (Hijikata 1929). However, as Yamazaki discerned, there were others who liked to punish those who profited from the boom: "They should suffer. The Japanese business community has been irresponsible since the war time. Thus only after great sufferings comes the rationalization of the business community" (Yamazaki 1929b, 95). Liquidationism had a moralistic appeal.

Later, during the Great Depression, some commentators such as Katsuta emphasized the cleansing effect of a panic. To promote *zaikai seiri* thoroughly, he argued that one has to maintain the prewar parity and have a panic to liquidate. During the depression, he said, "I want to promote the Great Depression greatly" (Nihon Ginko Chosa Kyoku 1968, 23, 621).

The new parity return group countered the prewar parity arguments as follows. First, the exchange rate stability was desirable, but the new parity return would serve that purpose better than the prewar parity return because raising the exchange rate could destabilize the exchange rate movement. Second, deflation was as much an evil as inflation, a point most clearly enunciated by Ishibashi. He declared that a hope for deflation was a "fallacy" (Ishibashi 1970–72, 6, 3–11). It would take longer time to adjust to deflation, and deflation would clash with nominal rigidities, thus stagnating corporate profits and the employment and income of the people. As for "international competitiveness," the prewar parity group confused internal value (expressed in terms of the domestic currency) with external value (expressed in terms of a foreign currency): the new parity return (devaluation) could restore "international competitiveness" without a decrease in the price level (deflation), an insight based on an understanding of the contemporary discussions in Western economics. Third, Yamazaki thought the "sentiment and face" argument was the "only and most powerful argument," hinting that there was no powerful "economic argument." However, he flatly denied it as a "useless" one (Yamazaki 1929a, 148): as France had done before, the new parity return was accepted. Of course, Japan was not as heavily damaged by the war as France was, but Japan went off the gold standard for more than a decade and experienced a financial panic. Considering the damage done to the economy by the prewar return, Japan could have chosen devaluation. As for the fourth point, Yamazaki said as follows:

> An idea that some pressure would be suffice to improve the Japanese industry applies only to the situation when the business community needs minor loss cut and liquidation; it would not apply to the period when one needs a major transformation of organizations and methods. If we can apply this idea, it follows that occasional appreciations would develop our industry. But no one would believe such a ridiculous idea. (Yamazaki 1929a, 151–152)

The Japanese business and the people who work in it would be affected: "the prewar parity return looks like justice since it brings sufferings, but it is indeed just the opposite of justice" (Yamazaki 1929a, 148). Also, as Ishibashi and Kamekichi Takahashi argued, even though *zaikai seiri* was necessary, the Japanese economy was too weakened to carry it out: it would require the new parity return to implement *saikai seiri*.

III. "Opening Up the Window into Storm"

The Hamaguchi-Inoue Deflation

Osachi Hamaguchi formed a government on July 2, 1929. Among the ten-point program of the Hamaguchi cabinet, point four "new thinking in diplomacy toward China" and point five "promotion of arms reduction" were about diplomacy and foreign relationship; points six through eight were about the economy, point eight being "resolute return to the gold standard"; and point nine was "social policy." Overall, the plan was to join the Washington-Genoa regime fully. Also, the cabinet understood the negative impacts of the prewar parity well, so the ten-point program included a social policy to deal with the unemployment. The appointment of Baron Kijyuro Shidehara as foreign minister and Junnosuke Inoue as finance minister revealed the nature of the Hamaguchi cabinet.[13]

The cabinet decided the prewar parity return in November 1929 and implemented it on January 11, 1930. Its economic policy was enthusiastically welcomed by the general public. Hamaguchi held the general election in February 1930, the governing *Minseito* winning 273 seats out of 466. This 57 seat gain from the last general election in 1928 gave Hamaguchi and Inoue a firm mandate for a return to the prewar parity.[14]

Shortly after the announcement of the decision, stock price went up, but it soon plunged back. The real gross domestic product (GDP) growth rate was virtually zero for 1930. It has been argued that the decision was ill timed and unlucky. Later, Inoue himself referred to it (Inoue 1930, 35–36), but this was not consistent with his "*zaikai seiri*," or liquidationist, position since he should have welcomed the cleansing effects of the depression. Indeed, it was suggested that Inoue actually welcomed the arrival of the Great Depression. As a testament to this perception, Inoue also argued that the recession was not as severe as it would have been without the prewar parity return (Inoue 1930, 29–30). He warned against a policy backlash: "if we prohibit the free exportation of gold, the exchange rate would plunge and bring a grave concern to the economy" (Inoue 1930, 54). He preached "nation's belief during recession time": "boom and recession happen for a wide variety of reasons and they come and go. Those who reap the benefit most during boom are those who have prepared in recession." During recession time, "people have to do whatever they have to do their best" (Inoue 1930, 62).

In reality, the government and the business community engaged in several countermeasures against the depression. Mergers and acquisitions among firms were encouraged, and the government-sponsored banks made loans to firms in need. The BOJ even lowered its interest rate. Within the government, *Shoko-sho* (the Ministry of Commerce and Industry, precursor to the Ministry of Trade and Industry) gained power. From 1929 to 1930, 19 cartels sprang up. The business community demanded that the government act as an "enforcer" to punish cartel outsiders rather than break the cartels. The landmark 1931 *Juyo Sangyo Tosei Ho* (Strategic Industries Control Act) was the legislation to control cartel breaking. Rajan and Zingales (2008) described the institutional dynamics during the Great Depression: the interests of corporations strengthened the control and regulation by the government. The same pattern happened in Japan: the interests of bureaucrats and those of the business community coincided to strengthen the control and restrict the competition.

New policy was accompanied by new policy ideas. The words "*Sangyo Gorika* (industrial rationalization)" became increasingly popular. Originally a German concept advanced by Walther Rathenau during the early 1920s, this idea did not appeal to the Japanese before the depression: after the depression, it appealed to the Japanese because this also meant mergers and acquisitions, and cartelization. Another idea in vogue was *Tosei Keizai Ron* (arguments for the controlled economy).

Over Kinyushutsu Saikinshi *(Resuspension of the Gold Standard)*

As Japan returned to the gold standard, the controversy changed its focus to the possible resuspension and the new parity afterward. The book by Teiji Katsuta and Kamekichi Takahashi, titled *Two Debates on the Desirability of the*

Re-suspension (Katsuta and Takahashi 1931), shows a milieu of this period. Originally featured in the Japanese newspaper *Jiji Shimpo*, the book comprised the articles and rebuttals by two journalists in an alternating order. Takahashi argued for the resuspension for three reasons. First, the Japanese economy had not yet adjusted to the violent change in the value of the currency caused by the return. Prices fell, but the production costs did not fall due to nominal rigidities; therefore, the firms lost their profits. On the other hand, the value of assets fell drastically, while the value of debts remained intact. Takahashi asked what policy was better than the resuspension under the circumstances. Second, *zaikai seiri* or reconstruction of the national economy would not be possible under the gold standard at the prewar parity. The economy might recover due to the recovery of the U.S. economy, but it could not be reliable (Katsuta and Takahashi 1931, 5). Third, resuspension and devaluation was to build a foundation for the recovery, enabling Japan to tackle "other fundamental measures" (Katsuta and Takahashi 1931, 6). However, the devaluation argument did not imply that Japan "needed no other policies or opposed to them" (Katsuta and Takahashi 1931, 23). Then Takahashi turned to the criticisms directed toward the resuspension argument. What he stressed most was that the resuspension and devaluation was not an inflationary policy: its purpose was to return to the economy as it was before deflation. He must have taken into account the public's anti-inflation sentiment. Also, he was right since devaluation policy did not allow further inflation.

Katsuta questioned the "abstract" and "ideational" nature and the "feasibility" of the new parity argument, allowing its theoretical validity. He admitted that "the previous opponents took the position of denying its theoretical effects, but that is a ridiculous argument. There is nothing wrong with their theoretical effects" (Katsuta and Takahashi 1931, 63). However, the proponents of devaluation explained only the new parity devaluation's "theoretical effects," not "the process through which these effects would materialize at all, technical difficulties of its implementation, and other measures." Katsuta's criticisms consisted of five parts. First, the new parity argument was based on the "mechanistic view of the business community," which did not fit into the "organic reality of the business community" (Katsuta and Takahashi 1931, 52). He stressed that the proponents of the new parity did not consider unintended effects by devaluation. Second, he attacked the idea that prices were determined by purchasing power parity, for it was an abstract concept, and there was no equilibrium (Katsuta and Takahashi 1931, 53). Third, he attacked its feasibility: "the devaluation would have an impact only when it is implemented suddenly, but it could not be done that way for all technical reasons." Fourth, Katsuta made the case that when devaluation was announced, it would "induce a panic beforehand with a rise in the interest rate, the fall in corporate bonds price, the fall in bank stock price, and the withdrawal of bank deposits."[15] Last, Japan's devaluation was purported to end deflationary depression, which was different from those executed in other European countries.

During this period, the focus of the controversy changed. Even the opponents could not counter the devaluation and new parity arguments theoretically. Therefore, their criticisms were directed against the feasibility and potential risks, as Katsuta argued. On the other hand, the new parity group had to argue cautiously that their policy was not inflationary. The public was still afraid of inflation amid deflation. Katsuta attacked an ambiguity in Takahashi's concept of inflation precisely because he thought that was the weakness of the new parity and devaluation argument.

V. The Takahashi Great Escape

Turning Point, 1931

The year 1931 was the turning point for the world economy. It was the year that a recession turned into the Great Depression. The direct cause was a series of financial and currency crises (Temin 1989, lecture 2; James 2001, chap. 2). As a fixed exchange system, the gold standard was likely to induce currency crises. It started with Austria in May when Kredit Anstalt, the biggest bank in Austria, went bankrupt. Then after the German financial sector was destabilized in July, a currency attack was mounted on the British pound sterling in August. Eventually, Britain gave up defending the indefensible and left the gold standard on September 21. The United States raised its discount rate to defend the dollar, contracting the economy further, while in hindsight there was no need to raise the discount rate. The Great Depression had begun.

The next target was Japan, and the speculative attack mounted against the yen. Finance Minister Inoue tried to defend the yen vehemently, yet that resulted in a depletion of the gold reserves. He denounced this speculation as *doru gai* (purchasing dollar) in moralistic terms, and his criticism of the *Zaibatsu* (Japanese conglomerate) generated anti-Zaibatsu, antibusiness sentiments among the general public, leading to political assassinations and coup attempts.[16] Needless to say, the speculative attack on the yen was rational behavior on the investors' part; therefore, the attack continued.

In the end, this currency crisis left Japan with no choice but to suspend the gold standard. Yet, there were two differences from the British case. One was the continuity of the controversy regarding the gold standard. The controversy had been over in Britain when Britain left the gold standard, while it was still hotly debated in Japan. The second difference was Inoue's stubbornness. The impending currency crisis should have forced Japan to change course immediately, but Inoue refused to follow the British example. Just at the same when Britain left the gold standard, the Mukden (Manchurian) Incident happened on September 18, 1931. This was a deliberate attempt by some faction of the Japanese military to challenge the establishment. Many thought that it was a perfect moment to change course, but Inoue did not act on any advice given to him. The military pressured the government in another form: in March and October, the attempted coup plans of army officers were exposed (the March and October Incidents).

Ultimately, it was politics that changed the course. The Imperial Diet members of the opposition party, *Rikken Seiyukai*, announced a resolution to suspend the gold standard on November 11, 1931,[17] yet on the same day, Inoue released his own statement, expressing his determination to maintain the gold standard. However, one minister in the Wakatsuki cabinet, Kenzo Adachi, revolted against the cabinet policy: he was trying to make a grand coalition with *Rikken Seiyukai* in favor of the suspension of the gold standard. Prime Minister Wakatsuki had to dissolve his cabinet on December 11, 1931.

On December 13, the new government was formed by *Rikken Seiyukai*, headed by Tsuyoshi Inukai, who appointed Korekiyo Takahashi as finance minister. On the same day, Takahashi suspended the gold standard on the advice from Eigo Fukai. This marked the beginning of the *Takahashi Zaisei* period, which would last until February 26, 1936.[18]

Toward Reflation Policies

Japan's "golden fetter" was broken. The exchange rate plunged by 40 percent, deflation stopped almost immediately, and stock prices jumped up. But Takahashi did not pursue any further policy action: even he thought the suspension was a temporary emergency measure. A couple of month after the suspension, deflation resumed and stock prices and production began falling (see Figure 4-1).[19]

The controversy over the gold standard continued with a change in emphasis. The suspension was no longer an issue, and the *Shin Kaikin-ha* wanted further policy actions, specifically, "reflation" policies. The word "reflation" had already been circulated before the spring of 1932.[20] In March and May, Tanzan Ishibashi wrote a long article titled "The Meanings, Method, and Effects of Inflation" (Ishibashi 1970–1972, vol.8) in his *Toyo Keizai Shimpo*. First, he answered the question of why a certain degree of inflation was necessary. He gave two reasons: (1) to restore the balance to the "great imbalance" between credit and debt caused by the "current financial disaster"; and (2) to

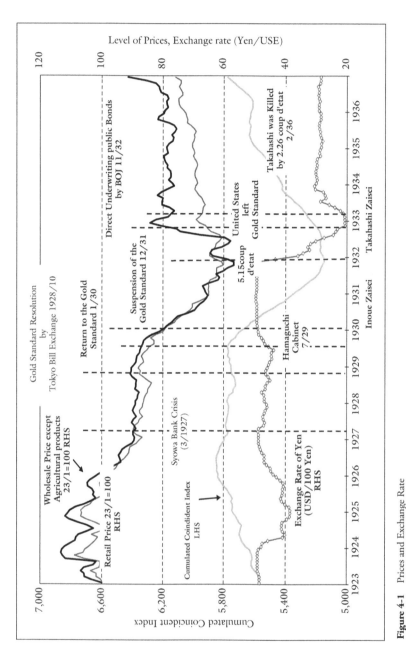

Figure 4-1 Prices and Exchange Rate

Source: Iwata et al. 2008. Reproduced with the permission of Gaskuhuin Daigaku Keizai Gakkai.

rescue the situation in which production stagnated and "people and facilities are left to idle fruitlessly." It should be noted that he wrote this article almost at the same time that Irving Fisher conceived of the debt-deflation theory of great depressions, with its emphasis on credit and debt (Fisher 1932, 1933). A certain degree of inflation was necessary to achieve the "normal course of economic activities," and Ishibashi warned that inflation here should not be taken as "supplying more money than needed to the development of economic activity." Reflation was the "stabilization (of the price), or inflation needed to compensate the damages caused by deflation" (Ishibashi 1970–1972, vol.8, 441–442). In modern parlance, his reflation was price level targeting like Fisher's.[21]

Second, Ishibashi articulated specific policy measures, citing three: interest rate policy by the BOJ, the open market operation policy by the BOJ, and fiscal policy by the government. Although he admitted fiscal policy, the government's purchase of goods and services to stimulate demand, had a large impact in theory, he thought that it was less likely that "the government project can be implemented in a sufficient scale, on time, and wisely, to stimulate the economy" (Ishibashi 1970–1972, vol.8, 448). He concluded that fiscal policy was not reliable. Furthermore, he understood that fiscal policy alone would not generate inflation: unless the BOJ bought government bonds, the amount of money would not increase, and without the increased money supply, there would be no inflation. Therefore, he preferred monetary policy by the BOJ, preferring an open market policy as the more direct one.

Third, Ishibashi elaborated the channels through which reflation policies worked by way of answering three criticisms direct against them. It also revealed what was discussed in popular economic discourse. Ishibashi encountered "numerous denunciations or hostile questions" against reflation policies, yet he said that "they are repeating what I have already answered without a thought." The first question is whether increased money supply would raise the prices. Ishibashi understood the concern that there was a prevalent "lack of confidence," so the very purpose of reflation policies was to ease this concern and generate some "hope" for the future. The effects might not work out soon but "would work as a cause and an effect cumulatively," with a change in price expectation and the onset of actual inflation.

The second question was related to Hajime Kawakami's question. Kawakami, the most renowned Marxian economist of the day, wrote a trenchant critique of relation policies in 1932 for *Toyo Keizai Shimpo* upon the invitation of Ishibashi (Kawakami 1982–1986, vol.19, 360–379). Kawakami picked up the "contradiction in capitalism": "capitalism necessarily requires a metal-based monetary standard," yet capitalists had to abandon that standard for the survival of capitalism. He also thought the real purchasing power of the workers would not rise since the rise in nominal income prices would be exactly offset by an increase in the price level. Furthermore, he attributed the cause of the depression to overproduction; therefore, "liquidation" (*Zaikai seiri*) was necessary as a remedy, while the price level in Japan was higher than the international price standard, which should fall to the prewar level. Kawakami combined the gold standard mentality and liquidationism perfectly. As such, he even lamented the death of Junnosuke Inoue since for Kawakami this meant that Japan lost a doctor who prescribed the right remedy for the disease. Ishibashi countered Kawakami's presumption: if wages rose exactly as much as the price level rose, workers' conditions per worker would remain the same, yet through reflation, the number of workers would increase; therefore, the workers as a whole would enjoy higher purchasing power.[22] In contrast to Kawakami who asserted the end of the Japanese economy as a fate, Ishibashi hoped that reflation policy would "save life which might be lost."

The third question involved hyperinflation. Ishibashi thought that hyper-inflation in Germany after World War I resulted from the "fiscal need for emergencies." What he proposed was different in that "its limitation has been set beforehand." Reflation could be controlled by the government or the central bank. "Those who insist that inflation would not stop after it begins do not think seriously" (Ishibashi 1970–1972, vol.8, 463). At this juncture, Ishibashi considered the present situation as the "transition phase" where inflation did not yet materialize, but an increased money supply was generating inflationary expectations: "the power of inflation has not yet stimulated firms, therefore it has not raised workers' income. Yet merchants and industrialists are anticipating inflation, accumulating the inventories and purchasing raw materials" (Ishibashi 1970–1972, vol.8, 463). In order to bring inflation from inflationary expectations, a "persistent" monetary expansion was required.

Two-Step Regime Shift: What Korekiyo Takahashi Did

One week after the last installment of Ishibashi's article appeared, Prime Minister Inukai was assassinated in another coup attempt on May 15 (the May 15 Incident). The government had already discussed possible actions within the government, and the discussion between the MOF and the BOJ accelerated. On November 25, 1932, the BOJ announced its direct underwriting of Japanese government bonds.[23] The performance was impressive: from 1932 to 1935, the average annual real GDP growth rate was 7.2 percent, and the average inflation rate was 2 percent (see Table 4-1). In international comparisons, Japan also fared better. The price level rose (Figure 4-2), and industrial production in Japan grew more than in other countries (Figure 4-3).

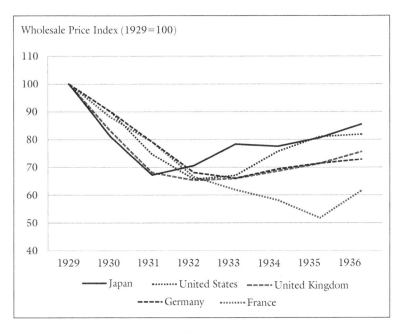

Figure 4-2 Wholesale Price Index during the Great Depression
Source: Data from Bernanke (2000a, 81).

Romer 2012 emphasized that ending the Great Depression required a regime shift. According to Iwata et al. (2008), the Takahashi reflation was a two-step regime shift. The first shift was going off the gold standard in December 1931. The second regime shift happened in 1932, regarding the BOJ's direct underwriting of Japanese Government Bond (*Chokusetsu Hikiuke*). Iwata, Okada, Adachi, and Iida held that the "change of the policy regime to a reflationary regime would first raise the expected rate of inflation, which in turn would raise stock and land prices, and then the actual rate of inflation. Finally, both the nominal and the real rate of economic growth would rise" (Iwata et al. 2008, 160). More specifically, according to Okada and Iida's (2004) study, which estimated the expected inflation rate and the expected real interest rate, the expected inflation rate jumped up in September 1931 and April 1932 (Figure 4-4): the former coincided with the British suspension of the gold standard and the outbreak of the Mukden Incident, which strengthened the public perception that Japan's departure from the gold standard was inevitable; the latter coincided with when Takahashi began talking about the direct underwriting of the JGBs, in March 1932.

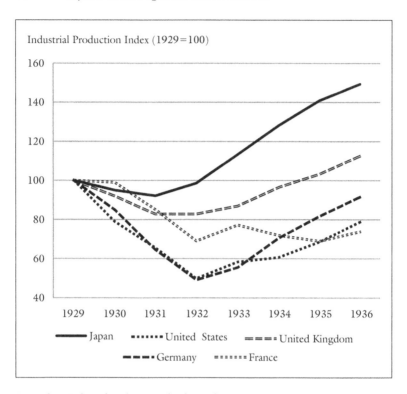

Figure 4-3 Industrial Production Index during the Great Depression
Source: Data from Bernanke (2000a, 83).

Later Chokusetsu Hikiuke, the BOJ's direct underwriting of JGBs, became severely criticized because it was abused by the military to support the war efforts, but as Figure 4-5 shows, Takahashi kept the ratio of public bonds held by the BOJ under control: 90 percent of the bonds underwritten by the BOJ were sold to the market so that the BOJ continued to control the base money.

Accordingly, Takahashi conducted fiscal policy carefully. First, he increased public expenditures but did not raise taxes. In January 21, 1932, he announced the postponement of Inoue's planned tax increase for the 1932 fiscal year: Takahashi was concerned with the damaged state of the economy, and he concentrated his efforts on recovering it. Net public expenditures amounted to around 3 percent of Japan's gross national product (GNP) in 1932 and 1933, the highest among the advanced economies (Shizume 2009, 141). Second, even though the budget deficit grew, Takahashi resisted pressures from the MOF bureaucrats to raise taxes: one MOF bureaucrat recalled

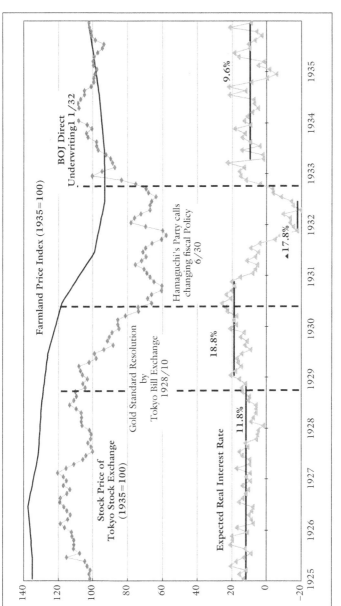

Figure 4-4 The Expected Real Interest Rate and Asset Prices

Source: Iwata et al. (2008). Reproduced with the permission of Gaskuhuin Daigaku Keizai Gakkai.

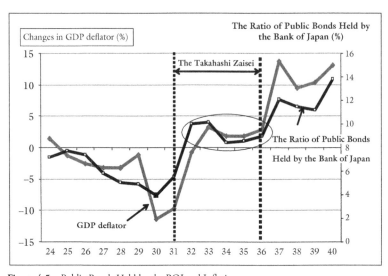

Figure 4-5 Public Bonds Held by the BOJ and Inflation

Source: Iwata et al. (2008). Reproduced with the permission of Gaskuhuin Daigaku Keizai Gakkai.

him saying that "it is better to cook a cow after it gets fat. Why do you want to cook a thin cow?" (Hirata et al. 1979, 21). Third, he began reducing the budget deficit and outstanding debt after June 1934 when the budget for 1935 fiscal year was discussed. The deficit-GNP was reduced from 2.9 percent in 1933 to 1 percent in 1936, and debt-GNP ratios were stabilized around 50 percent during his term. Shizume (2009) and (2011) argued that Japan's public finance was sustainable until 1931 but not after 1932, since the military virtually had veto power over the budget. It is true that Takahashi could not contain the rise of the military. Yet, he and other politicians were trying to regain power. Takahashi had broken with his old party, *Seiyukai*, since the party could not restrain its spending. Rather he aligned with *Minseito*, which had accepted Takahashi's economic policy of "controlled inflation." The general election was held on February 20, 1936, and *Minseito* won. The party politicians got together to form a government with Takahashi as a central figure. It was precisely at this moment that the army officers launched an attempted coup, assassinating Takahashi on February 26, 1936.

Why Takahashi Succeeded

Ben Bernanke once remarked that "Finance Minister Korekiyo Takahashi brilliantly rescued Japan from the Great Depression through reflationary policies in the early 1930s" (Bernanke 2003). Why did he succeed? Iwata et al. (2008) advanced a regime change hypothesis and examined other hypotheses to explain the success, namely, the fiscal policy hypothesis and the reduced nonperforming loans hypothesis. Due to its naming (*Zaisei* means fiscal condition in today's Japanese), many commentators tend naturally to associate the Takahashi reflation policy with its fiscal policy. This is not wrong but is misleading. First, the government under Prime Minister Wakatsuki had already increased fiscal expenditure in 1931 due to the Mukden Incident, but the timing coincided with Britain's suspension of the gold standard. Second, as Figure 4-2 shows, the real expected inflation rate decreased due to a rise in inflation expectations. Third, Takahashi reduced fiscal expenditure after the 1935 fiscal year; therefore, fiscal policy had the most impact in 1932 and 1933.

The second hypothesis is related to liquidationism and the bad loans problem. This hypothesis maintains that the Japanese economy recovered or that the Takahashi reflation succeeded because bad loans had already been wiped out by *Showa Kinyu Kyoko* (Showa Financial Crisis) in 1927. Adachi (2004) showed that the new bad loans began accumulating considerably during the Showa Depression, although bad loans caused by the post-World War I bursting of the bubble were resolved in *Showa Kinyu Kyoko*: deflation was a cause for newly accumulting bad loans during the Showa Depression.

This study also questioned the creative destruction during the Showa Depression. Figure 4-6 shows that the establishment of new firms declined during that period due to deflation. Relatedly, bank loans did not increase even though deflation stopped and prices and production began to rise (Figure 4-7). Bank loans lagged behind other economic indicators since the firms had accmulated free cash flow during the depression. The same applied to the U.S. situation (Figure 4-8), where bank loans did not increase for three years after the suspension of the gold standard.

What Might Have Been

Could Hamaguchi and Inoue have succeeded in returning to the gold standard had there been no Great Depression? Were they just unlucky? Obviously one cannot answer these questions with all certainty, but judging from the contrasting experience of Britain and France, Japan would have experienced further prolonged stagnation much like Britain even without the Great Depression. Also, with all major countries on the gold standard, an international recession might have happened anyway. France had been accumulating gold reserves during the 1920s, thus draining gold from the rest of the world (Irwin 2010). What would have happened if Japan took the French line, returning to the gold standard at a new parity? Unlike France, which returned

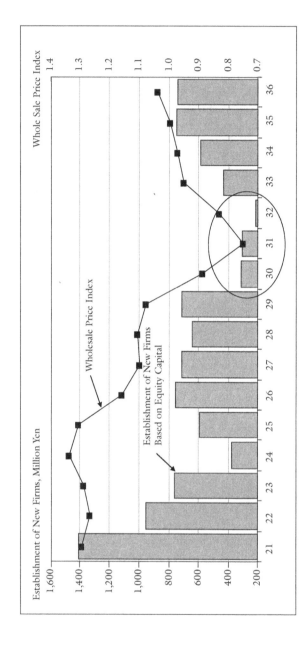

Figure 4-6 Deflation and Establishment of New Firms

Source: Iwata et al. (2008). Reproduced with the permission of Gaskuhuin Daigaku Keizai Gakkai.

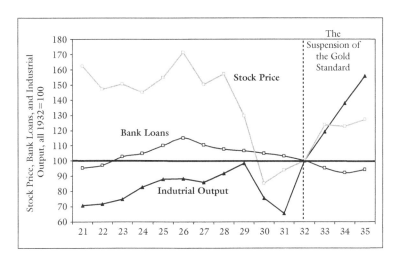

Figure 4-7   Bank Loans during the *Takahashi Zaisei* Period

Source: Iwata et al. (2008). Reproduced with the permission of Gaskuhuin Daigaku Keizai Gakkai.

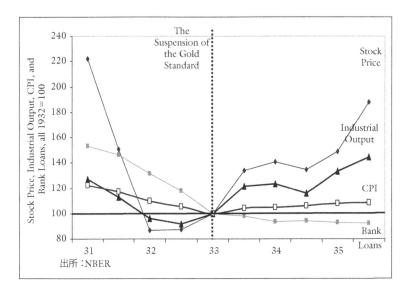

Figure 4-8   Bank Loans during the Recovery from the Great Depression in the United States

Source: Iwata et al. (2008). Reproduced with the permission of Gaskuhuin Daigaku Keizai Gakkai.

to the standard in 1928, Japan's timing was the worst; therefore, Japan would have experienced the Great Depression, albeit a lesser degree in its initial stage. Yet, as Britain went off the gold standard, Japan might have followed suit. In that case, the damage to the economy could have been a lot smaller.

Changing Ideologies and Regimes

Ending the Great Depression required "socialism in many countries" (Temin 1989), or the growth of the state (Higgs 1987). State regulation, control, and intervention increased in many countries, including Nazi Germany, and there was the New Deal policy in the United States and the rationalization movement in Britain. Shrinking international trade and the restriction of capital movement set in motion the slide to protectionism (Irwin 2011b). Japan seemed to have escaped the depression under the leadership of Finance Minister Korekiyo Takahashi, but during the crisis, in which people sought out "remedies," challenges to the establishment gained attractiveness and support among policymakers and the general public alike, leading to the popularity of the military. The invasion of Manchuria and the subsequent establishment of the puppet state there, Manchukuo, were enthusiastically welcomed by the people as the fundamental remedy of the current depression (Young 1998). Takahashi resisted such movement as much as he could, but after his assassination on February 26, 1936, in another attempted coup, the military had an upper hand, initiating a movement toward a militaristic regime. Though Tanzan Ishibashi continued criticizing the military, a truly brave act under the circumstances, his efforts ended in vain.

The demise of parliamentary politics strengthened the bureaucracy: after all, the military was the most powerful bureaucracy. MOF officials gained more authority over the budget, while Ministry of Commerce and Industry officials gained more authority and control over industry through industrial policy. As Chalmers Johnson put it, "economic crisis gave birth to industrial policy" (Johnson 1982, 114). Through the controversy over the return to the standard and the ensuing Showa Depression, the gold standard mentality and liquidationism receded, while another set of ideas, or "ideologies," emerged, among which were rationalization, state intervention of the national socialism sort, and developmentalism. What brought the downfall of Taisho Democracy and the rise of militarism were a series of macroeconomic failures that were supported by economic ideas.

In a nutshell, there was a competition among the regimes during this period (see Table 4.2): the Washington-Genoa regime, the Takahashi reflation, and the *Dai Toa Kyoei Ken* (Greater East Asian Coprosperity) regime (Adachi 2006). The Washington-Genoa regime was based on the cooperation

Table 4-2 Contrasting Regimes

Regime	Politics	Foreign Relations	Economic Policy
The Washington–Genoa Regime	Democracy	*Tai Eibei Kyocho* (Cooperation with the United Kingdom and United States)	Free market economy The gold standard Austerity
The Takahashi Reflation Regime	Democracy	*Eibei Kyocho* (Cooperation with the United Kingdom and United States)	Free market economy Managed currency Flexible exchange rate Macroeconomic management
Dai Toa Kyoei Ken (Greater East Asian Coprosperity) Regime	Authoritarianism	*Dai Ajia Syugi* (Pan-Asianism)	State controlled economy Controlled capital mobility Industrial policy

with the major powers, whose two pillars were the arms treaty and the gold standard. This regime was a deflationary regime and could not withstand the Showa Depression due to its adherence to the gold standard. The Takahashi reflation followed, succeeding in the recovery of the economy: the reflation regime was a combination of free market and macroeconomic management, and that regime tried to stay within the established international order.[24] At the same time, another regime was conceived by the military and the new generation of bureaucrats. The regime grew stronger in the course of the Showa Depression, eventually supplanting the Takahashi regime.

V. Conclusion

Japan before and during the Great Depression period provides us with a good model of what the government and central bank should do and should not do. The Japanese government under the Hamaguchi cabinet engaged in deliberate deflationary policy and failed. Also, the Japanese example provides us with a good illustration of the economic debate regarding the gold standard and the Great Depression: just by coincidence, Japan decided to return to the gold standard in November 1929, precisely when the stock market in the United States plunged, and implemented the policy in January 1930. Thanks to this coincidence, the economic debate on the depression centered on the desirability of the gold standard.

We examine economic policies and economic controversies from the 1990s to the 2010s in Chapters 2 and 3 and those from the 1920s to the

1930s in this chapter. The resemblance is striking. *Zaikai Seiri* was a liqui-dationist ideology and resembles the modern day *Kozo Kaikaku* (structural reform) ideology, while many of the arguments of *Shin Kaikin-ha* resemble macroeconomic ones. After all, the modern reflationists are the intellectual descendants of the original reflationsists, and they argue in an almost similar manner. Also, the debate was globalized: although the Western economists did not pay attention to the Japanese situation, with the exception of Gustav Cassel, some of Japanese policymakers and economists knew of the experiences of the Western world.

History is contested ground for today's policy discussions. The interepretaiton of the Showa Depression has been a important part of the economic controversies during Japan's Great Stagnation. The fiscal policy hypothesis has been used to argue for fiscal policy during Japan's Great Stagnation. The reduced nonperforming loans hypothesis has been also used during Japan's Great Stagnation period to rebut the effectiveness of monetary policy when banks had bad loans.

The most contested lesson from the Showa Depression is the interpretation of the Takahashi reflation itself. The tragic death of Korekiyo Takahashi, the rise of militarism, and the intensified inflation thereafter had a lasting effect on the years to come. The Takahashi reflation has been remembered as a failure, and the memory of the "failed" reflation policy lingers on today.

CHAPTER 5

Check 2015 Data

The Future Again?
The Assessment of Abenomics

I. Introduction

When Shinzo Abe resigned in disgrace in September 2007, no one expected his second coming. Yet he came back with a strong message for the Japanese economy: a policy package commonly known as "Abenomics."[1] The first time, it did not stick, and it was largely irrelevant, but this time, it is sticking, and it is having considerable consequences. Admittedly Abenomics is still in its early stages, and its future is still uncertain, but early signs have been promising. Stock prices have soared: for example, the Nikkei index has increased from ¥8,664 in November 14, 2012, to ¥15,071 in April 3, 2014, while the yen has depreciated from ¥81 per dollar to ¥103 during the same period. The effects are felt not only in financial markets but also in other markets. The real gross domestic product (GDP) growth rate has turned positive. The unemployment rate has decreased from 4.1 percent in November 2012 to 3.8 percent in June 2014. Even deflation has been receding. The change in the consumer price index (CPI), the so-called headline CPI, has increased from –0.2 percent in November 2012 to 3.4 percent in July 2014. The change in the CPI less all foods and energy, the so-called core CPI, has increased from –0.5 percent to 2.3 percent for the same period.[2] But, the consumption tax increase in April 2014 poses a great risk to the course of Abenomics. The growth rate has plunged back to a –6.7 percent annualized rate for April to June, and –1.9 percent annualized rate for July to September. The unemployment rate continues to decline to 3.5 percent in November 2014, but the change in the CPI has decreased to 2.4 percent in November 2014, and the change in the CPI less all foods and energy has decreased to 2.1 percent in November 2014. Toward the summer of 2014, people began talking about Abenomics being in trouble.[3]

There was a scheduled second consumption tax hike from 8 percent to 10 percent, effective from October 2015. The prime minister had to decide whether he should go ahead with the planned second hike before early December, 2014. The incoming economic figures showed that the economy was in recession. The annualized real growth rates for the second and the third quarters turned to negative, and the output gap widened to − 2.8 percent of Japan's GDP in the third quarter of 2014. In light of the deteriorating economic condition, the prime minister decided to delay the hike to April 2017. In order to delay the hike, he had to change the law, but many members of his own LDP party, the coalition partner, and the largest opposition party DPJ favor the consumption tax hike. And the bureaucracy, the Ministry of Finance in particular, was already expecting the hike. The BOJ unexpectedly announced another round of the QQE on October 31, 2014. Governor Kuroda cited a fall in oil price and a weakening demand of the Japanese economy due to the consumption tax hike for reasons to engage in the second round of the QQE. To break the political gridlock, the prime minister showed up on TV on November 18 and announced that he would dissolve the Lower House of the National Diet on November 21, and call an election due on December 14. In his speech, he admitted that the further consumption tax hike would threaten Japan's escape from deflation, the primary objective of Abenomics. The opposition parties and the media criticized the prime minister that the election did not have a justifiable reason, but calling the election was the only way for the prime minister to postpone the consumption tax hike. The prime minister asked the electorates whether he should continue his Abenomics. On December 14, 2014, the governing coalition parties secured 326 among 475 seats, and won the general election. However, the electorates did not really approve of Abenomics yet. According to the poll after the election, only 7 percent of the respondents thought that the prime minister's economic policy worked so far (Yomiuri Shimbun 2014). Abenomics has not yet won over the Japanese people.

This chapter offers a political, economic, and intellectual interpretation of Abenomics. First, the chapter chronicles the emergence of Abenomics. In the wake of the Lehman crisis, Japan's economic crisis deepened; the Liberal Democratic Party (LDP) government did not deal with it properly. In August 2009, the Democratic Party of Japan (DPJ) came to power with high expectations from the public but failed to revive the economy. Second, this chapter analyzes the official three-pronged economic policy of Abenomics. Abenomics has two faces: politics and economics; it is a product of political compromise among powerful LDP politicians, but it also makes sense as a policy to tackle deflation. Third, the chapter examines the possible risks and the prospects of Abenomics. Here again, the course of action depends on economic policy ideas, and success depends on whether Abe and his successors avoid the policy idea trap.

The chapter is organized as follows. The next section analyzes the political aspect of Abenomics. Abenomics is a political compromise among several factions within the LDP. More important, as Section III shows, Abenomics makes economic sense in its combination of policies to tackle deflation. However, this policy package has several risks and weaknesses: Section IV discusses them in a contemplation of the future of Abenomics. The last section concludes with an assessment of Abenomics up to the present time.

II. Political Face of Abenomics

Like any economic policy, Abenomics has two faces: politics and economics. Within politics, it is a product of compromise among powerful factions or groups within the governing LDP. One can name three of these: Prime Minister Abe and his close associates, the party politicians represented by Finance Minister Taro Aso, and those who are associated with the Ministry of Economy, Industry, and Trade, represented by Minister for Economic and Fiscal Affairs Akira Amari.[4] Putting it bluntly, Abenomics is a set of pet ideas from three powerful LDP politicians. Three arrows represent the pillars of the Abenomics policy. The first arrow materialized as "bold monetary easing," the second as "flexible fiscal policy," and the third as the "growth strategy."[5] However, there is at least one other group that is hidden under the rubric of Abenomics: that group comprises former mainstream members of the LDP, those who have supported fiscal consolidation under the agreement with the DPJ and Komeito Party in June 2012. It is no wonder that the economic policy that the Abe administration has adopted has the three arrows as a policy package. Everyone gets something out of this package, and this compromise minimizes the dissatisfaction of those who are involved.

As for the consumption tax hike, effective as of April 2014, Abe showed his reluctance to decide on the hike, delaying his decision until October 2013, precisely because he feared—rightly in my opinion—the hike would derail the efforts of his Abenomics project to lift Japan out of deflation. The act that sets forth the consumption tax hike has an "economic condition" clause, according to which the government can decide to postpone the starting date of the hike when the economy is in recession.[6] In reality, Abe's hands were already tied: one of the conspicuous initiatives of the growth strategy, a plan to provide women with subsidies to raise children, is financed through the consumption tax hike (Shimizu 2013, 9–10). Also, should he decide to postpone or stop the hike, he would have to create another act that would require the support of his own party members. The prime minister was popular, but not popular enough to decide against a fairly large number of his own party members: he had to concede to what the former majority of the LDP had decided about the consumption tax hike. The government set up a meeting to contemplate the hike from August 26 to August 31, 2013, inviting a wide range of so-called experts on the Japanese economy. Among the 60 meeting participants, the majority, about 70 percent, supported the hike, while only a handful opposed the hike for one reason or another.[7]

Left-leaning Western intellectuals, including Paul Krugman and Joseph E. Stiglitz, have embraced Abenomics, while the left-wing intellectuals in Japan have not, partly or mainly because Abe is considered a right-wing politician whose aspirations are to change the whole fabric of the post-World War II institutions, including the constitution. But there is an economic thought dimension to the left wing's opposition. As I have emphasize in this book, Japanese economic policy has been badly influenced by the questionable economic ideas which have been shared by many left-wing intellectuals and politicians. Unlike the left wing in the West, the Japanese counterparts did not learn a lesson from the Great Depression era,[8] and they are the intellectual descendants of the old economists who opposed Korekiyo Takahashi's reflation policy during the 1930s. According to the left-wing view of history, Takahashi's policy was a failure that ended with the rise of militarism and hyperinflation after the war, while in fact Takahashi was the staunchest opponent of the military, and his reflation policy delivered good results: inflation was maintained around 2 percent while he was in office. Also the left-wing interpretation of history has been supported by these intellectuals' aversion to monetary policy since the left-wing intellectuals think that money is a mere illusion and that an economic recovery engineered by monetary expansion would lead to a false dawn and, eventually, to a bubble.

Furthermore, the left-wing intellectuals in Japan are quite averse to the idea of promoting economic growth itself. During Japan's Great Stagnation, there has been a rise of antigrowth sentiment that has been teamed with the left-wing aversion to capitalism and the market economy. The *Asahi Shumbun*, the second largest circulation paper in Japan and a favorite among Japan's left-leaning intellectuals, carried an editorial opinion on January 1, 2012, titled "The Dawn of Post Growth." According to this article, after the 3/11 incident, it became apparent that economic growth dependent on nuclear energy and bubbles was no longer sustainable. Yet Japan has a huge amount of public debt, so the current generation should bear the burden in the form of public expenditure cuts and tax increases in the name of taking care of the future generation: the Japanese have to adjust themselves from a growth society to a "mature," post growth society. This newspaper once campaigned for an antigrowth policy during the 1970s with the slogan "Down with the GNP" (*Asahi Shumbun Keizaibu* 1971). It is no wonder that the *Asahi Shimbun* is the most vocal critic of Prime Minister Abe and Abenomics.

The DPJ reacted to Abenomics in a hostile manner. On November 17, 2012, Seiji Maehara, then minster for economic and fiscal affairs, criticized Abe's request for a reflation policy, stating that "his remark seems to dismiss the BOJ's independence." Likewise, then Prime Minster Yoshihiko Noda launched an attack on reflation policy during the election campaign in December 2012. This tactic backfired since it made "reflation policy" an election issue first time in the history of Japanese politics, which only highlighted the determination of Abe. Whenever Abe spoke about the inflation target of 2 to 3 percent or the necessity for the Bank of Japan (BOJ) to purchase long-term government bonds, the stock prices increased and the yen depreciated, which gave confidence to Abe on his policy. Against this background, what Abe has been trying amounts to stealing the thunder from the left-wing politicians. After the general election, as early as February 12, 2013, he asked leaders of major corporations, the chairs of three economic associations, *Keidanren*, *Keizai Doyu Kai*, and *Nihon Shoko Kaigisho* in Japan, to raise wages, salaries, and bonuses (Nihon Keizai Shimbun 2013). He kept asking the business community to raise them in order to tackle deflation. On April 27, 2014, Abe attended the May Day—the Japanese equivalent of International Labor Day—meeting organized by *Nihon Rodo Kumiai Sorengokai* (Japanese Trade Union Confederation): it was the first time in 13 years since Koizumi attended it. Abe gave a speech on the necessity of raising the workers' wages.

The reaction of the BOJ to Abe followed a typical BOJ pattern: initial rejection, followed by a gradual and grudging concession in form without substance. On November 11, 2012, Abe urged the BOJ for "bold quantitative easing since the policy action so far has been insufficient." He further emphasized that "if our party is in power, we welcome someone who would cooperate with the government to initiate a bold monetary easing with a view to achieve 2 to 3 percent inflation targeting," hinting at the desirable criteria for the soon-to-be appointed next governor of the BOJ after Shirakawa's term expired in April 2013 (Nihon Keizai Shimbun 2012). The next day, on November 12, 2012, in his speech at one meeting, Shirakawa retorted that "in an environment where neither prices nor wages have risen for a number of years, it is not realistic to believe that the general public's inflation expectations will go up all of a sudden, or that we can manage to lift these expectations somehow." According to him, "Consumers, with the perception that prices should not rise, are unlikely to accept price hikes by firms, who in return reduce costs including wages; hence, it will take longer for the economy to overcome deflation." He repeated his favorite argument that overcoming deflation should come from supply-side reforms: "After all, it is more important to generate material changes in the economy, including strengthening the economy's growth potential and achieving higher wages" (Shirakawa 2012b). Nevertheless, once Abe won the general election of the Lower House of the Diet, Shirakawa reluctantly agreed to introduce "Bukka Antei no Mokuhyo," a target for price stability of 2 percent, on January 22, 2013. Even then, he refused to cooperate with the government: in the Monetary Policy Committee meeting held on the same day, the plan was to increase the monetary base from the year 2014, not within the year 2013 (Shirakawa 2013). On February 5, 2013, Governor Shirakawa met Prime Minister Abe at the prime minister's office to express his intention to leave his job at the BOJ in March, before his term expired.[9] Upon the news, the depreciation of yen accelerated.

During Japan's Great Stagnation, Japan's place in the world has declined. For example, Japan's relative share of the global GDP has shrunk from 9.7 percent in 1988 to 5.4 percent in 2013.[10] The relative decline is common to all major Western countries, including the United States, and should not be a problem, but in terms of international security, the relative decline along with the relative growth of neighboring countries might pose a problem, especially with the rise of China. Deflation has been damaging to Japan's maintenance of its military capabilities: Japan's national defense budget has been fixed at around 1 percent of its nominal GDP; therefore, deflation has automatically stagnated the growth of military budgets. Indeed Japan's military budget peaked in 2002 and decreased until 2013. On the other hand, the military budget of China has been around 2 percent of its nominal GDP, and the Chinese economy has been growing, so the divergence between Japanese and Chinese military budgets is widening. On March 5, 2014, the first day of the National People's Congress, the Chinese government announced that it would double its military spending.[11]

The growing tensions in the Asian region have led to speculation as to the "true" nature of Abenomics. It would be an exaggeration to say that Abenomics came out of national security concerns only, but security concerns must be an integral part of prime minister's calculation. Indeed, security concerns are closer to his heart, and changing the constitution is his lifelong ambition, as is shown in his devotion of considerable efforts and energy to change the interpretation of the constitution regarding collective self-defense. At any rate, the prime minister being primarily concerned with national security is totally justifiable.

International receptions are also divided. Many policymakers and economists from Anglo-American countries and international organizations expressed approval of Abenomics, while those from China, Germany, and

South Korea either disapproved of or expressed some reservations about it. The prominent supporters include Paul Krugman, Joseph Stiglitz, Jeffrey Sachs, Ben Bernanke, Janet Yellen, Christina Romer, and Christine Lagarde. Their reactions are pithily summarized by what Paul Krugman said:

> Now comes Shinzo Abe. As Noah Smith informs us, he is not anybody's idea of an economic hero; he's a nationalist, a denier of World War II atrocities, a man with little obvious interest in economic policy. If he's defying the orthodoxy, it probably reflects his general contempt for learned opinion rather than a considered embrace of heterodox theory. But that may not matter. Abe may be ignoring the conventional wisdom on spending, and bullying the Bank of Japan, for all the wrong reasons—but the fact is that he is actually providing fiscal and monetary stimulus at a time when every other advanced-country government is too much in the thrall of the Very Serious People to do something different." (Krugman 2012)[12]

III. Abenomics as Economics

The Logic of Abenomics

Abenomics makes sense as a political compromise. But does it make sense economically? Any economic policy should have sound economic reasoning to be successful. For Japanese economic policy recently, Abenomics surprisingly makes sense as a policy to defeat deflation. As we see Chapters 2 and 3, the idea of reflation has been floating around but has largely been neglected by political and economic leaders; remarkably, Shizo Abe took it as *his* own policy. Therefore, as economics, Abenomics has a foundation in the reflationist ideas. As we see in Chapter 3, Japanese reflationists are of hybrid species: Koichi Hamada comes from an old Keynesian position of James Tobin stripe, while Kikuo Iwata is more willing to take modern macroeconomics positions with much emphasis on expectations and regime change.[13] Reflationsits' premises can be summarized as follows. First, they believe in the potentialities of the Japanese economy: even under a deflationary environment, it has grown more than 2 percent in real terms. Second, they believe that deflation is one of the major obstacles for Japan's full recovery and sustainable growth. Although they are the first to admit that Japan has a lot of other problems, deflation is not a minor problem, and it should be tackled with full force. Third, deflation has been happening only in Japan, and the Japanese people are expecting persistent deflation: deflationary expectation is self-fulfilling. Fourth, as a cause of deflation, explanations other than inept monetary policy are unconvincing. Fifth, the BOJ is responsible for monetary policy after all. Sixth, when the policy interest rate hits zero, the BOJ has to act ingeniously, particularly tackling deflation and deflationary expectation: it needs to introduce inflation targeting. These premises set apart Japanese reflationists from other economists and policymakers who are skeptical about the potential for the Japanese economy and monetary policy to defeat deflation.

Interpreted in a favorable light, the logic of Abenomics resembles Krugman (1998). To tackle deflation and deflationary expectation, one may (1) decrease the value of money constantly by increasing money supply, (2) increase the value of the goods and services and the people who produce them by purchasing goods and services temporarily, and (3) increase the value of goods, services, and people continuously by finding out new and better way to utilize them (structural reforms or the growth strategy). Now Krugman may not recommend structural reforms or the growth strategy as such, and this would certainly introduce confusion among the policymakers, the business economists, and the journalists since structural reforms are intended to raise the potential output, as opposed to the actual output. Nevertheless, it could be incorporated in the whole package to tackle deflation and deflationary expectations with some qualifications. This package is a clever one, since it gives something to everyone.

The transmission mechanism of Abenomics is summarized as follows, based on Iwata (2014) (see Figure 5-1).[14] It could be considered a big domino game. The key starting point is the increase in the expected inflation rate. Like a domino game, the first step is really the key to success, and the rest follows according to the logic of economics. If the first arrow, with some help from the second arrow, succeeds in generating enough inflationary expectations, the real interest rate must go down. Here it should be noted that the relevant interest rate is real, not nominal. The decrease in real interest rate has three consequences. First, it would affect asset prices, especially stock prices. As the present prices of stock variables reflect the information about the future, the reduction in real interest rate would translate into an improvement in the discounted present value of the corporate earnings in the future, which leads to an increase in stock prices in the present. Second, the real interest rate could influence investment, although the extent of the sensitivity of investment on real interest rate varies. Third, the reduction in the real interest rate would depreciate the yen. These effects, combined with an increase in government expenditures induced by the second arrow, would increase the aggregate demand, which would in turn decrease the output gap and increase demands for loans and labor. As a result, the inflation rate would go up, as would interest rates and nominal wages. As planned, the whole process of reflation would take one and a half to two years, depending on the time lag of monetary and fiscal policy, to have its full impact on the economy.

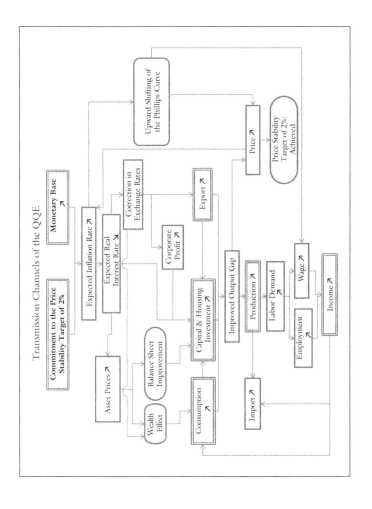

Figure 5-1 Transmission Channels of the Quantitative and Qualitative Easing (QQE)

Source: Iwata 2014. Reproduced with the permission of the Bank of Japan.

Tentative Assessments

The full assessment of Abenomics must wait several more years, but the British financial magazine *Banker* named Haruhiko Kuroda the "Central Banker of the Year 2014" in January 2014. Does he deserve the praise? Recent empirical studies show that Prime Minister Abe and Kuroda's BOJ have achieved the regime change. Seiji Adachi, director of economic research at Marusan Shoken Inc., has argued that the monetary regime has indeed changed, according to his own methodology of quantifying regime change (Adachi 2014). He has detected four regime changes since the 1980s: the first one happened after the Plaza Accord; the second one happened since 2003, when deflation receded; the third one happened around March 2011; and the fourth one has been happening from the start of the Abe administration to the present. Other than the third one, which was really a short-term liquidity provision during the emergency, these episodes coincided with a massive monetary expansion, with responses in the exchange rate, the stock prices, and the expected and actual inflation rates. Koiti Yano, associate professor of economics at Komazawa University, and his colleagues estimated the decreased expected real interest rate (Yano et al. 2014).

The flip side of the same coin of Japan's persistent deflation was the appreciating yen (McKinnon and Ohno 1998); therefore, the regime change in monetary policy must entail the breaking of the so-called ever-higher yen syndrome. Adachi examined the issue, concluding that policy regime changes are happening both in monetary policy and in exchange rates. Hausman and Wieland (2014) analyzed the issue in a similar line, categorizing policy regimes into low, medium, and high inflation regimes: they concluded that the first arrow is raising the probability of the medium inflation regime, although the BOJ's 2 percent inflation target is still not fully credible. De Michelis and Iacoviello (2014) showed that the first arrow has raised long-term inflation expectations, but at most by 1 percent. Using the money and credit growth indicators, Amisano, Colavecchio, and Fagan (2014) found that the deflation risk in Japan is declining. So far, Kuroda does deserve the praise.

IV. Risks and Prospects

Abenomics is in constant motion, and it is evolving. Also, the future is uncertain. This section discusses risks and prospects of Abenomics. As I explain later, I am more optimistic about the first arrow's prospects than about those of other two arrows: what matters most is the first arrow. Nevertheless, the other two arrows, particularly the third arrow, would be important in shaping what Japan would become.

IV.1 The First Arrow: Can It Reach the Mark?

Criticisms on the First Arrow

So far, the first arrow has been a dominant effect since the policy has been fully implemented and has been able to contribute the most to increasing the real GDP growth rate and reducing the unemployment rate in the short to medium run. Even with this apparent success of the first arrow, critics of Abenomics, many of whom are critics of expansionary monetary policy in the Great Stagnation era, die hard. At the end of 2013, the Nikkei asked 15 academic and business economists to name the best economics books of the year. The first choice was Hiroshi Yoshikawa's *Deflation* (Yoshikawa 2013) and that was followed by Kunio Okina's *Nihon Ginko* (BOJ; Okina 2013); both of these authors are highly skeptical about the efficacy of the first arrow.[15] The controversy continues. While reflationists are still in a minority position, critics take issues with reflation policy with a shifting focus. The following are representative criticisms.

1. Monetary policy is ineffective.
2. The BOJ cannot achieve the target rate of 2 percent.
3. Inflation would be a burden to pensioners.
4. Real wages would not increase.
5. Income disparity would be greater.
6. Reflation policy would lead to bubbles.
7. Reflation policy would lead to competitive currency competition.
8. The long-term interest rate would shoot up.
9. Reflation policy would lead to hyperinflation.
10. The BOJ should be worried with its balance sheet.
11. The BOJ should discuss the "exit strategy" as soon as it can.

The first criticism was popular until the launching of Abenomics, but it faded away as the inflation rate increased. As Chapter 3 shows, critics such as Noguchi Yukio, and Kunio Okina, who both have been around since the 1990s argued that Abenomics relies on cost-push inflation based on the increased import prices induced by devaluation, and that the effect of devaluation would wane in due course (Okina 2014). The upshot is that these critics do not believe that the increase in base money would affect the expected inflation, although there are several studies that show evidence of an increased expected inflation.

The second criticism is that the target rate of 2 percent would not be achieved within the roughly two year period that the BOJ set in April 2013. Critics argue that the BOJ should reach the exact target rate within the set period. This line of criticism is beside the point since an inflation target, in a usual sense, is defined not as a point target but as a certain range.[16] It is true that the BOJ is not explicit on this, but what matters more than the target is the commitment: the new reflationary BOJ regime, and Governor Kuroda and Deputy Governor Iwata in particular, have their reputations in history at stake. This does not mean that they are not going to make mistakes. On October 31, 2014, the BOJ announced the second round of the quantitative and qualitative easing, and decided to increase its base money from ¥60 to 70 trillion per year to ¥80 trillion per year, increase its purchase of the long-term Japanese government bonds, and triple the purchase of Exchange Traded Funds and Japan Real Estate Investment Trust. The BOJ should have engaged in this easing several months earlier since the consumption tax hike decreased the expected inflation rate: the BOJ miscalculated and underestimated the negative impact of the consumption tax hike on the inflation rate. They probably will make mistakes, but it is unlikely that they will not achieve the 2 percent target eventually.

The third criticism is about the "costs" of inflation and is specific to the pension system in Japan. In fact, the Japanese pensioners have been well taken care of. When the Japanese government introduced "macroeconomic scaling" to the pension system in 2004, the government decided not to have a deflation adjustment mechanism; therefore, the pension benefit would be scaled up with inflation, but would not be scaled down even if the benefit's real worth is increased by deflation. With inflation, pensioners will be compensated. A related issue is the management of the government-pension investment fund. An increase in stock prices during the year 2013 brought an increase in returns to the government-pension investment fund worth ¥10.2 trillion.

The fourth criticism is also a recent concern. Theoretically speaking, real wages could go up, stay the same, or go down depending on the circumstances. During the recession, the existence of unemployed resources would exert little upward pressure on factor prices; nominal wages are usually sticky in the sense that they would react to changes in the conditions slowly, while prices could increase, reflecting a change in inflationary expectations. In this case, the inflation rate goes up and the unemployment rate goes down, yet real wages could go down: this seems to be the initial stage of Abenomics. But eventually real wages are determined by the productivity of the workers; therefore, as long as the productivity is increasing, which has been the case even during the Great Stagnation, real wages would go up. Also, as far as the empirical regularities since the postwar period are concerned, Japanese real wages have been increasing in the inflationary period until 1997; after that, real wages have been stagnating.

The fifth concern is often addressed by people on the left. Abenomics has so far benefited two kinds of people: those who own stocks and those who have been unemployed or living on the margin of the market economy. The fall in the unemployment rate is good news for the latter, although they find only nonstandard jobs. Nevertheless, income and wealth disparity may widen, and people may need regular jobs. One must address these issues with another policy: income redistribution. I discuss this issue later in this chapter.

The sixth concern about a bubble is persistent. One cannot say with confidence whether a stock or land prices at one particular time represents a bubble or not, but this concern is strengthened by the experiences of not only Japan's Great Stagnation but also the Great Recession. Nevertheless, if the nominal growth rate exceeds the long-term nominal interest rate, bubbles may arise. According to the current consensus, if one has to deal with asset price boom, it must be dealt with by using other policy tools: this is the role for macroprudential and regulation policy.

The seventh concern was raised in the early phase of Abenomics, especially by policymakers from the emerging markets. In 2010, when the Federal Reserve Bank launched the second round of quantitative easing (QE), Brazilian Finance Minister Guido Mantega voiced his concern by popularizing the term "currency war," according to which the expansionary monetary policy of the developed countries would hurt the emerging countries by depreciating the formers' currencies. When an advance economy such as Japan reflates, however, it would increase not only exports but also imports, benefiting trade partners.[17] Also, Chapter 4 argues, the current consensus on the Great Depression teaches us what was needed for the world to escape from the Great Depression was simultaneous expansion of monetary policy: currency competition was necessary and is still in the time of recession.[18]

The eighth concern is extremely popular among the so-called *Shijyo Kankeisha* (market participants)—that is, bond traders. During Japan's Great Stagnation, they have been in a dominant position as the asset managers in Japanese financial institutions. As Chapter 4 shows, the long-term interest rate did not increase during the reflation process in the Great Depression period. It is true that the long-term interest rate must go up since Abenomics is the policy package to raise the inflation expectations and the potential growth rate,[19] but it may take time for Japan to return to the full-employment condition. With the success of reflation, returns on other assets should go up; therefore, financial institutions can profit from shifting their portfolios.

The ninth criticism has been circulated during the Great Stagnation and has been raised occasionally in the context of the eighth criticism. Yet, it should be recognized that the probability of Japan experiencing hyperinflation from deflation is very remote because, historically speaking, hyperinflation has happened in countries after the war or after revolutions when the productive capacity has been severely damaged. On the other hand, Japan's deflationary recession means resources have been underutilized. Also, Japan now has a formal inflation target: this should work as a safeguard against hyperinflation.

The tenth and eleventh criticisms are gaining attention. As the initial success of the first arrow becomes apparent, many critics are shifting their attention to the exit strategy. Kazumasa Iwata, the former deputy governor of the BOJ, has drawn attention to the BOJ's potential balance-sheet problem (Iwata and Fueda-Samikawa 2013; Iwata 2014), which has been reported by Gillian Tett (2013). They are worried about the potential balance-sheet loss incurred by a fall in the price of long-term bonds, caused by a rise in the long-term interest rate. This is not really a problem if, instead of considering the balance sheets of the government—in the narrow sense of that word—and the BOJ separately, we consider the balance sheets of the integrated government, which combines the traditionally defined government and the BOJ. When considered in terms of the integrated government, the potential loss to the BOJ should be exactly offset by the potential profit accrued to the government in the narrow sense, a point made by Bernanke (2003).[20] The old critics of reflation policy, such as Kunio Okina, have been arguing against an expansionary monetary policy, calling for an explicit "exit strategy." But in the end, the exit has already been posted in the form of the "inflation target."

Improving the First Arrow

Now the new BOJ view of the Japanese economy has emerged. According to this view, the Japanese economy has been undergoing a great transformation of industrial structure from a manufacturing-centered export economy to a service sector–centered, domestic demand-led one. It is still premature to talk about the final success. Although the first arrow has some success, compared with the Takahashi recovery during the 1930s, it has not done as much as Korekiyo Takahashi did. Also, it is not certain that the expected results, including the 2 percent inflation target, will materialize. With the consumption tax hike of April 2014, the short-term prospects are bleak: considering that almost all empirical studies cited here predict that the firepower of the first arrow may not be enough to reach the target, the BOJ should have acted soon. In the last analysis, the inflation target is the key: the current BOJ people could and would make mistakes in calculation, estimation, and judgment in the future, yet as long as they keep the target, they are obliged to achieve it.

This comes to the question of how one could improve monetary policy. Japanese monetary policy could be improved in three areas. First and foremost, the current regime does not have a full legal framework: the current BOJ law still does not have a clause on the inflation target. There is still a possibility that the current regime would be reversed, as happened in 2006. Therefore, a revision of the BOJ law to introduce an inflation target would strengthen the commitment to price stability. Second, one area for improvement is more technical but is practically important: there is room for discussing the precise definition of the target. Currently it is defined as the headline CPI less food prices, but it could be volatile, and the measurement error of up to 2 percent is known (see Chapter 1). In light of the 2006 experience when the BOJ terminated QE as the headline CPI hit 2 percent, it is better to redefine the target as the core CPI—that is, CPI less food and energy prices. Third, once the BOJ establishes an inflation target regime, it could begin contemplating other targets, such as a nominal GDP or a nominal GDP level target. After all, the purpose of raising the inflation rate is to stabilize employment and production.

IV. 2 The Second Arrow and Fiscal Consolidation

The Effectiveness of Fiscal Policy

Fiscal policy has been tried many times in Japan, but this has not succeeded in getting Japan out of the long stagnation. Yet Abenomics has revived a great interest in fiscal policy, partly because it has the political backing of the LDP politicians and the intellectual backing of the "*Kokudo kyojinka* (national homeland resilience)" movement. On the other hand, Japan's debt-GDP ratio has ballooned during the long stagnation, strengthening the impression that the fiscal consolidation must be carried out promptly. There has been a global debate over the desirability of austerity: this casts a long shadow on the Japanese discussion too. In the upshot, there are an increasing number of studies that show that fiscal policy may be more effective than has been presumed before the crisis; therefore, the second arrow of Abenomics just makes sense economically. But is fiscal policy in Japan effective?

Most of recent empirical studies on Japan answer that question in broadly negative terms, showing that the multiplier effect has been declining to as low as one. According to the short-run macroeconometric model of the Japanese economy made by the Economy and Social Research Institute of the Cabinet Office, the multiplier for public works has declined from 1.33 in 1991 to 1.07 in 2011. Other studies concur with these results (see Kato 2003 and Watanabe et al. 2008). The reasons for this declining multiplier effect can be multiple, such as Ricardian neutrality, non-Keynesian effects, and the Mundell-Fleming effect. Ricardian neutrality says that rational economic agents would correctly foresee an increase in the tax burden in the future; hence, they do not increase spending in case of an increased public expenditure. The Mundell-Fleming effect entails that the expansionary effects of fiscal policy would be offset by the reduction of net exports through the appreciation of the currency. However, the very existence of non-Keynesian effects is in doubt in the current literature (Blyth 2013). Also, an interesting study by Yasuyuki Iida at Meiji University argued that other effects, the neutrality and the Mundell-Fleming effects, are not detected from the data. In Japan, the so-called non-Ricardian households that cannot borrow from financial institutions or use up income within the period have rapidly increased from 10 percent in the 1990s to 30 percent in the late 2000s (Yano et al. 2010). Also, there is no evidence to support the idea that fiscal policy has caused an increase in the interest rate during the 1990s.[21] Instead, he advanced the supply-constrained hypothesis of public works (Iida 2013; Iida and Matsumae 2009): he showed that a 1 percent point increase in public works would decrease private work construction by a percentage point of 0.49. In other words, public work would "crowd out" half the private construction work. If this is true, the old-style pork barrel politics that the LDP has been famous for is no longer effective as a short-term stimulus. Indeed, as of 2014, there is a shortage of construction workers, and the prices for materials are increasing (Nikkei Business 2014). Nevertheless, Iida argued that the government could use other means of fiscal policy more effectively, specifically, tax cuts or direct payments to the people or public investment in the environmental health care and medical industries. It is true that the roads and infrastructure need repairs, and the country has to be prepared for earthquakes and other natural disasters. In the short term, public works investment might be effective, but that the effectiveness rapidly diminishes unless the direction of fiscal policy is reconsidered.

Fiscal Consolidation

The most important development is the consumption tax hike and fiscal consolidation. There was no clear commitment by Abe to raise the consumption tax when he became the leader of the LDP. On the contrary, his initial motivation to challenge the leadership suggests that he was opposed or at least unwilling to raise the consumption tax. However, he eventually decided to raise it. The major reason is political: the consumption tax hike had already been legislated, so if Abe were to change it, he would have to submit another law to overturn it. This would be politically costly, considering that many members of his own party, along with members of two other parties, have endorsed the hike, and other politicians are waiting for any mistake Abe might make.

Politics aside, what is the prospect for the fiscal consolidation of Japan, or to what extent is Japan's fiscal situation close to "crisis"? After all, Japan's outstanding gross government debt reaches ¥10 trillion in 2010 (Zaimusho Shukei Kyoku 2009). The word crisis has been much abused, but if it means that the Japanese government has to default or reschedule its interest payments, Japan is far from that situation. The most telling evidence is the premium on the credit default swap of Japanese government bonds, a surrogate of the likelihood of the default of Japan: it has peaked at 155.77 basis point on January 11, 2012, and has been declining since, reaching at 37 basis point on June 11, 2014. Admittedly this may take into account the efforts of fiscal consolidation since 2012, but economic recovery initiated by Abenomics is contributing, which is the first point worth emphasizing. Economically speaking, what matters most is not the size of the debt or deficit, but its relative importance to nominal GDP. In this sense, deflation could be deadly since it could stagnate nominal GDP. Japan's debt has ballooned during Japan's Great Stagnation. Therefore, getting out of deflation is the necessary condition for fiscal consolidation. Also, tax revenue depends on the growth of the nominal GDP.

Second, the amount of the Japanese government's assets is large: as of March 2013, the government's assets are worth ¥822 trillion, while the government's debt is worth ¥1,269 trillion, with the net debt being worth ¥447 trillion. Needless to say, some of these assets are not saleable, but many of them are financial assets. Some commentators like to point out that Japan is unlikely to default since its outstanding debt is owned by domestic residents. This is not true: as Reinhart and Rogoff's influential book of 2009 showed (Reinhart and Rogoff 2009), the composition of bondholders does not affect the probability of default. After Reinhart and Rogoff (2010), there was a preoccupation with the specific, threshold-like debt-GDP level at which the growth rate changes, yet it is now argued that what matters is the trajectory of the debt reduction rather than the size of debt itself (Pescatori et al. 2014). In this sense, the key to successful fiscal consolidation is economic growth.

Some are also wondering aloud why the Japanese interest rate has remained so low despite bold monetary easing by the new BOJ. As we see in Chapter 4, during the two episodes of deflationary depressions, the Great Depression and the Showa Depression, long-term interest rates remained low even after the launching of reflation policy. The main reason was free cash flow held by firms during the depression: when firms decide to start investing, they do not need to borrow funds. Therefore, the usual relationship between the nominal and real interest rates, what economists call the Fisher relationship, named after the great American economist Irving Fisher, does not hold in a strict sense when the economy is below capacity. But surely after reflation, the Fisher relationship would be restored, so should we not worry about the growing payment for debt services? The payment for debt services would increase, but then the nominal growth rate would increase as well, generating more tax revenues. As for the elasticity of tax revenue, it is around 1.1 in a typical inflationary environment, but the elasticity is 3 to 4 when the economy is a deflationary one.[22]

This does not mean that there is no need for fiscal reforms. On the contrary, Japan desperately needs fiscal reforms. However, there is an interesting trade-off between fiscal reforms and consolidation. Teulings (2012) argued that both fiscal reforms and consolidation involve costs in terms of consumption reduction and that in production, the implementation of one approach limits the other; therefore, the more the government goes for fiscal consolidation, the less scope there is for a fiscal reform. Unless we have reason to believe that Japan's default is imminent, it is better to prioritize reforms rather than consolidation.

IV. 3 The Third Arrow: Can It Even Fly?

The Long and Short of the Growth Strategy
The third arrow of Abenomics is named the growth strategy. Here again, economics and history can shed light on the issue. As Paul Krugman once said, productivity is a mysterious subject for economists (Krugman 1997). Another Nobel laureate, Robert Lucas Jr., also said economic growth is like "making a miracle" (Lucas 1993).[23] Thus, one can assume that the consensus among economists on growth policy is that it is a particularly difficult policy subject. The basic problem with Abenomics' growth strategy is that it does not recognize this difficulty of the problem.

Abe's plan, the Japan Revitalization Strategy (JRS), first issued on June 2013 and revised on June 2014, has four components: (1) the promotion of investment, (2) the strengthened utilization of human resources, (3) the creation of new markets, (4) and a global economic integration. These seem innocuous at first sight, but a closer look at the details reveals several characteristics.[24] First of all, there is no explicit discussion of what contributes to economic growth. One would like to see policy discussion based both on theory and on empirical evidence, like those of Aghion (2012) or Aghion and Durlauf (2007), but there is no policy paper yet to support the JRS. Second, one may discern two strands of economic policy philosophy in JRS, one emphasizes the active involvement of the government, reminiscent of industrial policy, and the other emphasizes more market-oriented reforms, reminiscent of "structural reforms." In a sense, the third arrow is a mixed bag of two ideas: the industrial policy myth and the structural reforms ideology. Third, there are, nonetheless, several policy initiatives that are worthwhile, such as joining the Trans-Pacific Partnership (TPP) and establishing the *Kokka Keizai Tokku* (National Special Economic Zone; NSEZ).

The best option is joining the TPP. The TPP has three characteristics, thorough trade liberalization in terms of the abolition of tariffs on principle, rule making and institution building in 21 areas, and multilateral negotiations.

Trade liberalization has the greatest potential as the foremost market-oriented reform. The estimates of benefits may vary: the Cabinet Office has said that the benefits are around ¥2.4 to ¥3.2 billion, while others have given higher estimates.[25] Rule making and institution building are also important since the trade structure is shifting from goods to services. It is important to note that interest group politics would distort the realization of these potentials, as Stiglitz (2014) warned us: his concern is that the negotiation over the "non-tariff barriers," or regulatory policy, would lead to major corporations' "race to the bottom." However, it is very difficult for the United States and Vietnam to agree on the harmonization of labor standards to promote the interests of major corporations, and it is also very difficult for the United States, Australia, and New Zealand to agree on the harmonization of food safety standard: the multinational negotiation could counter the influence of interest groups.

As for NSEZ, one should reexamine the previous example of the Keizaiku Tokku (the Special Economic Zone) introduced by the Koizumi administration. Hoshi and Kashyap (2011, 2012) analyzed the economic effects of the Special Economic Zone and determined the effects to be virtually null: "Many special zones were established but only few of them had sizable impact. Worse, many local promotion zones ended up diverting business from other areas" (Hoshi and Kashyap 2011, 33). Therefore, the proponents of the new version of NSEZ, such as Heizo Takenaka, are now arguing that the government has to implement deregulation more deeply and vigorously in these NSEZs (Takenaka 2014). More specifically, Takenaka proposed to replicate what he succeeded with in the past: setting up a council in charge of reforms and implementing the reforms with the leadership of the prime minster and the support of the experts. The framework was legislated in December 2013.

Is Japan's Growth Potential Declining?
The government, the BOJ, and private research institutions estimate Japan's growth potential to be declining from 2 percent in the 1990s to 0.5 percent in the 2010s. As the aging and decline of the population proceeds, the growth potential could decline, but it would change very slowly, taking five to ten years. Therefore, it is very difficult to believe that the growth potential of the Japanese economy has declined so rapidly. There is also a technical issue of filtering, especially the use of the Hodrik-Prescott (HP) filter, which is explained by Paul Krugman beautifully:

> The use of the HP filter presumes that deviations from potential output are relatively short-term, and tend to be corrected fairly quickly. This is arguably true in normal times, although I would argue that the main reason for convergence back to potential output is that the Fed gets us there rather than

some "natural" process. But what happens in the aftermath of a major financial shock? The Fed finds itself up against the zero lower bound; it is reluctant to pursue unconventional policies on a sufficient scale; fiscal policy also gets sidetracked. And so the economy remains below potential for a long time. Yet the methodology of using the HP filter basically assumes that such things don't happen. Instead, any protracted slump gets interpreted as a decline in potential output! (Krugman 2012)

It is true that Japan's real growth rate has declined on average from 3.8 percent in 1974 to 1990, to 1.3 percent in 1991 to 2000, and 0.74 percent in 2001 to 2012. A closer inspection, however, shows that Japan has achieved an average growth rate of around 2 percent in 1995 to 1997, 2000 to 2002, and 2003 to 2008, all punctuated by a series of macroeconomic policy mistakes, the consumption tax hike of 1997, the termination of the zero interest rate policy in 2000, and the termination of QE. Again this comes back to the problem of supply versus demand explanations of the Great Stagnation. Surely, the long stagnation must have decreased its potential output growth rate, but the current consensus seems too low. In any case, this is the estimate: the true potential of the Japanese economy will be found after Japan sets its macroeconomic policy right.

Implementing the Third Arrow

Martin Wolf, chief economics editor at *Financial Times*, wrote a column on the assessment of Abenomics in its first year, arguing that its first arrow may succeed in overcoming deflation, but achieving 2 percent output growth is not "impossible" but is "ambitious" (Wolf 2013). His reasoning is based on the simple calculation that the working population is shrinking by 0.7 percent and that female participation rates could be increased a little more but not much; therefore, productivity should increase by around 2.5 percent, which has been unprecedented among the developed economies.[26]

The goal looks ambitious, but as we explained earlier, Japan has been achieving 2 percent real growth rate when macroeconomic policy did not interrupt. Thus 2 percent does not look so ambitious, yet clearly, after the Japanese economy completes the reflation process, the growth potential should rise, and the third arrow surely should be effective.

There is room for reform within the existing legal institutions. Haidar and Hoshi (2014) looked at one of Abenomics' few explicitly stated goals: to elevate Japan into the top three on the World Bank's Doing Business ranking of Organisation for Economic Co-operation and Development (OECD) countries. Haidar and Hoshi categorized reforms into four categories, depending on the necessity of legal changes and the strength of political resistance, concluding that by "just doing the reforms that do not require legal changes and are not likely to face strong political opposition, Japan can improve the ranking from the current 15th among high-income OECD countries to #9." However, it is more difficult to move into the top three: it would require all kinds of reforms, including the ones that require both making legal changes and overcoming strong political resistance.

Improving the Third Arrow
It must be admitted that even if we follow all of Haidar and Hoshi (2014) recommendations, Japan needs more improvement on the third arrow front. To improve the third arrow further, one has to contemplate what contributes to economic growth in a more systematic manner. The literature on modern growth theory emphasizes that the engine of growth is "doing something new," including innovations and improvements. These innovations do not have to be disruptive or drastic, but they require new entrants who can bring in new ideas into the economy. Aghion and Durlauf (2009) distinguished between two cases, one in which a country is far away from the technology frontier and the other in which a country is near the frontier: developed countries such as Japan are supposed to be near the frontier. Regardless of the level of economic development, the following four factors are important: (1) the protection of property rights, (2) the development of finance, (3) the education of the labor force, and (4) the stability of macroeconomic conditions. It is important to note that monetary and fiscal policy can contribute to economic growth through the stabilization of the price and, hence, the real interest rate.

As a country approaches the frontier, the trial and error increases; therefore, it is imperative to increase the opportunities for trial and error as a policy. In addition to the aforementioned four policies, for the developed countries, the following additional five policies are recommended: (5) competition and new entry in product markets, (6) higher education, (7) equity finance, (8) democracy, and (9) decentralized firm organization. Equity finance enables firms to raise funds in an uncertain environment. Democracy is here related to the promotion of entry. Acemoglu and Robinson (2012) and Zingales (2012) emphasized that the openness of political systems to an outsider is the key to continued innovations. Also, corporate organization should be decentralized to increase the information flows within the organization. More specifically, the recommended set of policy would be as follows:

Policy 1. Competition and open-up policy
Policy 2. Higher education improvement
Policy 3. Financial and stock market promotion
Policy 4. Macroeconomic stability

For policy 1, the abolition of entry barriers is the most effective. Using a framework similar to Aghion and Durlauf (2009), Aghion and Griffith (2005) showed that competition among the firms would increase the growth rate for a country near the technology frontier. Also, the study showed that the "competition for new markets" has been increasingly more significant than the "competition within a market." Also, another empirical study finds out that the scope and extent of competition law is positively correlated with the degree of market competition (Hylton and Deng 2007).[27] This also explains why trade liberalization policy is desirable. As for policy 3, the best policy is an increase in stock price. Reflation policy works as both policies 3 and 4. In 2013, initial public offerings in Japan had reached ¥18.1 billion, making Japan number one in Asia and the number two in the world for initial public offerings, and this trend is continuing.

Yet there is another area in which Japan has not yet reached the "knowledge frontier": that area is policy. The Japanese government has been lagging behind the state-of-the-art policy practices of the developed countries, and for that matter, the BOJ is lagging behind too. The adoption of explicit inflation targeting is one of the major policy innovations, and that effort has succeeded so far. In other areas, there is room for improvement. For example, Japan does not have a proper system of tax collection in the form of an internal revenue service and an individual tax and social security number system. Corporate tax in Japan remains high in part because the tax authority in Japan cannot collect taxes on an individual basis. Also, Japan has not introduced the radio spectrum auction that was already implemented in other countries after the 1990s. Policy innovations in these areas should be the focus of the third arrow since this truly requires government action before the government can ask the private sector to do more.

IV. 4 The Remaining R: The Weakest Link of Abenomics

The most worrying aspect of Japan's Great Stagnation is its deleterious impact on future generations. The hardest hit segment of the society during the Great Stagnation is the youth. The youth, 15 to 24 years old, unemployment rate soared from 4.1 percent in January 1990 to 10.9 percent in June 2010. Recent changes in the employment system have been affecting younger people the most since the declining demand for labor clashed with Japan's long-term employment system. What one has to worry about is the so-called depression babies phenomenon. According to Malmendier and Nagel (2011), the macroeconomic environment would affect people's attitude toward risks. For instance, members of the generation who experienced high rates of return on stock in their youth have a lower risk aversion, are more willing to participate in the stock market, and have a higher ratio of stock in their portfolio than do other generations. Those who experienced high inflation like to refrain from investing in stocks and prefer more inflation-proof assets. Giuliano and Spilimbergo (2014) showed that a recession could have a long-lasting effect on the beliefs of a generation: those who experienced a recession while they are young tend to believe success has more to do with luck than with effort and to support more redistribution by the government.

There is not yet an equivalent systematic study on Japan, but several opinion surveys showed a disturbing social trend. According to Pew Research Center's Global Attitude Project, the Japanese had very low trust in the market economy, compared with the people of other countries, in a 2007 survey: when asked to agree or not with the statement "people are better off in freer markets," only 49 percent of Japanese people agreed, while 70 percent of Americans and 75 percent of Chinese agreed. When asked to agree or not with the statement that the "state should take care of the very poor," only 59 percent of Japanese people agreed, while 70 percent of Americans and 90 percent of Chinese agreed (Ohtake 2010).[28]

Although the economic recovery would benefit the hardest hit segment of the society, Japan needs a serious redistribution policy. On broader issues of redistribution, Japan has serious problems. First, the redistribution system is skewed toward the so-called group-based one, as opposed to an individual-based one: although ideally the government should support only the poor individuals, it actually redistributes income to groups including rice farmers, older people, small and medium companies, and the residents at rural areas (Hatta 2009, 470–476). This is inefficient and unjust. The pension system is a perfect example: as a pay-as-you-go system, it has been severely affected by aging and depopulation. On principle, Japan's redistribution system should shift to an individual-based one using the earned income tax credit or the negative income tax.

Clearly, Japan's redistribution system needs a wholesale reform. But can Abe deliver? So far, the Abe administration has done very little on this front except that it has toughened the monitoring of welfare recipients. Redistribution policy is entangled deeply in politics and values. The very system that he has to change is the product of long-time LDP politics, so any attempt at reform has to deal with interest groups and politicians: older people vote more than do younger people. Also, more conservative members of the LDP who harbor traditional values on family tend to take a tougher approach to the poor. This combination of politics and a clash of values may prevent the government from tackling the wholesale reform.

IV.5 The Shape of the Next Regime to Come

Reflationary regime is by definition transitional. As we discuss in Chapter 5, during and after the Great Depression, political and intellectual dynamics led to the emergence of controlled economies all over the world. There is still a distinct possibility that Japan would go down that road this time, unless countered by promarket reform forces. In a time of crisis, one can easily overemphasize the use of intervention, and historically Japan has an intellectual tradition of interventionism. In this sense, the third arrow may determine the shape of the next regime, although the third arrow itself may not be significant.

Table 5-1 shows two contrasting ideals for Japan's choice of regime, the open regime and the closed regime. The difference in the two regimes rests on each regime's policy, philosophy, or idea. The open regime emphasizes rules and frameworks under which new entry is encouraged: the private sector's initiatives are preferred to the government's. Redistribution follows rule, not discretion. On the other hand, the closed regime emphasizes the discretion and planning of the government and the interests of certain industries and corporations. These are ideals, so the next regime would be likely to be a mix of the two in some areas. Against this distinction, it is clear that the first arrow fits in the open regime. Because the second arrow is skewed toward public works, it favors a certain industry. If the third arrow purports to support a specific industry, the arrow would lead to the closed regime, but if that arrow supports new entrants and competition, it would lead to the open regime.

Table 5-1 Contrasting Two Regimes

	Open Regime	Closed Regime
Principle	Rule, framework-based	Discretion, planning from the top
Market or Business	Promarket	Probusiness
New Entrants	Welcome	Cautious
Monetary Policy	Framework-based, inflation targeting, nominal GDP level targeting	Discretion-based, "*Sogo handan* (judgment by the BOJ)"
Main Policy	Competition policy	Industrial policy
Main Policy Tools	Tax cuts	Subsidies
Redistribution Policy	Rule-based: Negative income tax, basic income	Discretion-based
Structure of Policymaking	Decentralized	Centralized
Economics	More economics	Less economics

In determining the future regime, again idea and perception matter. In this case, perception of the Koizumi-Takenaka structural reform matters. When asked, public supports deregulation and reform,[29] but the intellectual appeal of structural reforms seems to be waning as is shown in the declining number of references to structural reforms recently (Figure 2-1). Structural reform ideology may have worked as a "bad" idea in the previous period since it diverted public attention from macroeconomic issues to the "structural factors." But when reflation is under way, market-oriented reforms are sorely needed. The biggest irony is that the intellectual appeal of structural reform is weakened when we need it most.

V. Conclusion

Immediately after the launch of Abenomics, Christina Romer called it a "policy regime shift" (Romer 2013). This is true and explains why the first arrow matters most. First, the first arrow is the real innovation in Japanese macroeconomic policy, which breaks away from the exiting policy idea trap. Some commentator said that Abenomics is a rehash of old policy, just on large scale: "For all the buzz about status-quo-shaking reforms, bold ideas, and a revolution in competitiveness, Abenomics sure looks a lot like what Japan has been doing for 20 years now—just on a bigger scale and with a splashier marketing campaign" (Pesek 2014, 186). This is correct for the other two arrows, but it is not so for the first arrow since the first arrow has never been implemented in the past. The BOJ had engaged in a large-scale, QE-type expansionary monetary policy but had not committed to any specific price target, and the BOJ terminated the policy prematurely in 2006. Second, there is a saying in macroeconomics that "it takes a heap of Harberger Triangles to fill an Okun gap" (Tobin 1977, 468), which means that any summation of microeconomic gains (Harberger's triangle) cannot beat macroeconomic gains in terms of the magnitude (Okun's Law). If Japan achieves a 2 percent inflation rate, the unemployment rate must fall, and the growth rate must increase. The exact amount is uncertain, yet this effect is more certain than the third arrow. Third, one can expect positive spillover effects to other areas such as reforms and redistribution. The reduction in the real interest rate induced by the first arrow would lead to increased investment, which is a major source of productivity-enhancing innovation. Also, with the tightened labor market, firms would look for labor-saving inventions, and the government is under pressure to change institutions. It is telling that Japanese policymakers have now begun discussing the use of female workers and a foreign workforce earnestly, although it would still take some time for the Japanese to agree on this front. As for redistribution, reflation is at least decreasing the unemployment rate, and thus the poverty rate.

The recovery from 2012 initiated by Abenomics has many similarities with *Takahashi Zaisei*: more than anything else, it is a "regime shift" in monetary policy (Romer 2014; also see Chapter 5). The similarities are not a coincidence: certain policymakers have been deliberately learning from and trying to reengineer the precedent of *Takahashi Zaisei*. The most prominent among them is Kikuo Iwata, a representative Japanese reflationist and now deputy governor of the BOJ. Also, the Takahshi reflation teaches us that the bad loans problem was a secondary issue compared with deflation, and bank loans did not have to increase for deflation to stop and inflation to resume.

Yet, there are several important differences. Abenomics has not yet succeeded as much as the *Takahashi Zaisei* did. This may reflect differences in the nature of regime changes: the Takahashi reflation involved changes in all three respects: the exchange rate, the monetary policy, and the fiscal policy regimes, while the Abe reflation did not change the exchange rate system, although it may break the ever-higher yen syndrome. Also, Takahashi refused to raise any tax during the reflation phase, with one small exception, while Abe raised the consumption tax in April 2014. This could shake people's perception of Abenomics as being a reflation regime. Third, public expenditure in the form of public works may not be as effective as before: with the supply-constraints of the construction sector growing, the efficacy of old LDP-style fiscal policy is increasingly in question.

Could Abenomics succeed? The answer depends on two things: interests and ideas. Economic reforms would take time, and it takes extra time to tackle economic reforms in Japan since it involves dealing with the powerful bureaucracy and interest groups. Therefore, the longer Abe stays in power, the better the chances are that the economic reforms part of Abenomics will succeed. Success also depends on whether Abe and his successors can learn from the past mistakes and break from the policy idea trap that has pervaded Japan's economic policymaking during Japan's Great Stagnation. As I have argued in this book, the economic policy of Japan has been influenced by several "bad" economic ideas; among them are three policy ideas: the BOJ doctrine, the Ministry of Finance view (the modern treasury view), and the industrial policy myth stand out. In a sense, Prime Minister Abe has succeeded in fighting against the BOJ doctrine; therefore, it is no surprise that the first arrow has the greatest chance of success. As for the second arrow, the consumption tax increase could just be premature, and it could repeat the mistake of 1997, when the government raised the consumption tax from 3 to 5 percent. As for the third arrow, it is still uncertain since this is a mixed bag of structural reform ideology and the industrial policy myth: if the former gains momentum once again, another round of market-oriented reforms is possible, but if the industrial policy myth prevails, it could turn out to strengthen the government's control of the economy. When the first and second arrows succeed, what Japan will need most is reform, and the course of this does affect lives of the Japanese in the long run.

Even with the success of Abenomics, the Japanese would face serious challenges. They would include worldwide problems such as the rising inequality, the rise of the computerized machines, the long-run growth prospects, and the local problems that include demographics. Getting out of deflation and long stagnation is just a way to get back to the normal status of the economy. But with the success of Abenomics, the Japanese could afford to tackle other problems earnestly.

CHAPTER 6

Concluding Remarks: Beware of Japanization

I. Introduction

What lessons should we draw from the whole episode of Japan's Great Stagnation? Knowing what happened in Japan is the best way to avoid repeating it, and some have already learned the lessons, while others have not. As for the lessons learned, the Federal Reserve Board (FRB) avoided falling into deflation in 2004, and some governments and central banks, after the Lehman shock, tried to avoid deflation. Also, unlike Japan, central banks dealt with the financial panic of 2007–2008 more or less quickly, although the bankruptcy of Lehman Brothers itself and the triggering of the panic are debatable.

In other areas, the governments and central banks did not learn from Japan's experience. Faced with a potential Great Depression-like crisis, Christina Romer, then chair of the Council of Economic Advisors, came up with the right amount of public expenditure needed to subdue the Great Recession: $1.7 to $1.8 trillion for three years, yet the Obama economic team did not adopt it (Scheiber 2012). The European Central Bank (ECB) raised its deposit facility—key policy interest—rate in April 2011 from 0.25 to 0.5 percent. Furthermore, from 2010 onward, the governments in major advanced economies, including Japan, began pursuing an austerity policy out of concern for the sovereign debt crisis: this premature setback has deepened the Great Recession and slowed the recovery (Blyth 2013).

As of August 2014, the Great Recession is not really over. It is clearly not over for the European countries. The United States has managed better than others have, but there is a growing discussion about the sluggish labor market conditions and "secular stagnation" (Teulings and Baldwin 2014). At this still critical juncture, learning from Japan's Great Stagnation should be relevant.

The studies on the causes of Japan's Great Stagnation are voluminous.[1] Although economists have been divided on the causes and although there is no complete consensus on them, several consensuses emerged after a great deal of literature and debates. One of them points to macroeconomic policy failures made by the government and the Bank of Japan (BOJ). Those failures have been repeated for a long time. I first ascertain what those failures are in Section II, and then I turn to the question of why the failures have been repeated in Section III. Section IV summarizes what can be found in this book, drawing lessons for the world. The last section is the conclusion.

II. What Went Wrong in Japan: Four Mistakes That Japan Made

Mistake 1: The Ever-Higher Yen Syndrome

In a chronological order, the first failure was in macroeconomic policy with a view to the exchange rate in 1985. I have argued that Japan's Great Stagnation has been caused by a series of macroeconomic policy mistakes, presenting the perspective of the "Thirty Years' Crisis." The malfunctioning of the Japanese macroeconomic policy started with the Plaza Accord of 1985. After that, macroeconomic policy went astray, and fiscal and monetary policymakers have been preoccupied with directing the exchange rate in a certain direction: first they tried to appreciate the yen, and then they attempted to tame the supposed damages caused by the appreciation. This had long-lasting psychological ramifications among the Japanese policymakers, economists, and the public: first they were afraid of the appreciation (*endaka kyofusho*, yen appreciation-phobia), and then after the effects of the appreciation turned out to be minor, they came to believe that the Japanese economy could withstand it. The reason the Japanese economy could overcome the appreciation of the yen was purely accidental: there was a considerable decline of the crude oil prices at the same time, so the terms of trade were favorable to the Japanese economy (Hamada and Okada 2009), but that was not recognized then.

Mistake 2: Policies toward the Bubble

The second failure was allowing the rapid increase in the prices of assets such as stocks and land during the late 1980s and the fall of those prices, the so-called bubble and its bursting. Here, however, failure should be carefully discussed. Some argue strongly that central banks should take asset prices into account in the conduct of monetary policy. This view—known as the BIS view, named after the view of the economists at the Bank for International Settlements—has gained more respect, especially after the Great

Recession. However, there is in no way a consensus on this matter. The current consensus still emphasizes that the purpose of central banks should be the stabilization of prices and, to the same or a lesser degree, the stabilization of production and employment, while there is no consensus as to the desirability of asset prices as a target of central banks. Rather, the majority of the economics professionals and central bankers still believe that the asset price should not be a target of central banks. In the end, the asset price inflation, or the bubble, collapsed. This was in part the result of the deliberate "*Bubble Tsubushi*" (bursting bubble) policies of the Ministry of Finance (MOF) and the BOJ from 1989. The question remains whether these deliberate counter-bubble policies were reasonable. By definition, a bubble is a deviation from the fundamental value of assets; therefore, it should collapse eventually, but it is questionable whether the MOF and the BOJ should have taken such a strong measure to burst the bubble. As we have argued, there may be a justification for monetary policy acting against asset price inflation, but it is reasonable to conclude that a "too strong tightening policy leading to the collapse of the boom itself is out of the question" (Jinushi 2007).

Mistake 3: Too Little, Too Late

Third, policy responses after the bursting of the bubble were problematic, to say the least. Bubbles come and go throughout history and all over the world, and there is nothing peculiar about the fact a bubble happened in Japan. In fact, a bubble must happen whenever and wherever there is an asset, an asset market, and expectations for future growth,[2] although its likelihood depends on particular sets of institutions and regulations.[3] But what is peculiar about the Japanese bubble was its aftermath: policy responses have been poor. In the late 1980s, many countries, including Nordic countries, experienced bubbles and their collapses, but the Japanese experience stood out in its length of stagnation afterward, even though the size of the bubble in Japan was just a little greater than the average size of those affected by bubbles (Harada 2003, chap. 2). Reinhart and Rogoff (2009) identified the bigger cases of the financial crises in post-World War II history, calling them the "Big Five" crises (Spain, 1977; Norway, 1987; Finland and Sweden; and Japan, 1992). Yet "among the eighteen bank-centered financial crises following World War II, the 'Big Five' crises have all involved major declines in output over a protracted period, often lasting two years or more. The worst postwar crisis prior to 2007, of course, was that of Japan in 1992, which set the country off on its 'Lost Decade'" (Reinhart and Rogoff 2009, 215). In its magnitude, Japan's case is just above the average, but in duration, it is longer and is thus called the "extraordinary experience of Japan (with its seventeen consecutive years of real housing price declines)" (Reinhart and Rogoff 2009, 226). More specifically, the historical average of decline in real house prices for the post-World War II but pre-2007 banking crises is −35.5 percent in magnitude and six years in duration, but if one excludes Japan, the length becomes five years (Reinhart and Rogoff 2009, 227); in terms of real equity prices, Japan is again just above the average (−55.9 percent decrease over 3.4 years) (Reinhart and Rogoff 2009, 228). As for the unemployment rate and the gross domestic product (GDP) growth rate, Japan has done better than the average, but the unemployment figure is tricky to interpret since the Japanese government has been subsidizing firms to keep employers. Japan's prolonged stagnation has less to do with the bubble itself and more to do with poor responses after the bursting of the bubble.

Japan's policy responses were the typical ones of doing "too little, too late," of "stop and go" approaches, and of not simultaneously coordinating the policy mix. Figure 6-1 shows the conduct of fiscal and monetary policy from the mid-1990s to the present time, in which fiscal policy is defined as a year-to-year change in public investment, while monetary policy is defined as a change in monetary base. Even during the Koizumi-Takenaka recovery period from 2001 to 2006, fiscal policy was contractionary, while monetary policy was expansionary; after the Lehman shock, from 2009 to 2010, fiscal policy became expansionary, yet monetary policy became contractionary. As this shows, policymakers kept making problematic decisions throughout the period, up to and including the Great Recession.

Using the policy rule during Japan's good macroeconomic years of 1975 to 1985, before the bubble, as a benchmark to evaluate the macroeconomic performance of following years, Toshiki Jinushi at Kobe University argued the following: (1) During the bubble years, more than usual fiscal tightening was combined with more than usual monetary expansion. (2) After the collapse of the bubble, monetary policy became too tight since it hit the zero interest rate lower bound, while the conduct of fiscal policy "was about usual in the early 1990s, but then expanded, contracted, and again expanded, all in a more than usual pattern, during the late 1990s" (Jinushi 2007, 178). The more than usual contraction here refers to the Hashimoto administration's fiscal policy from the last half of 1996 to the first half of 1997 involving the consumption tax hike. Jinushi concluded that "monetary and fiscal policy have rarely been used in a coordinated manner either to be contractionary or to be expansionary during the periods of great economic fluctuations of the emergence of a bubble and its collapse and the subsequent long stagnation. I must say this is lamentable" (Jinushi 2007, 178–179). During Japan's long stagnation, Japan has not conducted an expansionary policy mix, which it should. Now one may see part of the reason why Abenomics succeeded in its

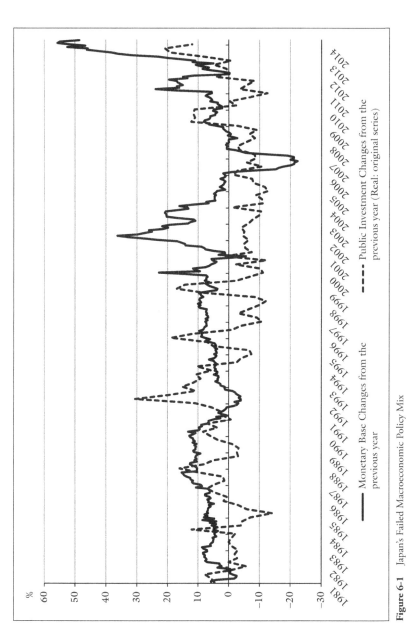

Figure 6-1 Japan's Failed Macroeconomic Policy Mix

Sources: Data from Cabinet Office and the BOJ.

initial stage: it has a coordinated macroeconomic policy for the first time in recent history. One may also see why the consumption tax hike effective as of April 2014 poses a danger to the future prospects of Abenomics.

Mistake 4: Other Mistakes

Fourth, Japanese policy makers went astray in policy areas other than macroeconomic policy. During most of the 1990s and continuing into the early 2000s, the most hotly debated issue was the disposal of the bad loans problem. But it is problematic to consider it as a macroeconomic policy. At first, it was assumed that the bad loans problem could have macroeconomic consequences through lending channels since bank loans had declined during the 1990s: people talked about "*Kashi Shiburi*" (unwillingness to lend money) on the banks' side, or the credit crunch, as the problem of Japan's Great Stagnation. But it turned out that there was not enough evidence to support the "*Kashi Shiburi*" hypothesis; there was only the period of financial crisis from 1997 to 1998 (Hayashi and Prescott 2002; Yoshikawa 2003).[4] The research focus has shifted to "*Oigashi* (zombie or forbearance lending)" to firms whose profitability and productivity are low and firms that should have already exited the market: the so-called zombie firms. Takeo Hoshi at Stanford University is the leading proponent of the "*Oigashi*" hypothesis (Hoshi 2006; Cabarello, Hoshi, and Kashap 2008). This has been gaining some popularity among the economists, but it is far from being the consensus. Kyoji Fukao at Hitotsubashi University, Japan's leading expert on the productivity study, pointed out that the zombie lending hypothesis does explain the productivity slowdown in manufacturing, which accounts for half of the slowdown of the total factor productivity growth rate, and that as far as listed companies are concerned, industrial metabolism of nonmanufacturing has remained low, not only after the 1990s but also before the 1990s. Fukao concluded that "even if the zombie problem had existed, that explains only a tiny part of the stagnation of the TFP during the 1990s Japan" (Fukao 2012, 194).

What is certain about the bad loans problem is the fact that both the regulatory authority—the MOF was in charge of the supervision of the financial sector—and the Japanese banks postponed the disposal of the bad loans (Iwata 1998; Takahashi 2000, 2003; Muramatsu 2005). The bad loans problem has two aspects: private financial institutions and the regulatory authority. However, in the early 1990s, the former "didn't have a rule about cutting losses (i.e., setting up an allowance according to their loss as in accounting)," while the latter did not act to check on the financial institutions (Takahashi 2003, 40). As we see in Chapter 2, the bad loans problem was recognized as early as 1991. The MOF had already conducted the inspection of the financial conditions of the *Jusen* companies (private nonbank financial companies for housing loans set up by private banks) from 1991 to 1992, revealing that the *Jusen* had accumulated a large number of bad loans; in one of the companies, 59.8 percent of all loans had turned out to be bad (Iwata 1998, 5). In later years, the MOF did not pursue the consistent policy of its resolution, and this prolonged resolution cost more public money. Yoichi Takahashi, an MOF official in charge of financial inspections from 1993 to 1994, speculated that the "government had to pour 'public funds' in 60 trillion yens [sic] to solve the bad loan problem in October 1998." He further speculated that the amount of injected public funds had been one tenth of of 60 trillion yen if proper disposal measures had been taken during 1992–1994 (Takahashi 2003, 40). In this sense, the MOF failed in dealing with the bad loans issue as promptly as it should have done.

In other policy areas, Japan's Great Stagnation was the Age of "Structural Reform." As we see in Chapter 2, the meaning of this term varies a great deal, depending on the writers. In the early 1990s, Japan put an enormous amount of energy into political reform: it coincided with the eruption of political scandals such as the Recruit and the Tokyo Sagawa Kyubin incidents, and people tended to attribute the cause of "what is going wrong" in 1990s Japan to something "fundamental and inherent" to Japan. If the structural reform is understood as a so-called supply-side policy, that is, deregulation, privatization, or trade liberalization, tax reform should be of macroeconomic importance: on this front, Japan lowered its income and corporate taxes and implemented several microeconomic measures. The Cabinet Office (Cabinet Office 2010) reported that regulatory reforms have been conducted in telecommunications, transportation, energy, finance, food and beverage, and so on, with a cumulative increase of consumer surplus amounting to ¥25 trillion as of 2008 from the early 1990s. As Figure 6-2 shows, in terms of regulation in product markets, Japan has advanced in its deregulation from 1998 to 2003. It is true that Japan's deregulation efforts have stalled since 2003, and the markets are more regulated than those in the United States, the United Kingdom, and Canada but are less regulated than those in Sweden (Saito 2013; OECD 2014). Despite those supply-side reform efforts, the Japanese economy has been stagnating for a long period.

Explanations for Mistakes Reexamined

This leads to the question of what exactly contributed to Japan's Great Stagnation. One does not have to take a sole-causal view of it, but economists

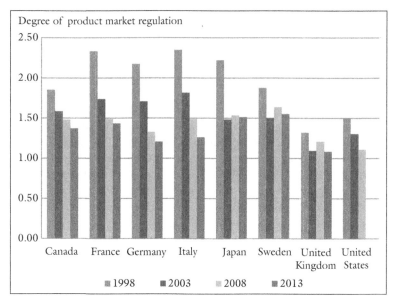

Figure 6-2 Product Market Regulation
Source: Data from OECD (2014).

have been divided on this issue, as we see in Chapter 3. Based on Miyao (2006), Kataoka's (2010) study summarized the explanations as follows:

1. Demand-side A: stagnation of consumption and investment through insufficient monetary easing and persistent deflationary expectations
2. Demand-side B: decreased public expenditures through fiscal tightening
3. Demand-side C: shortage of investment through a bank's "*Kashishi-buri* (unwillingness to lend)" or problems in the financial sector
4. Supply-side A: stagnation of the productivity of the firms
5. Supply-side B: slow adjustment of industrial structure
6. Supply-side C: inefficient resource misallocation due to "*Oigashi*" and unproductive public works (Kataoka 2010, 154).

No doubt the list can be extended. Demand-side A is the position taken by the "reflationists." Popular business economists such as Richard Koo combine demand-side B with demand-side C, stressing the deteriorated balance sheet as the cause of long stagnation and the restoration as the remedy for it. The foremost proponent of supply-side A is Fumio Hayashi (Hayashi and Prescott 2002), but further studies showed a more complicated picture of Japan's productivity slowdown. First, a large-scale joint study headed by Hayashi (Hayashi 2007) drew the following set of conclusions: (1) "the slow-down in the TFP growth rate during the 1990s was smaller than Hayashi and Prescott (2002)" (Hayashi 2007, 81); (2) "the average of the Solow residuals has declined from the 1980s to the 1990s, while pure technological progress rate has not declined" (Hayashi 2007, 48); (3) "according to the zombie lending hypothesis, it is supposed that the stagnation of TFP in Japan occurred mainly in non-manufacturing sector" (Hayashi 2007, 72), yet "many studies have shown that TFP growth rate slowdown has been more serious in manu-facturing than in non-manufacturing sector[s]" (Hayashi 2007, 81), casting doubt about the zombie lending hypothesis; (4) "even during the 1990s stag-nant growth period, technological change in consumption goods sector has been stagnating, while that in investment goods sector has been continuing, which has promoted the growth rate potentially" (Hayashi 2007, 146–147). The reasons these potentials were not realized were greatly owed to "factors other than technology" (Hayashi 2007, 147).

Needless to say, many studies show that the TFP growth rate has declined; therefore, this requires explanations. Hayashi and Prescott (2002) pointed out the reduced working hours and regulations that protect declining indus-tries, which could be considered policy failures. Also, as Chapter 3 shows, supply and demand interact with each other; therefore, it is too simplistic to attribute the cause of Japan's Great Stagnation to either of them. In an overview, Hayashi criticized the demand-side explanation for its dubious logic and nonexplicit use of the model (Hayashi 2007, 6–7), and surely his research has advanced the important subject of the relationship between sup-ply and demand. Fukao (2012), another representative study on productivity in Japan, analyzed the influence of the TFP growth rate on demand. However, the basic premise of the correlation between the TFP growth rate and GDP growth rate can be interpreted in other ways. Comin and Gertler (2006), for example, argued that the TFP could be influenced by demand factors.

In the end, the following remarks by Charles Yuji Horioka are still valid:

> there is no easy answer to the question of whether demand-side factors or supply-side factors were more important, but my reading of the data and of the literature convinces me that demand-side factors were probably more important and that the single most important cause of the prolonged slow-down of the Japanese economy in the 1990s was the stagnation of private fixed investment, which in turn was caused by overinvestment in plant and equipment during the bubble economy of the late 1980s, the collapse of asset

prices during the postbubble period, and an inadequate policy response to these events. In particular, I feel that policy mistakes during the bubble period (e.g., overly expansionary monetary policies) as well as during the postbubble period (e.g., overly contractionary fiscal and monetary policies and the inadequacy of government actions aimed at resolving the financial crisis and the non-performing loan problem) are largely to blame. (Horioka 2006)

What Might Have Been

As for the role of the BOJ and monetary policy, referring to Braun and Waki (2006) and Inoue and Okimoto (2008),[5] Hayashi concluded: "The main cause of the Lost Decade was first the decreased TFP growth rate, and second stagnated investment. Monetary policy should be responsible for deflation, although the stagnation of GDP was inevitable under different sets of monetary policy." Assuming that the BOJ had followed the modified Taylor rule, and assuming also that the TFP growth rate had declined as much as Hayashi and Prescott (2002) assumed, Braun and Waki (2006) showed that long stagnation and deflation during the 1990s could be explained. This modified Taylor rule "has a two percentage point higher constant term" (Hayashi 2007, 9). In other words, if the BOJ had adopted the 2 per cent inflation target, the nominal interest rate would have been 2 percent higher, and deflation would have been avoided. In fact, the BOJ did exactly the opposite. Daniel Leigh (2009) estimated the "implicit inflation target" of the BOJ went down: "Regarding the implicit inflation target, the results provide evidence of a downward drift in the target from about 2.5 percent in the early 1980s to about 1 percent by 1995 (Leigh 2009, 11)."

In January 2013, the Initiatives on Global Markets Forum hosted by Chicago Booth School of Business asked 38 distinguished economists for their opinions about the following sentence: "The persistent deflation in Japan since 1997 could have been avoided had the Bank of Japan followed different monetary policies." Of the respondents, 53 percent said that they "agree" or "strongly agree." Weighted with confidence, 79 percent said likewise.[6]

A Comparison with Sweden

In order to understand what Japan could have done, a brief comparison with the Scandinavian case, especially the Swedish one, is useful. Sweden experienced a credit-fueled property boom, its collapse, a severe banking crisis, and a contraction: the real GDP growth rate became negative from 1991 to 1993, but with a swift and resolute management of the bad loans problem, Sweden overcame the aftermath of the bubble quickly and escaped from the crisis, returning to a positive growth rate in 1994. Against the backdrop of the successful resolution of the bad loans problem was a proper macroeconomic policy mix. Sweden had pegged its currency, the krona, to the European currency unit (ECU) until May 1991. Yet as the economy began to stagnate in the aftermath of the bursting of the bubble, the prospect of a currency crisis loomed large toward the fall of 1992, and Sweden decided to return to a flexible exchange regime on November 19, 1992. As a result, the krona depreciated 30 percent against the U.S. dollar from 1992 to 1993. This gave the Swedish policymakers the autonomy they needed to engage in an expansionary monetary policy. Sweden needed a nominal anchor as a guide for the conduct of monetary policy, so the country introduced an inflation target of 2 percent on January 15, 1993, and planned to hit the target in two years (Sveriges Riksbank 1993).

Lars Jonung, a renowned Swedish macroeconomist, summarized seven factors that contributed to the successful management of the economy after the banking crisis (Jonung 2009).[7] They are the following:

> (1) The importance of political unity behind the resolution policy, (2) a government blanket guarantee of the financial obligations of the banking system, (3) swift policy action where acting early was more important than acting in exactly the right manner, (4) an adequate legal and institutional framework for the resolution procedures including open-ended public funding, (5) full disclosure of information by the parties involved, (6) a differentiated resolution policy minimizing moral hazard by forcing private sector participants to absorb losses before government financial intervention, and (7) the proper design of macroeconomic policies to simultaneously end the crisis in both the real economy and the financial sector. (Jonung 2009, 1)

As Jonung rightly points out, some of these Swedish characteristics may not be exported to other countries. Sweden was a small open economy under the pegged exchange rate regime. When the crisis happened, the "Swedish financial system was much more transparent than is currently the case in most countries" (Jonung 2009, 17), and "Sweden has a long tradition of confidence in its domestic institutions, in its political system and in its elected representatives" (Jonung 2009, 18).[8] Also, in Sweden, the bureaucrats can rotate from the MOF to the Sveriges Riksbank and vice versa, facilitating information sharing and swift decisions (Kasuya 2005). No doubt some of Japan's political and institutional settings have prevented the Japanese policymakers from taking swift and decisive actions. But what characterizes Japan's failure has more to do with the lack of macroeconomic knowledge.[9]

III. Why Failures?

In discussing policy failures, one cannot agree more with the following statement: "To understand the 'why' question, we must turn to politics" (Grimes 2001, xv). If policy failure comes from the failure of politics or policymakers, the simplest answer would be the incompetence of policymakers, yet the very fact that policy failures have been repeated over an extended period of time would suggest a hypothesis that there is something wrong with Japan's policymaking process itself, rather than with individual policymakers. This could be called the structural problem of the policymaking process hypothesis. Then other hypothesis should be also contemplated.

Political scientists tend to point out the structural or systematic deficiency of the policymaking process. William Grimes, a political scientist at Boston University, represents this view:[10] the upshot of his view is that "Japan's macroeconomic pathologies have included an excessive reliance on monetary policy to solve large-scale macroeconomic problems and an extreme aversion to loosening fiscal policy. These pathologies were not the result of incompetence or corruption on the part of policy makers (many of them among Japan's 'best and brightest'); rather, they were structural in nature, the products of a policymaking process in which political leaders, the Ministry of Finance, and the Bank of Japan competed to advance their own versions of national interest" (Grimes 2001, xvi). Specifically, he stresses the lack of independence of the BOJ, arguing that it has distorted the macroeconomic policy mix in that the MOF had shifted its burden of conducting macroeconomic policy to the BOJ. The distortion of the macroeconomic policy mix is consistent with the observation that the Japanese macroeconomic policy mix did not work during the Great Stagnation.

The structural deficiency in the Japanese policymaking process must be taken seriously, and no doubt Grime's explanation has hit on the important point. Yet there are problems with this type of explanation. First, the status of the independence of the BOJ should be examined more carefully. In the process of the deregulation of financial markets, including the relaxation of interest rates, the policy target rate has shifted from the official discount rate to the overnight call rate: with this change, it is argued, the BOJ had gained its de facto independent status even before the BOJ law was revised in 1998 (Kamikawa 2005). Second, it does not predict the performance of macroeconomic policy after the BOJ gained de jure independence as well: the BOJ raised the interest rate from zero in August 2000, went back to the zero interest rate policy and introduced quantitative easing (QE) in March 2001, and terminated the QE in March 2006 with its interest rate hike in June 2006. Also, it did not keep up with other central banks by expanding its balance sheet after the Lehman shock, resulting in the rapid appreciation of the yen afterward. In light of the subsequent developments, it is difficult to say that the performance of the independent BOJ is better than that of the dependent one. Third, as Grimes pointed out, politicians, the MOF bureaucrats, and the BOJ officials have "their own versions of national interests" that should have been explored further.

This harkens back to the problem of ideas, which should be understood as a wide variety of beliefs, cognitive biases, ideas, institutional memory, "models," and way of thinking, as we discuss in Chapter 1. For instance, why did the MOF resist implementing the expansionary fiscal policy in the early 1990s? As the decade continued, the debt accumulated, and there emerged a growing sense of fiscal policy ineffectiveness; yet, it is difficult to understand why the MOF resisted in the early 1990s. Why did they place a particular priority on a balanced budget and fiscal consolidation, even in the midst of a recession? The intervention into the foreign exchange market at the time of the Plaza Accord was intended to divert the criticisms from the United States regarding the trade disputes. This was heavily influenced by politics, and even though every policy is politically determined, politics matters, especially to international relations. But one cannot portray the Japanese policymakers as pushed by their American counterparts to reluctantly appreciate the yen: those in charge of the exchange rate policy at the MOF were not passive agents; they were willing participants in the Plaza Accord. As far as their recollections are concerned, those in charge were not concerned with the macroeconomic consequences of their policy action; rather, they were elated to be a participant in the major international event, and they were proud of being a member of the major powers (Takita 2006).

Turning to the BOJ, why did it allow deflation to happen in the late 1990s? It is quite natural to ask "*why* Japanese policymakers in general—and the Bank of Japan in particular—responded so slowly and so erratically in the face of deteriorating economic questions" (Harrigan and Kuttner 2005, 102; emphasis is original). The "simplest" answer is that "the Bank of Japan behaved appropriately given the information it had available at the time, but was caught off-guard by the severity and speed of the disinflation" (Harrigan and Kuttner 2005, 102). This has indeed been the official answer provided by the BOJ economists: "the BOJ's policy at that time was basically optimal under uncertainty about the policy multiplier, but that the policy was not optimal under uncertainty about the inflation process and a more aggressive policy response would have been needed" (Fujiwara et al. 2007, 31). Also, the study by the FRB economists suggested that the "bottom line of this analysis is that Japanese monetary policy during 1991–1995 appeared appropriate based on the expectations for the economy that prevailed at that time," although "inadequate allowance for downside risk was built into monetary policy, as evidenced by the fact that once actual inflation and growth numbers came in weaker than expected, interest rates ended up being higher than were called for under the Taylor rule" (Ahearn et al. 2002, 20). Yet, at best "this story becomes less convincing after 1993" (Harrigan and Kuttner 2005, 102). Also, as Chapter 3 shows, even in the early 1990s, the BOJ's conduct of monetary policy did not lack severe critics, and the BOJ economists engaged directly with them in controversies, the prime example being the money supply controversy between Kikuo Iwata and Kunio Okina. It is true that those critics did not anticipate full-fledged deflation, but the concerns about asset price deflation and recession were real. It is difficult to conclude that, as Harrigan and Kuttner (2005, 102) claimed, "the Bank of Japan behaved appropriately given the information it had available at the time."

Then the next answer turns on the historic "conflict between the Bank of Japan and the Ministry of Finance." This has to do with the structural deficiency of the policymaking process: the lack of coordination between them has contributed to the failure of the macroeconomic policy mix. Yet, this lack of coordination has been strengthened by the institutional memory of the BOJ. As we see in Chapter 4, during the Great Depression, the BOJ purchased the Japanese government bonds directly from the government, which helped Japan escape from the Great Depression. Nevertheless, this episode has been remembered in the BOJ as a cause for high inflation after Korekiyo Takahashi's assassination on February 26, 1936, and this episode has an extraordinarily bad reputation: the official history of the BOJ, *Nihon ginko hyakunenshi* (The centennial history of the Bank of Japan), described this direct purchase as the "most deplorable event in the long history of the Bank" (Nihon Giko Hyakunenshi Iinkai 1986, 26). Moreover, this memory of accelerated inflation caused by government's pressure was further strengthened by the experiences of the 1970s high inflation.

However, there is one more hypothesis: "simply that the Bank of Japan's policies were constrained by a rigid adherence to certain economic doctrines" (Harrigan and Kuttner 2005, 103).[11] They include the lack of the concept of "real interest rate," adherence to the nominal interest rate policy, and liquidationist (creative destruction) thinking. The most problematic of all was their understanding of "price stability." The BOJ before the new regime did not seem to be concerned with deflation, although it was indeed concerned with inflation. The BOJ raised its policy interest rate in August 2000 against advice from the government and international organizations. The BOJ thought that the subsequent recession was just "unlucky" since it coincided with the bursting of the information technology bubble in the United States. But the Japanese economy at that time was under deflation. Again, in March

2006, the BOJ terminated its QE and raised the policy interest rate in July 2006. The headline consumer price index (CPI) has just touched 2 percent, but after the end of QE, the inflation rate plunged back to deflation. The rise of the "good deflation" argument around the early 2000s within the BOJ signaled that the BOJ understood price stability as a very low inflation rate or even slight deflation.[12] Although the BOJ defeated two-digit high inflation during the 1970s successfully, there may be a bias for the BOJ to accept mild deflation.

The BOJ's "adherence to certain economic doctrines" reflects its own history. Ex-BOJ economist Kunio Okina argued that central banks' behavior could be understood from their "traumas" (Okina 2013, chap. 2).[13] Although he does not explicitly spell out the "traumas" of the BOJ, there are three candidates. First is the Showa Depression. Although the Takahashi reflation was a success, it was remembered as a failure due to high inflation after World War II. Second is the Great Inflation of the 1970s (Kataoka and Wakatabe 2011; Wakatabe 2013). The BOJ cooperated with the government in the early 1970s, allowing the money supply to increase. Third is the creation of the bubble economy in the 1980s. The BOJ officials learned from the episode that they should prevent asset price inflation from happening. In all cases, the BOJ cooperated with the government in an expansionary direction, and the BOJ perceived that the cooperation failed. The outlook of the modern BOJ comes from officials who are too afraid of general inflation and asset price inflation and who are reluctant to cooperate with the government.

The biggest failure of all is the persistence of policymakers in not learning from the past. Congleton (2004) proposed that "Insofar as policy mistakes are unavoidable during times of crisis, the standing procedures for dealing with crisis should allow policy mistakes to be discovered and corrected at relatively low cost (Congleton 2004, 198)" Constitutionally speaking, this is the reason why we have elections, but this has not worked well in Japan.

Revealingly, Heizo Takenaka, the most successful economic minister during Japan's Great Stagnation, perceived that the stagnation was caused by a series of policy mistakes. In a paper that was published just one month before he became the minister for economic and fiscal policy, he pointed out the "policy crisis" as a cause for the stagnation during the 1990s (Takenaka et al. 2001). As Chapters 2 and 3 show, he has been inconsistent on several occasions and made several mistakes, but in the end he delivered results.

IV. Beware of Japanization: Lessons for the World

By way of conclusion, lessons from Japan's Great Stagnation can be summarized as follows.

Lesson 1: Beware of Deflation

Japan's Great Stagnation has been characterized with deflation. It is true that the degree to which deflation has contributed to the stagnation is still debatable, but the case for not having deflation is paramount. As Japan's example shows, the conduct of monetary policy becomes more difficult once the nominal interest rate hits the zero lower bound, and it is extremely difficult to end deflation once it sets in. Recovery can happen even under the deflationary environment, but it would be weak and not sustainable. The FRB has so far managed to learn from history, but the European situation is worrying. Jaime Caruana, head of the BIS said, "The historical evidence indicates that deflations have often been associated with sustained growth in output. The Great Depression was more the exception than the rule (Evans-Pritchard 2014)."[14] In his speech, he referred to "good deflation," a robust growth period with mild deflation that is caused by imports from China and other emerging markets (Caruana 2014). Other BIS studies referred to deflation in the late nineteenth century. This kind of reaction has already been made in Japan. Some economists downplayed the danger of deflation, citing the example of late nineteenth century deflation (Sakakibara 2003).

As of October 2014, the Eurozone needs to worry about Japanization. The Eurozone has not yet reached deflation, although the inflation rate is close to 0.4 percent, and in some countries such as Greece, Italy, and Spain, the percentage changes in CPI have now begun hitting the negative region. Accordingly, the real GDP growth rate has declined to a mere 0.2 percent. A money-based indicator for deflation risk tells us that the Eurozone is now increasingly becoming a low inflation regime: "Model estimations conducted with information up to the end of 2013 show that the risks of a low inflation regime have been increasing in the course of the last six quarters of the sample in the euro area, while they have remained substantially unchanged in the US and even declined in Japan" (Amisano et al. 2014, 16).

Against this backdrop, the reactions of the Europeans are worrying. Mario Draghi, the current president, promised to do "whatever it takes," defending the euro in 2011–2012, cutting the deposit facility rate to negative in June 2014, and announcing the plan to purchase asset-backed securities in September 2014, but he has not yet engaged in full-blown QE. Needless to say, the ECB has been constrained by its institutional framework. The institutional constraint is obvious in that the ECB has member countries and cannot purchase the government bonds of the member states. But it has been constrained by policy philosophy, most notably by that of Bundesbank. It has been known that Bundesbank has been traumatized by the experience of hyperinflation in the early 1920s, although it was the deflationary depression,

[handwritten margin note: Germany wanted full structure in place before Euro. France said work things out when they happen. Eg Greece But lack the Tools!]

the Great Depression, which led to the collapse of the Weimar republic and gave rise to the Nazism.[15]

Lesson 2: Beware of Bad Ideas

Chapter 3 lists nine ideas circulated during Japan's Great Stagnation.

1. Liquidationism, or policy nihilism: A boom needs the subsequent recession to "cleanse" the economy through selection of bad projects, firms, and industries; therefore, countercyclical policy is not desirable.

2. Macroeconomic ineffectiveness doctrine or structural reforms ideology: Japan's stagnation is structural in nature and could not be solved by macroeconomic policy; therefore, the restoration of the economy requires measures other than macroeconomic policy—that is, structural reforms.

3. "Only fiscal policy works" doctrine: When macroeconomic policy works, the main tool must be fiscal policy, and public works are preferable to tax cuts. This is likely to be combined with the old understanding of the liquidity trap and the argument in item eight.

4. Austerity doctrine—modern treasury view: Fiscal consolidation should be the first and foremost goal of economic policy. In its extreme version, this entails fiscal policy ineffectiveness, and monetary policy would not solve the consolidation.

5. Good deflation doctrine: Deflation is good since the prices are decreasing.

6. Structural explanations for deflation: The causes of deflation are globalization, economic integration with China in particular; decreased population or working population; or stagnant bank loans due to the bad loans problem.

7. Monetary policy ineffectiveness doctrine—the BOJ doctrine: Money supply cannot be controlled, the price level cannot be controlled, the concept of real interest rate is useless, or the quantity theory of money cannot hold since there is an infinite demand for money under the zero interest rate environment (he money supply would be sucked into the hands of households and firms like a star would be sucked into a black hole).

8. Belief in industrial policy—modern MITI view: The government has to, and can, effectively target and support specific industries for economic growth.

9. Antigrowth sentiment—limits to growth doctrine: Economic growth is undesirable, and impossible for the Japanese economy.

The world may not see all nine ideas: clearly, the "belief in industrial policy" is not shared by other Western countries, but certainly some of the bad ideas will be circulated. For example, we have already seen the "good deflation" doctrine and "structural explanations for deflation" advocated by Caruana (2014). Christina and David Romer have written an important paper warning about the "monetary policy ineffectiveness" doctrine (Romer and Romer 2013). Romer and Romer (2013) detected that, like the Great Depression before, the doctrine has emerged in the policy discussion of Fed officials. Even Bernanke, Janet Yellen and William Dudley, who are considered to be advocates for policy action, occasionally refer to two sets of ideas. The tools for monetary policy are limited, and they involve four potential costs: they "could impair the functioning of securities markets," "reduce public confidence in the Fed's ability to exit smoothly from its accommodative policies," create "risks to financial stability," and cause "the possibility that the Federal Reserve could incur financial losses" (Bernanke 2012b [quoted in Romer and Romer 2013, 59]). As they note, Bernanke concluded that "the costs of nontraditional tools, when considered carefully, appear manageable (Bernanke 2012b [quoted in Romer and Romer 2013, 59])." This was just before he launched the second round of the QE, and thus he was not subscribing to the BOJ-like monetary ineffectiveness doctrine, yet there are reasons to be concerned.

At this critical juncture, many economists are talking about secular stagnation. Liquidationism has not yet set in, but as the stagnation prolongs, there is a distinct possibility that this defeatism or policy nihilism will creep into the media discourse. Also, as it has happened in Japan, once there is a perception that macroeconomic policy is ineffective, attention turns to "structural factors." This might lead to misdirected efforts such as deregulation amidst a deflationary environment, although reforms combined with macroeconomic stabilization is desirable.

Lesson 3: Beware of the "Policy Idea Trap"

The time of crisis is a time of controversy. Bad economic ideas are contained as long as the macroeconomic situation is going well, while they tend to be resurrected during crisis time. As I argue in Chapter 1, these "bad ideas" have been shared not only among policymakers but with economists and the media.

Chapter 2 shows the logic behind the policy dynamics of Japan's Great Stagnation. It started with one policy mistake, but it was followed by a series of mistakes. The Plaza Accord brought the precipitous appreciation of the yen, which had negative consequences for the economy. To counter these negative impacts, the government and the BOJ changed their policy stance, which generated asset price booms. To "correct" this mistake, they completely reversed the policy stance once again, this time to prick the bubble. Then came the lesson of the recent experience: the government and the BOJ should have responded to asset price deflation with an expansionary policy, but they chose not to repeat the same mistake. Instead, they tried out another solution, deregulation and liberalization, which eventually evolved to become a policy slogan, "structural reforms." However, those structural reforms could not deliver the recovery without macroeconomic policy: macroeconomic failures such as doing "too little, too late" and an uncoordinated policy mix created the perception among the public that macroeconomic policy did not work. The Japanese policymakers should have corrected macroeconomic mistakes with proper macroeconomic policy.

For Western countries, the bad loans problem would not be as severe as in Japan: those countries have rules and regulations to deal with such loans. But preoccupation with "structural" or "system" issues could take any form other than the bad loans problem. At crisis time, macroeconomic policy is extremely important, yet preoccupation with systemic problems might distort the proper response. All sorts of lags exacerbate the response problem.

The longer the economy stagnates, the bigger the problems are. I touch on the perils of long stagnation in Chapter 5. People and institutions can adjust to deflation and stagnation, but this adjustment is dangerous and has negative effects on the economy and the society as a whole. Entrepreneurship, or what Keynes called animal spirits, breeds on "optimism," even a groundless one (Coehlo 2010; Ohtake 2010, 33–34). Like deflation, once defeatism has crept into the society, it would be difficult to get out of it. This would set a long process of decline into motion.

In the end, the most troublesome idea is the antigrowth sentiment. As we see in Chapters 3 and 5, there is a growing antigrowth sentiment in Japan: some even condemn the current dismal condition of the society on the growth-oriented mentality. It might be worthwhile to conceive a different society based on no growth, but usually those who suffer from negative or low growth rate are the poor, the unemployed, and the weak. After all, Japan has experienced 20 years of negative or low growth.

It is better to avoid falling into such a policy idea trap. Beware of Japanization.

Notes

Preface

1. The entire volume of this government-sponsored project is available on the Internet, although it is written in Japanese (http://www.esri.go.jp/jp/prj/sbubble/menu.html). Hamada, Kashyap, and Weinstein (2011) is a coproduct of the project but is independent of the Japanese version. See also Cargill and Sakamoto (2010), Garside (2012), and the works cited in the following chapters for the literature.

Chapter 1

1. It is telling that Japanization was used in a positive manner in the late 1980s, against the background of the ascendance of the Japanese management style as one that should be imitated by other countries. For example, *Collins Dictionary of Business* (HarperCollins 2006) defines it as "the adoption by organizations elsewhere of work organization and employment practices usually found in large Japanese companies."
2. Posen (2003a) seems to be among the first to use the term Japanization in its relationship to other developed countries' policy.
3. For more recent examples, see the exchanges on the Internet among Avent (2012a, 2012b), DeLong (2012), Noah (2012), and Modeled Behavior (2012).
4. This growth performance partially reflects the surge in consumption before the consumption tax hike, effective as of April 2014, but the investment was also robust.
5. This has been shared by Fingleton (2012) and Krugman (2012). Fingleton even tried to argue that Japan was not a failure but a success story, but his reasons are problematic because he cited the "low" unemployment rate, the appreciated yen, and the current account surplus as the good signs of the Japanese economy. Examining Japan's GDP per working population among those aged from 15 to 64, Krugman modified his perception. Yet he maintained that "there were two long periods of depressed output relative to trend, one in the mid-1990s, and another, much worse, between 1997 and 2007." His explanation

remained the same as before: Japan has been trapped in a "liquidity trap." See Chapter 2.

6. The output gap may be underestimated when one uses the Hodrik-Prescott filtering method. See Krugman (2012c).

7. This may offer another reason for a central bank to aim at an inflation target of 2 percent.

8. The latest figure was released in July 2014: http://www.mhlw.go.jp/toukei/saikin/hw/k-tyosa/k-tyosa13/dl/03.pdf.

9. There are no reliable data on female prostitution in Japan, yet based on his own fieldwork research and interviews of around one hundred female prostitutes, Ogiue (2012) found that 43 percent of interviewees become a prostitute to pay for the costs of living and 31 percent of them become a prostitute to pay for credit card debts. Some cases of mental illness have been reported, but the majority of them became prostitutes out of poverty.

10. OECD, Income Distribution and Poverty, OECD StatExtracts. http://stats.oecd.org/Index.aspx?DataSetCode=IDD

11. The number for 1990 is available in the following: http://www1.mhlw.go.jp/toukei/ksk/htm/ksk030.html.

12. According to the *Syotoku Saibumpai Chosa* (Survey on Income Redistribution) conducted by the Ministry of Health, Labor and Welfare, the Gini coefficient (at disposable income, posttax, and transfer) is 0.3814 in 1998 and 0.3791 in 2010. http://www.mhlw.go.jp/file/04-Houdouhappyou-12605000-Seisakutoukatsukan-Seisakuhyoukakanshitsu/h23hou_1.pdf.

13. See, for example, Quiggin (2012) and Mirowski (2013).

14. Furner and Supple (1990) classified knowledge into "professional, or disciplinary, knowledge; informed opinion, or practical knowledge; and cultural beliefs and values regarding the economic order" (Furner and Supple 1990, 12). These categories do not correspond one-to-one with the three A–C categories listed in this section, since economists have not only professional knowledge but also other informed opinions or cultural beliefs.

15. Or they may bring in new ideas. The process for new ideas is still an unexplored issue. Rodrik (2014) referred to Leighton and López (2012), emphasizing the role of political or policy entrepreneurship. Like economic entrepreneurs, political or policy entrepreneurs seek out opportunities to influence policy for their own benefits. These benefits may involve not only personal gains, material or otherwise, but also public gains or psychological satisfaction from the sense of achieving public gains.

16. The elasticities approach is based on the concept that the balance of payments would respond to the exchange rate, depending on the elasticities, i.e., the responsiveness of the demand for changes in prices, of a wide variety of goods. It supposes that the balance of payments would decrease when the exchange rate for that country appreciates, given a certain condition.

17. I explored this theme in my 2009 book (Wakatabe 2009), which examined the Great Depression, the Great Inflation, Japan's Great Stagnation, and the current Great Recession.

Chapter 2

1. For other accounts of the Japanese economy since the 1980s, see Kuroda (2005), Cargill and Sakamoto (2008), Naikakufu Keizaishakai Kenkyusyo (2009), and Garside 2012.
2. It is not easy to trace the first usage of the term "Ushinawareta Junen (Lost Decade)" in the media discourse. The term became widely used around 1998, near the end of 1990s, but in 1995, one anonymous columnist at *Nikkei Kinyu Shimbun* had already that the 1990s could be the "Lost Decade" unless the problems of the banking sector were dealt with ("Ushinawareta 10 nen ha Gomen [No Thank You for the "Lost Decade,"]," *Nikkei Kinyu Shimbun*, December 4, 1995).
3. On the Plaza Accord, see Volker and Gyohten (1992), Funabashi (1989), Kondo (1999), and Takita and Kashima Heiwa Kenkyujyo (2006). Takehiko Kondo was a deputy vice minister of finance for international affairs at that time. Takita used primary sources provided by ex-Ministry of Finance (MOF) officials, including *Ousetsu Roku* (Records of Meetings) written by Makoto Utusmi, who was at the Japanese Embassy in Washington, DC, from 1983 to 1986.
4. The effect of the Louvre Accord was limited because it did not stop the appreciation of the yen, which had increased from $1 = ¥153 in February 1987 to $1 = ¥125 at the end of 1987 (Kuroda 2005, 86–87).
5. The use of some cases is questionable. One municipality, Kuroishi City, Aomori prefecture, made a golden *Kokeshi* (Japanese doll). See Komine (2010), 1, 237. Another municipality, Tsuna Machi, Hyogo prefecture, purchased and displayed a gold ingot worth $100 million. Takeshita himself defended his policy that those "projects" generated a lot of tourists revenues (Takeshita 1991, 223)
6. Yasuda Kaijyo Insurance Company bought Gogh's Sunflower at ¥5.3 billion. Other purchase, all in 1989, included a Renoir (¥540 million), a Modigliani (¥1.1 billion), and a Picasso (¥7.5 billion) (Naikakufu Keizaishakai Sogo Kenkyusho 2011, 1, 347–348).
7. Criminal cases committed by the so-called *Jiageya* (landshark) who pressured small landowners to sell their lands were reported widely. The Japanese movie *Marusa no Onna 2* (A taxing woman's return), directed by Juzo Itami and released in Japan in 1988, vividly portrayed the atmosphere of this period.
8. One such incident was called the Recruit Affair, named after a personnel company Recruit: whose president Kosei Ezoe gave unlisted shares of Recruit Cosmos, Recruit's subsidiary company, to politicians, bureaucrats, and journalists from 1984 to 1985. Share of Recruit Cosmos went open to the public, in the end realizing profits worth of ¥600 million to those who received stock. It was reported by the media in 1988.
9. As we see in Chapter 3, this perception was shared by economists such as Yukio Noguchi (Noguchi 1992).
10. Yoshio Nakamura, Miyazawa's cabinet secretary in 1992, testified that Miyazawa constantly read the *Financial Times* (Matsushima and Takenaka 2011, 448, 453–454).

11. Hayashi and Prescott (2002) attribute one of the causes of the Great Stagnation to this law.

12. The book was the joint work of eminent scholars at that time: it has now been revealed that the economics part was virtually written by Motoshige Ito and Heizo Takanaka. See Mikuriya and Serizawa (2014).

13. There is no English version of the Hiraiwa report.

14. Originally, those who drafted the report included an increase in public works and countercyclical measures, but those measures were deleted faced with the resistance form the MOF (Naikakufu Keizaishakai Sogo Kenkyusho 2011, 514).

15. Another blow to the MOF was the entertainment scandal reported in 1995: high-ranking MOF officials were entertained by two credit unions.

16. According to Kume's (2002, 2009) study, which analyzed the newspaper coverage of *Jusen* problem, the public's reaction was an emotional one.

17. Strangely, there was no explicit comparison with other central banks in *Chuo Ginko Kenkyukai* (Research Taskforce on Central Bank), the meeting privately commissioned by the prime minister to deliberate the revision of the BOJ. However, on its seventh meeting, on October 17, 1996, many members of the taskforce voiced concerns over the BOJ putting too much emphasis on price stability, thereby jeopardizing economic growth. Therefore, the latter half of Article 2 was added as follows: "Currency and monetary control by the Bank of Japan shall be aimed at achieving price stability, thereby contributing to the sound development of the national economy" (Mabuchi 1998, 277).

18. On the contrary, Hayami believed otherwise. Kunio Okina recalled an exchange between Hayami and the BOJ staff. When a staff member explained the desirability of the depreciation of the yen for the Japanese economy, Hayami angrily replied: "I know the logic, but I want you, as a central banker, to have a faith that the appreciation would strengthen the economy" (Okina 2011, 210n3).

19. This is the only option available to the government to protest the BOJ's decision under the new law.

20. According to Okina, when the question of the direct purchase was discussed, Hayami shot back: "this is not a matter of theory, but a matter of belief" (Okina 2011, 210n3). Incidentally, Hayami was a devout Christian of the Protestant stripe.

21. The internationalization was initiated around the time that the BOJ celebrated its 100th year of founding, in 1982. John B. Taylor of Stanford University and Allan Meltzer of Carnegie-Mellon University were academic consultants of the Institute for Monetary Studies, having attended several conferences held by the BOJ. Both of them recommended a more expansionary monetary policy for the BOJ. Meltzer (2001) made the following policy recommendation: "The main policy conclusion calls on the Bank of Japan to pursue a more expansive policy to end deflation. This policy would depreciate the yen, but it would end the deflation that is costly to Japan and its neighbors." Taylor 2001 concluded that both an interest policy rate rule and quantity theory "approaches suggest that monetary policy has been the key factor in generating the different inflationary experiences."

22. Under deflation, the nonbank corporate sector had accumulated free cash flows. With the onset of inflationary expectations, firms would not need loans to finance their investment. Therefore, the increase in bank loans is not necessary during reflation. During the Great Depression, bank loans increased three or four years after deflation ended (Iwata 2004). This shows the BOJ's preoccupation with the banking sector.

23. Adachi (2013) rebutted these four points. For example, one could argue that the price level targeting of 1930s Sweden to combat deflation was a precursor to inflation targeting (Berg and Jonung [1999]; cf., for a different interpretation, Straumann and Woitek [2009]). Also, in the early 1990s, New Zealand, a pioneer inflation targeter, tried to reflate the economy when there was a fear of deflation.

24. He was a former CEO of Tonen General Oil Company, but he was unique among Japanese CEOs of his generation in that he had a formal training in economics, with master of arts in economics from Harvard University. He is also well connected to many powerful politicians, such as Koizumi and Abe. For his activity as a board member, see his own vivid memoir Nakahara and Fujii (2006).

25. He consulted Fumio Hayashi, Yuji Shimanaka, John B. Taylor, Bennett T. McCallum, and Milton Friedman.

26. Nakahara corresponded with Milton Friedman on several occasions. On March 28, 2001, he reported the start of the QE as the "Copernican turnaround of the Bank of Japan's monetary policy from the 120-year old interest rate targeting to reserve targeting cum inflation targeting." Friedman replied to Nakahara on April 2, congratulating him (Milton Friedman Papers, File 157, Hoover Institution, Stanford University). Friedman diagnosed that a "decade of inept monetary policy by the Bank of Japan deserves much of the blame for the current parlous state of the Japanese economy," proposing the increase in base money by open market operations to revive the Japanese economy in 1998 (Friedman 1997).

27. His career was unique for a Japanese academician: he first worked for the Japan Development Bank, a government financial corporation, and then moved to academia. When he went to Harvard in 1981, he befriended important American economists, including Larry Summers and Jeffrey Sachs, later becoming a visiting associate professor at Harvard in 1989. Reputedly, it was during his first exposure to the American policymaking process that he set his mind to becoming a policy entrepreneur.

28. The Council's Secretariat is under the supervision of the minister of state for economic and fiscal policy. Consulting with four members of the council, Takenaka could virtually determine the agenda.

29. Keiichi Ohmura, professor of finance at Waseda University and then at the Cabinet Office, remarked that "I have been doing this job for about one year and seven months, but there are many things that surprised me. Put it simply, we have reached the consensus as to the current status including the bad loans problem and so on just recently. Therefore, naturally, there was no consensus as to what to do beforehand. This time, with the change in the minister, there emerged a consensus" (Hamada et al. 2003, 267).

30. The transcript was not made public until ten years later; therefore, his advocacy for inflation targeting was not known among the general public.

31. Takenaka was advised by Yoichi Takahashi, one of his most trusted advisors. Takahashi, career Ministy of Finance bureaucrat, studied at Princeton from 1998–2001, where he frequently attended Ben Bernanke's workshop and learned that inflation-indexed bonds are used in the United States.

32. Hamada and Noguchi (2005) analyzed the opinions of three major newspapers, Yomiuri, Asahi, and Mainichi. Asahi and Mainichi did not take deflation seriously, and Mainichi even accepted the "good deflation" doctrine. However, Asahi became more concerned with deflation as the attention to deflation became apparent.

33. Fukui graduated from the Faculty of Law of the University of Tokyo in 1957, having been selected and groomed as the "prince" of the BOJ. He was supposed to succeed Matsushita in 1998, yet he had to resign from the BOJ, taking responsibility for the scandals of his subordinates.

34. According to Watanabe and Yabu (2011), "roughly 60 percent of the funds supplied to the market through yen-selling foreign exchange interventions were offset (i.e., sterilized) by monetary operations by the Bank of Japan, while the remaining 40 percent were not offset. Moreover, the funds that were not offset remained in the market for some time. This result contrasts with the situation before this period, when 100 percent of the funds of foreign exchange interventions were offset, showing that the extent to which interventions were not sterilized during January 2003 to March 2004 was quite considerable" (Wanatabe and Yabu 2011, 18).

35. Hoshi and Kayshap argued that this was not effective (Hoshi and Kayshap 2011, 2012).

36. For an account that is sympathetic toward the "Rising Tide" faction, see Takahashi (2007, 221–230; 2008). He was a close advisor to Takenaka and Nakagawa during the debate. For an account that is sympathetic toward the "Fiscal Hawks" faction, see Shimizu (2007).

37. Hidenao Nakagawa, then the secretary general of the LDP, and Shinzo Abe, then the cabinet secretary, voiced their concern. However, Kaoru Yosano, then the minister for economic and fiscal affairs, who could have protested officially, was sympathetic toward the BOJ.

38. The evaluation of the QE varies, but Honda argued that the QE was effective in raising investment and production through Tobin's q channel. See Honda (2014). Using structural vector autoregression, Hayashi and Koeda (2014) show that the QE can increase inflation and production.

39. Rumor has it that on one occasion he said that "every reform we had to do has been carried out by this person, so I have nothing left to do," pointing to Heizo Takenaka.

40. This is not informative since the Japanese use more cash than other nations do, so the money-GDP ratio has been historically high in Japan.

41. Instead, however, they tried to set up *Kokka Senryaku Kyoku* (Bureau of National Strategy), but they did not legislate it.

42. Kazuo Mizuno, a well-known business economist who wrote a book titled *Hyakunen Defure* (Deflation for one hundred years [Mizuno 2003]), was appointed as deputy director general for economic research at the Cabinet Office in September 2010 and councillor at the Cabinet Secretariat in November 2011. He was a growth and deflation pessimist who believed that Japan could not grow anymore and could not end deflation.
43. Yoshiyasu Ono, economist and close advisor to Kan, was appointed as *Naikakufu Sanyo* (advisor to the Cabinet Office) in February 2010 and then as *Sogo Keizai Shakai Kennkyu-sho Shocho* (president of the Economic and Social Research Institute, the Cabinet Office) in October 2010.
44. See the memoranda written by Chairman: http://www.cas.go.jp/jp/fukkou/pdf/kousou1/gityou.pdf.
45. Popular commentators such as Kazuyo Katsuma and Tsukasa Jonen contributed to this.
46. The DPJ had a fairly large number of members in the National Diet who voiced concerns about deflation, but they failed to influence those in the upper echelon of the party who decided policy.
47. The implications of this for other central banks, such as the European Central Bank, is discussed in Chapter 6.
48. Governor Shirakawa's testimony before the Budget Committee in the Lower House of National Diet on February 2, 2012.
49. The break-even inflation rate in Japan jumped from a negative range to a positive range after February 14, 2012.
50. On the political process of the consumption tax hike, see Ito (2013) and Shimizu (2013).
51. Yamamoto studied economics and the University of Tokyo under the supervision of Ryutaro Komiya, and has known Kikuo Iwata for a long time. After having worked at the MOF, he became a member of the House of Representatives from 1993. He has been advocating reflation policy and the revision of the BOJ law to make inflation targeting the BOJ's mandate early on. See Yamamoto 2010.
52. *Nihon Keizai Shimbun*, April 14, 2013.
53. Volker and Gyohten 1992 did not reveal his concern about the domestic economy upon the Plaza Accord. Also, he said he did not believe in the effect of foreign currency intervention, and did not know the Mundell-Fleming model (Naikakufu Keizaishakai Kenkyusho 2001, 3, 517).
54. Judging from his memoirs, one cannot get a sense that Takeshita understood basic economic principles. He recalled that he "learned" economic policy, industrial policy to be exact, and the importance of seeing politics from the economy, when he was an undersecretary of the MITI in 1963 (Takeshita 1991, 28). He was the chief cabinet secretary of the Sato administration in the 1970s when Richard Nixon announced the suspension of the gold convertibility of the dollar. He confessed that "Frankly speaking, we including Prime Minister Sato did not understand the international currency problem" (1991, 68). When Kakuei Tanaka took power, he was appointed as the deputy secretary-general of the LDP. He observed that inflation during the Tanaka administration was caused

by expansionary public works and the Oil Shock: there was no reference to monetary policy (88–89). As a finance minister in the Ohira administration, he worked for fiscal consolidation. Later as prime minister, he tackled to introduce consumption tax. He toyed with an idea of restricting private property rights regarding land in order to deal with the land issue (176).

55. During World War II, Miyazawa attended Osamu Shimomura's lectures on Keynes's general theory in the MOF (Mikuriya and Nakamura 2005, 188). Later Shimomura became a member of the brain trust of Hayato Ikeda and the architect of the *Shotoku Baizo Keikaku* (National Income Doubling Plan).

56. Koichi Kato, a LDP politician and Miyazawa's most trusted aide at that time, recalled Miyazawa's confrontation with Takeshita in one meeting at the LDP around 1985: Miyazawa abused Takeshita to his face in front of a large number of people. Miyazawa said, "Did you know what you have done?" The criticism was so severe that many who were present thought that Miyazawa's career was over (Naikakufu Keizaishakai Kenkyusho 2011, 3, 433).

57. As a person who experienced postwar high inflation, Miyazawa was fearful of inflation.

58. This does not mean that there was no contemporary critic; on the contrary, there were many. See, for example, Noguchi and Tanaka (2001).

Chapter 3

1. It was modeled after *The Economist* in the United Kingdom, but there has been no relationship between the two.

2. Fujimaki (2002) listed 16 economists.

3. Thus he has been much vilified. While Takenaka was a minister, several powerful LDP politicians often demanded that he resign the job.

4. I owe this insight to Posen (2003).

5. He was born in 1932, and he received his doctorate in economics from the University of Tokyo in 1962. He spent most of his career at the Economic Planning Agency, until his retirement in 1992. After his retirement, he was the director of the now defunct Research Institute of Long Term Credit BOJ until 1998.

6. Born in 1943, Miyao graduated from Keio University, receiving PhD from the MIT. After taking several positions at the University of Toronto, the University of California, and the University of South California, he became a professor at Tsukuba University in 1985. As an expert on urban economics, he commented first on urban and land issues in Japan and then moved to the broader issue of Japan's Stagnation.

7. Atsumi (2006) listed 15 different definitions of structural reforms during the Koizumi administration era.

8. "The etymology of structural adjustment appears to await scientific study" (Fisher 1995, 21).

9. As a radical student activist, he wrote several articles and a book on State monopoly capitalism, and translated Leon Trotsky's works into Japanese. While he was

at Harvard, he befriended with radical economists including Samuel Bowles and Herbert Gintis.

10. When he was asked by Takenaka to join the expert team for the nonperforming loan issue, the so-called Takenaka Project Team, in October 2002, he declined the offer, referring to the impossibility of reform (Takenaka 2006, 59). Takenaka did not name the person in question, but it was believed to be Ikeo (Ono 2005, 45).

11. He specifically referred to Ito et al. (1988).

12. The effectiveness of Japan's industrial policy has been questioned in the literature. See Beason and Weinstein (1996), Miwa (2004), and Okita (2010, chap. 7) for a comprehensive survey. Nakatani was doubtful about the efficacy of industrial policy (Nakatani 1996, 129–130).

13. Although the opponents referred to the movement of unemployment rate in the United States, they did not seem to understand that the unemployment rate is affected by macroeconomic policy.

14. He eventually received his PhD in economics from Osaka University. He wrote a book on his term as a government minister (Takenaka 2006). The award-winning Sasaki (2013) offers a highly critical—perhaps too critical—account of Takenaka's life and work.

15. His first work, Takenaka (1984), which was based on his thesis, was about the economics of research and development and other investment decision making using the rational expectation approach to investment.

16. Nakasone suggested it on August 9, 1972. "Yen Saikirisage wo Fusegu tame ni wa Chosei Infure mo" (We may need adjustment inflation to prevent yen's reappreciation) *Asahi Shimbun*, Tokyo, August 10, 1972, 9).

17. The *Asahi Shimbun* quickly criticized Nakasone's "*Chosei Infure Ron*" in its editorial titled "Chosei Infure Yonin Ron ni Hantaisuru" (We oppose the adjustment inflation argument) (*Asahi Shimbun*, Tokyo, August 13, 1972, 5).

18. For example, Kazuhide Uekusa, a very popular business economist during the period, had to sell a demand-side policy as a supply-side one. See Uekusa (1998).

19. At the same time, Hoshi supported an expansionary monetary policy using inflation targeting (Arai and Hoshi 2004).

20. As a friend of Heizo Takenaka, Sachs assured Takenaka of the appropriateness of "structural reform" policy when he visited Japan in May 2001 (Takenaka 2006, 252).

21. For the concept of the liquidity trap in the history of macroeconomic thought, see Boianovsky (2004).

22. When he met Takenaka himself, Takenaka explained his policy as a "supply-side" one in that structural reform would stimulate demand by strengthening the growth prospect. Krugman retorted: "Well, maybe. But the plan does seem like a leap in the dark—radical measures taken because they might work, not because there is solid reason to believe that they will work" (Krugman 2001).

23. Bernanke would be later to be reminded of his words compared with his action. See Sumner (2010). Krugman (2012a) and Ball (2012) argued that Ben Bernanke changed his mind; Krugman said that Bernanke was assimilated by the

Fed Borg, named after a popular enemy that appeared on the television series *Star Trek*.

24. See Bernanke and Gertler (1989, 1990, and 1999). Also Nobuhiro Kiyotaki at Princeton University and John Moore at the London School of Economics have developed their models in a similar vein (Kiyotaki and Moore 1997). It is likely that Kiyotaki, a son of banker in Osaka, came up with the model from his observation of the Japanese economy after the burst of bubble.

25. The entire discussion is available in Japanese: http://warp.ndl.go.jp/info:ndljp/pid/1022127/www.mof.go.jp/singikai/kanzegaita/giziroku/gaic150416.htm

26. During his speech, he jokingly said that because he proposed using government money, he would be stripped of his PhD.

27. For an overview of the debate on "inflation targeting" in Japan, see Fujiki (2004) and Noguchi (2014).

28. The dissemination of the Krugman proposal among the general public owed much to the development of the Internet. Hiroo Yamagata, who is a prolific writer, a consultant at the Nomura Research Institute, a critic, a translator, and a public intellectual, translated Krugman (1998b) immediately after it was uploaded to Krugman's homepage. He also translated Krugman (1998a) and Svensson (2003) into Japanese.

29. More business economists supported fiscal policy, but they were very skeptical about the effectiveness of monetary policy and inflation targeting at the same time. That was the case for Kazuhide Uekusa and Richard Koo, both of whom were at the Nomura Research Institute, the largest private think tank in Japan.

30. For his model in detail, see Aoki and Yoshikawa (2002). His model should be called Robertsonian rather than Keynesian since Dennis H. Robertson thought demand saturation was the cause of the Great Depression (Robertson 1937).

31. The joint appeal was published in an article in *Nikkei Shimbun* (Ito and Yoshikawa 2003). The article listed four specific proposals including monetary expansion with an inflation target, depreciation of the yen, resolution of the bad loans problem, and fiscal policy inducing structural reforms. Judging from its content, the article was probably written by Takatoshi Ito. Other cosigners included Motoshige Ito, Masahiro Okuno, Kiyohiko Nishimura, Tatsuo Hatta, Yoshio Higuchi, Mitsuhiro Fukao, and Naohiro Yashiro.

32. Of course, in a real world, there would be no infinite supply of money to begin with. Therefore, it is impossible to verify Ono's policy implications.

33. For a different interpretation of the Swedish experience, see Straumann and Woiteck (2009), who claimed that Sweden adopted exchange rate targeting. Regardless of the interpretation, it is important that Sweden did whatever it thought necessary to end deflation. See Chapter 4 as well.

34. Tachibanaki (1998) claimed Japan became more unequal, judging from growing Gini coefficient. Ohtake (2005) argued that about 60 percent of the increased Gini coefficient could be explained by the aging of the population. However, it was later shown that as the unemployment of the youth increased, the income disparity among the youth increased.

35. The reality was different since postredistribution income inequality during the Koizumi-Takenaka period stayed the same or declined, but the data available at that time showed a growing inequality trend before the Koizumi-Takenaka period. See Chapter 1.
36. In the case of Anglo-American economic discourse, Hayek looms large. See Wapshot (2011).
37. Another economist who became known to the public during the period was Irving Fisher. His 1933 paper has been frequently cited and referred to as the earliest theory of debt deflation induced by deleveraging. It was cited by those who advocated fiscal policy, including Richard Koo, who referred to him but curiously downplayed Fisher's main proposal of monetary policy. Also, Fisher's remark that the "stock market reached a permanently high plateau" in 1929 and the eventual financial loss due to the crash did not help uphold his reputation.
38. This part is drawn on Wakatabe (2014a).
39. The term had already been used in the prewar period, and it was reputedly influenced by Oskar Lange (Lange 1935), who in turn was inspired by Kei Shibata (Shibata 1933). See also Bronfenbrenner (1956), and Dimand and Wakatabe (2011).
40. The division between two economics was so visible that the history of the Department of Economics at the University of Tokyo, in its commemoration of the 50th year of its founding, had two separate roundtable retrospective discussions, one for Marxian economics oriented majority, and the other for the minority "Modern Economics" (Tokyo Daigaku Keizaigakubu 1976).
41. Martin Bronfenbrenner described it as "schizophrenia," since modern economists taught the merits of free trade in classroom, while the same supported protectionist measures in a government committee. The effectiveness of industrial policy in Japan has been questioned in the recent literature. See, e.g., Beason and Weinstein (1996).
42. This critical remark against structural reforms should not be taken as a negation of deregulation, privatization, or political and economic reforms in general: as is discussed fully in Chapter 5, the Japanese economy needs market-oriented reforms in many fields. But we do need growth policy *and* stabilization policy: the latter is necessary in the time of recessions and is also prerequisite to growth policy; if reforms entail costs, it is better to ease these costs.

Chapter 4

1. This was the title of the British Academy conference held on April 16–17 in London. The conference papers were published first in volume 26 of the *Oxford Review of Economic Policy* and then in book form (Crafts and Fearon 2013).
2. He analyzed and learned from the Great Depression as early as 2001 (Iwata 2001). Iwata (2004) is a product of a joint study project headed by Iwata, whose gist is translated into English in Iwata et al. (2008). Wakatabe (2014b) is a part of this project.

3. Temin (1976) criticized Friedman and Schwartz (1963), arguing that at the initial phase, the Great Depression was caused by a sudden decrease in autonomous spending, while money did not play an active role from 1929 to 1931.

4. The literature is voluminous. Other classics include Eichengreen and Sachs (1985), Temin (1989), Eichengreen (1992), Bernanke (2000a), and James (2001). For more popular accounts, see Hall and Ferguson (1998) and Ahmad (2009).

5. The classic paper is Sargent (1982).

6. The simplest theoretical discussion using the IS-LM framework of the Great Depression with a comparison of the spending hypothesis (Keynesian), the money hypothesis (Monetarist), and the deflationary expectations hypothesis may be found in Mankiw (2009).

7. De Long (1990) listed Joseph A. Schumpeter, Lionel Robbins, Friedrich A. von Hayek, and Seymour Harris among the proponents. One version is the business cycle model in which misplaced overconfidence in the rate of return by an entrepreneur leads to investment boom, which turns into depression as the true rate of return is revealed. With the advancement of real business cycle theory or dynamic macroeconomics, there has been a revival in liquidationism of this sort. As for the empirical evidence, or lack thereof, see Cabarello and Hammour (2000). For the contrary view regarding Hayek and Robbins, see White (2008).

8. Takenaka (2014) characterized the era from 1918 to 1932 as a "developing democracy."

9. Literally traslated, *Kin Kaikin* means the lifting of embargo on the exportation of gold. In the literature, see Wakatabe (2014b) and the literature cited there.

10. See Irwin (2011a) for Cassel's contributions.

11. See Ikeo (2014, 60–62), for the background.

12. When the so-called Young committee, headed by American Owen D. Young, who was involved in the Dawes Plan, convened in February 1929, it proposed to restrict the member states of the newly established Bank for International Settlements to countries with stable currency. Japan was allowed to join it as an exception, but this requirement shook the Japanese policymakers. Japan needed to borrow the pounds sterling equivalent of ¥230 million from Anglo-American bankers, which was the amount of the outstanding debt that Japan incurred in the Russo-Japanese War of 1904 to 1905. Yet Anglo-American bankers demanded the stabilization of the yen. The Zaigai Seika had declined precipitously from ¥1.3 billion and ¥34 million in the end of 1919 to ¥91 million in March 1929 and ¥83 million in June 1929 (Ito 1989, 212–213).

13. The appointment of Inoue was taken as a surprise since he expressed his skepticism toward the prewar parity return. Yet, he was never opposed to the prewar return in principle; therefore, he could have thought that Japan could return to the gold standard with careful preparation.

14. Some argue that Hamaguchi and Inoue decided on the prewar parity since it required changing the law to implement the new parity. But as the fact that they held a general election and won shows, they could have changed the law if they wanted to change it.

15. Katsuta welcomed a panic; therefore, his concern with a panic is not consistent. At other place, he said that the prewar return was not a cause for the depression: "the

return may have accompanied the recession, but it did not result in the recession. The return induces an outflow of species, which in turn dampen the prices, and the recession came" (Katsuta 1930b, 29). But this is also not consistent since if the outflow was the cause of the recession, he should have welcomed the return at the new parity.

16. Baron Takuma Dan, president of the Mitsui holding corporation and friend of Inoue's, was assassinated by a terrorist on March 5, 1932.

17. Three of the *Shin Kaikin-ha,* Kamekichi Takahashi, Yamazaki, and Obama, were involved in this statement, which was drafted by Takahashi, although it was further revised by others (Ando 1965, vol. I, 94).

18. The *Takahashi Zaisei* period was interrupted for a short interval, from July 8, 1934, to November 27, 1934, when Sadanobu Fujii was appointed.

19. There is no reliable data on the unemployment rate. One estimate shows it was 5.3 percent in January 1931 and that it peaked at 7.2 percent in July 1932. This was calculated from *Nihon Keizai Tōkei Nenkan* from Toyo Keizai Shimposha by Seiji Adachi.

20. The first usage is probably "'Reflation' or Bankruptcy" in *The Economist*, February 13, 1932. It also turned up in the *Hansard* of the British House of Commons on April 20, 1932.

21. Fisher proposed the desirable price level target aiming at the price level of mid-1920s in the United States, and *The Economist* proposed the target aiming at the price level in 1928.

22. On another occasion, he analyzed the cases in which a rate of change of nominal income was not the same as the inflation rate (Iahibashi 1970–72, 8, 179–184).

23. It is an exaggeration to say that Ishibashi or other Shin Kaikin-ha affected the policymaking process, yet Korekiyo Takahashi, extremely well-read and versatile in English, referred to "Mr. Fisher and the workshop at the University of Chicago," "Keynes," the "Macmillan committee report," and "Hawtrey" in the speech he gave in April 1933 (Takahashi 1936, 559, 567–568, 570). By the "workshop at the University of Chicago," he probably meant the Harris Foundation Conferences held at the University of Chicago in 1931 and 1932, which Fisher attended.

24. Smethurst (2009) argued that Takahashi appreciated the market economy, acknowledging its defects at the same time. For example, Takahashi understood that the disparity of income and wealth was the major problem and contemplated some remedies: "since his days as Hara's finance minister following World War I, [he] advocated the creation of a system to create a fairly equal distribution of wealth between capitalists and workers. He decried the widening gap between rich and poor in interwar Japan" (Smethurst 2009, 305).

Chapter 5

1. It is the name that Hidenao Nakagawa, a strong supporter of Abe, used back in 2006. Nakagawa used it in the Lower House meeting of the National Diet on October 2, 2006. http://kokkai.ndl.go.jp/cgi-bin/KENSAKU/swk_dispdoc. cgi?SESSION=9564&SAVED_RID=1&PAGE=0&POS=0&TOTAL=0 &SRV_ID=9&DOC_ID=2453&DPAGE=1&DTOTAL=397&DPOS=1&S ORT_DIR=0&SORT_TYPE=0&MODE=1&DMY=11669

2. This includes the impact of a consumption tax increase introduced in April.

3. Robert Feldman quoted in Jonathan Sobel, "Abenomics: Off Target," *Financial Times*, August 25, 2014.

4. Amari, born in 1949, is an LDP politician with a close relationship with the Ministry of Economy, Industry, and Trade, one of "*Shoko Zoku*," lobbyist-politicians: he served as the minster of the Ministry of Economy, Industry, and Trade from 2006 to 2008.

5. According to the old legend, the warlord Motonari Mori (1497–1571) once asked his three sons to break an arrow. They broke it easily. Then he asked them to break the three arrows bundled together. His sons could not break them. He taught his sons the virtue of sticking together to survive the warlord period. The house of Mori survived the warlord and Edo periods, becoming a powerhouse for leading the Meiji restoration in 1868. Abe comes from the Yamaguchi region where the house of Mori ruled during the Edo period.

6. The clause was inserted to accommodate the demand from some DPJ politicians who were afraid of the negative impacts of the tax hike.

7. The official name of the meeting is *Kongo no Keizai Zaisei Dokonado ni Kannsuru Shuchu Tenken Kaigo* (Meeting for Intensive Examination of the Future Economic and Fiscal Conditions). All presentations and summaries are available on the following site: http://www5.cao.go.jp/keizai-shimon/kaigi/special/tenken/index.html

8. Strumthal 1944 is the classic account of the reactions of the left-wing forces during the Great Depression and the lessons they learnt. Although the book was translated in Japanese, the lessons were not learnt.

9. As we chronicle in Chapter 2, political struggle delayed the appointment of Governor Shirakawa one month later than was usual: his term became effective as of April 2008.

10. The figures are all in a purchasing power parity basis. See http://www.quandl.com/economics/gdp-as-share-of-world-gdp-at-ppp-by-country.

11. Edward Wong, "China Announces 12.2% Increase in Military Budget," *New York Times*, March 5, 2014.

12. On another occasion, Krugman said: "I have no stake in Abe's success politically, and no sense of whether he knows what he's doing. But the case for a coordinated fiscal-monetary push seems overwhelming given the intellectual framework all of us, I think, more or less share" (Krugman 2013c).

13. Hamada's expertise on international monetary economics also matters greatly. Contrary to the beggar-thy-neighbor argument, he argued that under the flexible exchange rate system, an expansionary monetary policy by two countries could be mutually beneficial.

14. A similar diagram is drawn by Goushi Kataoka, an economist at Mitsubishi UFJ Research and Consulting (Kataoka 2013, 211).

15. Hiroyuki Maeda "Ekonomistuto ga erabu Keizaitosyo besuto 10" (Economists pick top ten economics and business books of the year), *Nikkei Shimbun*, December 29, 2013.

16. On March 5, 2013, upon the Iwata confirmation hearing, Keisuke Tsumura, a DPJ Diet member, questioned Iwata about what Iwata would do if the BOJ fails

to achieve the 2 percent target within two years. Tsumura has worked for the BOJ.

17. As of July 2014, Japan has a trade deficit. McCullum (2003) did predict the development of a current account when Japan reflates.

18. See also Ito (2013) and Eichengreen (2013). Eichengreen (2013) argued that emerging market countries could engage in contractionary fiscal policy to offset the effect of advanced countries' expansionary monetary policy.

19. Abenomics would lower the risk premium on Japan's government bond.

20. Bernanke (2003) concluded: "one could make an economic case that the balance sheet of the central bank should be of marginal relevance at best to the determination of monetary policy." The remaining issue is the institutional structure to assure the transfer of profit and loss between the government in a narrow sense, and the BOJ. For this, Bernanke (2003) has offered a solution in the form of the "bond-conversion."

21. As Iida recognizes, it is not straightforward to delineate the Mundell-Fleming effect from data. The usual explanation that emphasizes a change in the interest rate in the Mundell-Fleming effect is a theoretical expediency. In reality, fiscal policy is transacted in an incremental way: a small increase in fiscal expansion would cause a slight upward pressure on the interest rate, which in turn would lead to a slight appreciation of the currency. In this case, there is no discernable increase in interest rate, yet the Mundell-Fleming effect is at work.

22. In reality there have been changes in the tax system in Japan. A report by the Cabinet Office estimates the elasticity for tax revenues, corrected for changes in the tax system, as follows: 1.47 for 1981–1990, 0.38 for 1991–2000, and 3.1 for 2000–2009. The averages are 1.61 for 1981–2009 and 1.69 for 1991–2009. See Naikakufu (2011).

23. For economists' consensus on economic growth, see Weil (2013).

24. The full list is accessible at http://www.kantei.go.jp/jp/singi/keizaisaisei/pdf/en_saikou_jpn_hon.pdf and http://www.kantei.go.jp/jp/singi/keizaisaisei/pdf/en_saikou_jpn.pdf.

25. The numbers depend on assumptions. Petri and Plummer (2012) concluded that the benefits would be around ¥9 billion, assuming that both Japan and South Korea join the TPP, and all nontariff barriers are abolished. Todo (2013) estimated that the growth rate would increase by 1.5 percent, including the indirect effects on growth by knowledge creation.

26. As for his other comment on "structural imbalances," the coexistence of financial surpluses of firms and the low shares of household disposable income and consumption, it is important to note that this phenomenon began in 1997 when deflation started. Firms tend to hold huge free cash flows under deflation. It may not be so "structural" after all.

27. However, this conclusion is tentative, and the correlation is not strong.

28. See the following: http://www.pewglobal.org/2007/10/04/chapter-1-views-of-global-change/. Young people do not seem to possess a positive image about Japan: according to a survey by Lifelink, a nongovernmental organization focused on youth suicide, among 200 undergraduate and graduate students who are looking for a job, 69 percent said that "the honest people lose in Japan" and 65 percent

said that "the Japanese society does nothing when one needs help." The survey showed a growing support for a lifetime employment system among the youth, not because they want to stay in a company until their retirement but because they believe it is the safest way for survival. This survey may be biased in its sample. For the survey, see http://www.lifelink.or.jp/hp/Library/201310shukatsu.pdf.

29. According to an opinion survey conducted jointly by *Nihon Keizai Shimbun* and TV Tokyo in the late June 2014, after the revised version of the JRS was announced, 46 percent of the respondents said they rate the reform highly, while 29 percent said they do not. *Nihon Keizai Shimbun*, June 29, 2014.

Chapter 6

1. Muramatsu and Okuno (2002); Iwata and Harada (2002); Iwata and Miyagawa (2003); Hamada et al. (2004); Ito, Patrick and Weinstein (2005); Hayashi (2006, 2007); ESRI (2009, 2011); Kataoka (2010); Hamada et al. (2011); and Garside (2012).

2. This does not mean that one should embrace bubbles in a more positive manner than is considered. However, if innovative activity is driven by psychological "biases" such as euphoria and overconfidence rather than by rational calculation, one could take another perspective on bubbles. On the basis of insights from the American economy during the 1990s, Ricardo Cabarello and his colleagues at Massachusetts Institute of Technology analyzed "speculative growth" in which asset boom and rapid economic growth could happen concurrently (Cabarello et al. 2006).

3. Reinhart and Rogoff (2009) suggested that financial liberalization such as freer international capital mobility after the 1980 has contributed to the recurrent banking crises all over the world: "In eighteen of the twenty-six banking crises . . . the financial sector had been liberalized within the preceding five years, usually less. In the 1980s and 1990s, most liberalization episodes were associated with financial crises of varying severity" (Reinhart and Rogoff 2009, 155). However, these recurring crises might have something to do with the development of financial markets. Hirano and Yanagawa (2010) argued that there would be no bubble in the least developed and the most developed stages of financial development, while there would be bubbles in the middle stage. In both the least- and most-developed stage, the nominal interest rate would exceed the nominal growth rate, but in the middle stage, the nominal growth rate could exceed the nominal interest rate. Therefore, as a country develops financially, there would be more bubbles. They argued that this corresponds to the recent situation of emerging and developed economies.

4. Ogawa (2003) argued that there was a credit crunch for medium and small size firms. As Sakuragawa and Sakuragawa (2009) pointed out, one cannot discern the presence of the credit crunch in macroeconomic data in most of the 1990s, but there is a possibility that a credit crunch and zombie lending happened at the same time.

5. Inoue and Okimoto (2008) was first published as chapter 7 of Hayashi (2007).

6. http://www.igmchicago.org/igm-economic-experts-panel/poll-results?Survey ID=SV_bvjcAG4fti8BdBj. Among them, Barry Eichengreen of University of California Berkeley, Anil Kashyap of Chicago, and Maurice Obstfeld of University of California Berkeley said that they "strongly agree" with a certainty of 10 out of 10.

7. However, proponents of the structural view tend to downplay or neglect this important macroeconomic dimension of dealing with the banking crisis. See Katz (2008).

8. See also Ergungor and Cherny (2009): they stress four principles of effective crisis resolution, transparency of asset losses up-front and honest communication about the extent of public intervention, politically and financially independent receivership, maintenance of market discipline, and restoration of credit flows.

9. According to Kato (1994), "the ministry's special education and training systems are designed not only to help bureaucrats study academic disciplines to enable them to qualify as policy specialists, but also to nurture the same attitudes about policy-making. Obtaining an economic education while working in the administration does not make them strict interpreters of economic theory. The bureaucrats often emphasize the importance of common sense rather than theoretical consistency or elegance. They have a deep suspicion of neoclassical economic theory, which tends to regard the financial behavior of the government sector as a function of the market economy. They claim they nurture their own sense that guides their decisions through their experiences in public financial management and knowledge gained from their experience within the organization" (Kato 1994, 58).

10. For another example, see Amyx (2004). She emphasized the institutional inertia that has been strengthened by network-based regulation and policy authorities, especially the MOF.

11. This was first suggested by Posen (2003).

12. Scott Sumner of Bentley University thought that the BOJ has been "successful" in its commitment to "price stability": one has to remember that the BOJ has achieved a zero or slightly deflationary CPI increase rate throughout the period (Sumner 2009). In this sense, the BOJ had a deflation target, and it has worked well.

13. DeLong (1997) noted that the American policymakers' preoccupation with the Great Depression prevented them from pursuing a more effective macroeconomic policy to deal with the Great Inflation of the 1970s.

14. http://www.telegraph.co.uk/finance/comment/ambroseevans_pritchard/10814728/ECB-is-delighted-by-the-splendid-prospect-of-deflation.html

15. The historical museum of Bundesbank in Frankfurt features a history of hyperinflation and an interactive computer game in which an increased money supply could lead to hyperinflation (*Economist* 2008).

Bibliography

Abe, Shinzo. 2007. *Utsukushi kuni he* [Toward a beautiful country]. Tokyo: Bungei Shunju.
———. 2013. *Atarashi kuni he: Utsukushi kuni he kanzenban* [Toward a new country: Toward a beautiful country]. Complete ed. Tokyo: Bungei Shunju.
Acemoglu, Daron A., and James A. Robinson. 2012. *Why Nations Fail: The Origins of Power, Prosperity, and Poverty.* New York: Crown.
———. 2013. "Economics versus Politics: Pitfalls of Policy Advice." *Journal of Economic Perspectives* 27 (2): 173–192.
Adachi, Seiji. 2004. "Showa kyoko ni okeru furyo saiken mondai to kinyu sisutemu no tenkan" [Bad loans problem and the transformation of the financial system in the Showa crisis]. In *Showa kyoko no kenkyu* [Studies on the Showa Depression], edited by Kikuo Iwata, 219–248. Tokyo: Toyo Keizai Shimposha.
———. 2006. *Datsu defure no rekishi bunseki: Seisaku rejimu tenkan de tadoru kindai nihon* [Historical analysis of overcoming deflation: Modern Japan seen through regime shifts]. Tokyo: Fujiwara Shoten.
———. 2013. "Kinyu seisaku kettei purosesu to kinyu seisaku ronso no keifu" [Chronology of the monetary policy-making process and debates]. In *Mazu defure wo tomeyo* [Stop deflation first], edited by Kikuo Iwata, 67–108. Tokyo: Nihon Keizai Shimbunsha.
———. 2014. "Kinyu Seisaku no Regime Tenkan to sono Koka" [Monetary policy regime change and its effects]. In *Tettei bunseki Abenomics* [Abenomics analyzed], edited by Yutaka Harada and Makoto Saito, 57–79. Tokyo: Chuo Keizaisha.
Aghion, Phillipe. 2012. "From Growth Theory to Growth Policy Design." http://www2.lse.ac.uk/researchAndExpertise/units/growthCommission/documents/pdf/Aghion_GrowthDoc_Apr2012.pdf
Aghion, Phillipe, and Steven Durlauf. 2009. "From Growth Theory to Policy Design," Commission on Growth and Development. http://www.growthcommission.org/storage/cgdev/documents/gcwp057web.pdf
Ahamed, Liaquat. 2009. *Lords of Finance: Bankers Who Broke the World.* New York: Penguin.
Ahearn, Alan, Joseph Gagnon, Jane Haltmaier, Steve Kamin, Christopher Erceg, Jon Faust, Luca Guerrieri et al. 2002. "Preventing Deflation: Lessons from Japan's Experience in the 1990s." International Finance Discussion Papers 729, Board of

the Governors of the Federal Reserve System. http://www.federalreserve.gov/pubs/ifdp/2002/729/ifdp729.pdf

Akerlof, George. 1970. "The Market for 'Lemons': Quality Uncertainty and the Market Mechanism." *Quarterly Journal of Economics* 84 (3): 488–500.

Akerlof, George, William Dickens, and George Perry. 1996. "The Macroeconomics of Low Inflation." *Brookings Papers on Economic Activity*, no. 1, 1–59.

Amisano, Gianni, Roberta Colavecchio, and Gabriel Fagan. 2014. "A Money-Based Indicator for Deflation Risk." Universität Hamburg, DEP (Socioeconomics) Discussion Papers. http://www.wiso.uni-hamburg.de/repec/hepdoc/macppr_3_2014.pdf

Amyx, Jennifer A. 2004. *Japan's Financial Crisis: Institutional Rigidity and Reluctant Change*. Princeton, NJ: Princeton University Press.

Ando, Yoshio, ed. 1965. *Showa keizaishi heno Shogen* [Testimonies on the Showa economic history]. Tokyo: Mainichi Shimbunsha.

Aoki, Masahiko, ed. 1984. *The Economic Analysis of the Japanese Firm*. Amsterdam: North-Holland.

———. 1988. *Information, Incentives, and Bargaining in the Japanese Economy*. Cambridge: Cambridge University Press.

———. 2008. *Watashi no rirekisho* [My curriculum vitae]. Tokyo: Nihon Keizai Shimbunsha.

Aoki, Masanao, and Hiroshi Yoshikawa. 2002. "Demand Saturation-Creation and Economic Growth." *Journal of Economic Behavior and Organization* 48 (2): 127–154.

Arai, Yoichi, and Takeo Hoshi. 2004. "Monetary Policy in the Great Recession." RIETI Discussion Paper Series 04-E-024. http://www.rieti.go.jp/jp/publications/dp/04e024.pdf

Asahi Shimbun Keizaibu. 1971. *Kutabare GNP* [Down with the GNP]. Tokyo: Asahi Shimbunsha.

Aso, Taro. 2013. "Q & A after the Cabinet Meeting," January 29, 2013. https://www.mof.go.jp/public_relations/conference/my20130129.htm.

Atsumi, Yasuhiro. 2006. "'Koizumi Kozo Kaikaku' naru Syogainen ni tsuite no Kosatu" [Thoughts on several concepts regarding Koizumi structural reform]. PRI Discussion Paper Series 06-A28. https://www.mof.go.jp/pri/research/discussion_paper/ron162.pdf

Avent, Ryan. 2012a. "Japan's Tragedy." *Free Exchange* (blog), *Economist*, August 3. http://www.economist.com/blogs/freeexchange/2012/08/lost-decades

———. 2012b. "Japan's Tragedy, Continued." *Free Exchange* (blog), *Economist*, August 6. http://www.economist.com/blogs/freeexchange/2012/08/lost-decades-0

Ball, Laurence M. 2012. "Bernanke and the Zero Bound." Working Paper 17836. National Bureau of Economic Research, Cambridge, MA.

Beason, Richard, and David E. Weinstein. 1996. "Growth, Economies of Scale, and Targeting in Japan (1955–1990)." *Review of Economics and Statistics* 78 (2): 286–295.

Berg, Claes, and Lars Jonung. 1999. "Pioneering Price Level Targeting: The Swedish Experience 1931–1937." *Journal of Monetary Economics* 43 (3): 525–551.

Bernanke, Ben S. 2000a. *Essays on the Great Depression*. Princeton, NJ: Princeton University Press.

————. 2000b. "Japanese Monetary Policy: A Case of Self-Induced Paralysis?" In *Japan's Financial Crisis and Its Parallels to U.S. Experience,* edited by Ryoichi Mikitani and Adam S. Posen. Washington, DC: Institute for International Economics. http://www.iie.com/publications/chapters_preview/319/7iie289X.pdf

————. 2002. "Deflation: Making Sure 'It' Does Not Happen Here" (transcript). November 21. Federal Reserve Bank. http://www.federalreserve.gov/boarddocs/speeches/2002/20021121/default.htm

————. 2003. "Some Thoughts on Monetary Policy in Japan" (transcript). Before the Japan Society of Monetary Economics, Tokyo, Japan, May 31. http://www.federalreserve.gov/BoardDocs/Speeches/2003/20030531/

————. 2012a. *The Federal Reserve and the Financial Crisis: Lectures.* Princeton, NJ: Princeton University Press.

————. 2012b. "Monetary Policy since the Onset of the Crisis." At the Federal Reserve Bank of Kansas City Economic Symposium, Jackson Hole, Wyoming, August 31, 2012. http://www.federalreserve.gov/newsevents/speech/bernanke20120831a.htm

Bernanke, Ben S., and Mark Gertler. 1989. "Agency Costs, Net Worth, and Business Fluctuations," *American Economic Review* 79 (1): 14–31.

Bernanke, Ben S. and Mark Gertler 1990. "Financial Fragility and Economic Performance." *Quarterly Journal of Economics* 105 (1): 87–114.

————, and Mark Gertler. 1999. "Monetary Policy and Asset Price Volatility." In *1999 Symposium: New Challenges for Monetary Policy*, 77–128. Kansas City, KS: Federal Reserve Bank of Kansas City.

Bernanke, Ben S, Thomas Laubach, Fredrick S. Mishkin, and Adam Posen. 1999. *Inflation Targeting: Lessons from the International Experience.* Princeton, NJ: Princeton University Press.

Blanchard, Oliver. 1997. *Macroeconomics.* Upper Saddle River, NJ: Prentice-Hall.

Blanchard, Oliver, and Michael Kremer. 1997. "Disorganization." *Quarterly Journal of Economics* 112: 1091–1126.

Blinder, Alan S., and Alan B. Kreuger. 2004. "What Does the Public Know about Economic Policy, and How Does It Know It?" *Brookings Papers on Economic Activity,* no. 1, 327–386.

Blyth, Mark. 2002. *Great Transformations: Economic Ideas and Institutional Change in the Twentieth Century.* Cambridge: Cambridge University Press.

————. 2013. *Austerity: The History of a Dangerous Idea.* Oxford: Oxford University Press.

Boianovsky, Mauro. 2004. "The IS-LM Model and the Liquidity Trap Concept: From Hicks to Krugman" annual supplement. *History of Political Economy* 36:92–126.

Braun, R. Anton, and Yuichiro Waki. 2006. "Monetary Policy during Japan's Lost Decade." *Japanese Economic Review* 57 (2): 324–344.

Bremmer, Brian 2004. "Commentary: Don't Let Japan's Mr. Dollar Get Away with It," *Bloomberg Businessweek*, March 21, 2004. http://www.businessweek.com/stories/2004-03-21/commentary-dont-let-japans-mr-dot-dollar-get-away-with-it (accessed on May 1, 2014)

Bronfenbrenner, Martin. 1956. "The State of Japanese Economics." *American Economic Review* 46 (2): 389–398.

Brynjolfsson, Erik, and Andrew McAfee. 2014. *The Second Machine Age: Work, Progress, and Prosperity in a Time of Brilliant Technologies.* New York: Norton.

Cabarello, Ricard J., and M. L. Hammour. 2000. "Creative Destruction and Development: Institutions, Crises, and Restructuring." NBER Working Paper 7849. National Bureau of Economic Research, Cambridge, MA.

Cabarello, Ricard J., Takeo Hoshi, and Anil Kashyap. 2008. "Zombie Lending and Depressed Restructuring in Japan." *American Economic Review* 98 (5): 1943–1977.

Cabinet Office. 2010. "Kisei Seido Kaikaku no Keizai Koka" [Economic effects of regulatory and institutional reforms]. http://www5.cao.go.jp/keizai3/2010/10 seisakukadai06-0.pdf

Caplan, Bryan. 2002. "Systematically Biased Beliefs about Economics: Robust Evidence of Judgmental Anomalies from the Survey of Americans and Economists on the Economy." *Economic Journal* 112:433–458.

———. 2003. "The Idea Trap: The Political Economy of Growth Divergence." *European Journal of Political Economy* 19:183–203.

———. 2007. *The Myth of the Rational Voter: Why Democracies Choose Bad Policies.* Princeton, NJ: Princeton University Press.

Cargill, Thomas F., and Takayuki Sakamoto. 2008. *Japan since 1980.* Cambridge: Cambridge University Press.

Caruana, Jaime. 2014. "Global Economic and Financial Challenges: A Tale of Two Views." Bank for International Settlements. https://www.bis.org/speeches/ sp140409.pdf

Cassel, Gustav. 1921. *The World's Monetary Problems: Two Memoranda.* London: Constable.

———. 1922. *Money and Exchange after 1914.* London: Constable.

———. 1924. "The Restoration of the Gold Standard." *Economica,* no. 9, 171–185.

———. 1926. "The Japanese Currency." *Ginko Tsushin Roku,* 81 (83): 492–498.

Chen, Joe, Yun Cheong Choi, Kota Mori, Yasuyuki Sawada, and Saki Sugano. 2012. "Recession, Unemployment, and Suicide in Japan." *Japan Labor Review* 9 (2): 75–92.

Choudhri, Ehsan U., and Levis A. Kochin. 1980. "The Exchange Rate and the International Transmission of Business Cycle Disturbances." *Journal of Money, Credit, and Banking* 12:565–574.

Christensen, Lars. 2011. "Market Monetarism." *Historinhas* (blog). http://thefaintof heart.files.wordpress.com/2011/09/market-monetarism-13092011.pdf

Comin, Diego, and Mark Gertler. 2006. "Medium-Term Business Cycles." *American Economic Review* 96 (3): 523–551.

Congleton, Roger, D. 2004. "The Political Economy of Crisis Management: Surprise, Urgency, and Mistakes in Political Decision Making." In *The Dynamics of Intervention: Regulation and Redistribution in the Mixed Economy,* edited by Peter Kurrild-Klitgaard, 183–203. Vol. 8 of *Advances in Austrian Economics.* Bingley, UK: Emerald Group Publishing Limited.

———. 2009. "On the Political Economy of the Financial Crisis and Bailout of 2008–2009." *Public Choice* 140 (3–4): 287–317.

Cowen, Tyler. 2011. *The Great Stagnation*. New York: Dutton.

———. 2012. "Will a More Expansionary Monetary Policy Give Rise to a Bubble?" Marginal Revolution, August 14. http://marginalrevolution.com/marginal revolution/2012/08/will-a-more-expansionary-monetary-policy-give-rise-to-a-bubble.html

Crafts, Nicholas, and Peter Fearon, eds. 2013. *The Great Depression of the 1930s: Lessons for Today*. Oxford: Oxford University Press.

DeLong, J. Bradford. 1990. "'Liquidation Cycles': Old Fashioned Real Business Cycle Theory and the Great Depression." NBER Working Paper 3546. National Bureau of Economic Research, Cambridge, MA.

———. 2012. "A Question from the Floor; Understanding Japan's Options in the Early 1990s." *Grasping Reality with Both Invisible Hands* (blog). August 1, 2012. http://delong.typepad.com/sdj/2012/08/a-question-from-the-floor-understanding-japans-options-in-the-early-1990s.html

De Michelis, Andrea, and Matteo Iacoviello. 2014. "Raising an Inflation Target: The Japanese Experience with Abenomics." Unpublished manuscript. https://www2.bc.edu/matteo-iacoviello/research_files/ABENOMICS_PAPER.pdf

Dickinson, Frederick R. 2013. *World War I and the Triumph of a New Japan, 1919–1930*. Cambridge: Cambridge University Press.

Dimand, Robert W., and Masazumi Wakatabe. 2011. "The *Kyoto University Economic Review* (1926–1944) as Importer and Exporter of Economic Ideas: Bringing Lausanne, Cambridge, Vienna, and Marx to Japan." In *The Dissemination of Economic Ideas*, edited by Heinz D. Kurz, Tamotsu Nishizawa, and Keith Tribe. Cheltenham, UK: Edward Elgar.

Economist. 2004. "Toshihiko Goldilocks." *Economist*, February 14. http://www.economist.com/node/2429154

———. 2008. "Charlemagne: Don't Play Politics with the Euro: The Lessons of German History Haunt the Single Currency." *Economist*, March 8. http://www.economist.com/node/10809039

Eggertsson, Gauti B. 2008. "Great Expectations and the End of the Depression." *American Economic Review* 98 (4): 1476–1516.

Eggertsson, Gauti B., and Paul Krugman. 2012. "Debt, Deleveraging, and the Liquidity Trap." *Quarterly Journal of Economics*, 127 (3): 1469–1513.

Eichengreen, Barry. 1992. *Golden Fetters: The Gold Standard and the Great Depression, 1919–1939*. New York: Oxford University Press.

———. 2009. "The Last Temptation of Risk." *National Interest Online*, April 28.

———. 2013. "Currency War or International Policy Coordination?" *Journal of Policy Modeling* 35 (3): 425–433.

Eichengreen, Barry, and Kevin H. O'Rourke. 2009. "A Tale of Two Depressions." Vox, April 6. Last modified June 4, 2009. http://www.voxeu.org/index.php?q=node/3421

Eichengreen, Barry, and Jeffrey Sachs. 1985. "Exchange Rates and Economic Recovery in the 1930s." *Journal of Economic History* 45 (4): 925–946.

.

Eichengreen, Barry, and Peter Temin. 2003. "Ideology and the Shadow of History: A Perspective on the Great Depression." In *The Economic Future in Historical Perspective*, edited by Paul A. David and Mark Thomas, 339–362. Oxford: Oxford University Press.

Ergungor, Emre, and Kent Cherny. 2009. "Sweden as a Useful Model of Successful Financial Crisis Resolution." Vox, March 19. http://www.voxeu.org/article/resolving-banking-crisis-should-we-follow-sweden-s-example

Evans-Pritchard, Ambrose. 2014. "ECB Is Delighted by the Splendid Prospect of Deflation," *The Telegraph*, May 7, 2014.

Faini, Riccardo, and Gianni Toniolo. 1992. "Reconsidering Japanese Deflation during the 1920s." *Explorations in Economic History* 29:121–143.

Federal Reserve Board. 2012. "Press Release," January 25, 2012. http://www.federalreserve.gov/newsevents/press/monetary/20120125c.htm

Fingleton, Eamonn. 2012. "The Myth of Japan's Failure." *New York Times*, January 6.

Fisher, Irving. (1911) 1997. *The Purchasing Power of Money: Its Decentralization and Relation to Credit, Interest and Crises*, New York: Macmillan. Reprinted in *The Works of Irving Fisher*, edited by William J. Barber. The Pickering Masters 4. London: Pickering and Chatto.

———. (1928) 1997. *The Money Illusion*, New York: Adelphi. Reprinted in *The Works of Irving Fisher*, edited by William J. Barber. The Pickering Masters 8. London: Pickering and Chatto.

———. (1932) 1997. *Booms and Depressions: Some First Principles*, New York: Adelphi. Reprinted in *The Works of Irving Fisher*, edited by William J. Barber. The Pickering Masters 10. London: Pickering and Chatto.

———. 1933. "The Debt-Deflation Theory of Great Depressions." *Econometrica* 1 (4): 337–357.

Fisher, Stanley. 1995. "Structural Adjustment Lessons from the 1980s." In *Structural Adjustment: Retrospect and* Prospect, edited by Daniel M. Schydlowsky, 21–31. Westport, CT: Praeger.

Fourcade, Marion. 2009. *Economists and Societies: Discipline and Profession in the United States, Great Britain, and France, 1890s to 1990s*. Princeton, NJ: Princeton University Press.

Friedman, Milton, and Rose Director Friedman. 1980. *Free to Choose: A Personal Statement*. New York: Harcourt Brace Jovanovich.

Friedman, Milton, and Anna Jacobson Schwartz. 1963. *A Monetary History of the United States, 1867–1960*. Princeton, NJ: Princeton University Press.

Fujiki, Minako. 2004. "Inflation Targeting Discussions in Japan." CJEB Working Paper 219. Center on Japanese Economy and Business, Columbia Business School, New York.

Fujimaki, Hideki. 2002. *Genba ni Deta Keizaigakushatachi* [Economists on the policy field]. Tokyo: Chuo Daigaku Syuppankai.

Fujiwara, Ippei, Naoko Hara, Naohisa Hirakata, Takeshi Kimura, and Shinichiro Watanabe. 2007. "Japanese Monetary Policy during the Collapse of the Bubble Economy: A View of Policy-making under Uncertainty." IMES Discussion Paper

2007-E-9. Bank of Japan. http://www.imes.boj.or.jp/research/papers/english/07-E-09.pdf

Fukai, Eigo. 1928. *Tsuka Chosetsu Ron* [The control of money]. Tokyo: Nihon Hyoronsha.

Fukao, Kyoji. 2012. *"Ushinawareta 20-nen" to Nihon Keizai* [The Lost Two Decades and the Japanese economy]. Tokyo: Nihon Keizai Shimbun Shuppansha.

Fukuda, Tokuzo. 1930. *Kosei Keizai Kennkyu* [Studies on welfare economics]. Tokyo: Toko Syoin.

Funabashi, Yoichi. 1989. *Managing the Dollar: From the Plaza to the Louvre.* 2nd ed. Washington, DC: Institute for International Economics.

Furner, Mary O., and Barry Supple. 1990. "Ideas, Institutions, and State in the United States and Britain: An Introduction." In *The State and Economic Knowledge: The American and British Experiences,* 3–39. Cambridge: Cambridge University Press.

Gao, Bai. 1997. *Economic Ideology and Japanese Industrial Policy.* Cambridge: Cambridge University Press.

Garside, W. R. 2012. *Japan's Great Stagnation: Forging Ahead, Falling Behind.* Cheltenham, UK: Edward Elgar.

Giuliano, Paola, and Antonio Spilimbergo. 2014. "Growing Up in a Recession," *Review of Economic Studies* 81 (2): 787–817.

Gordon, Robert J. 2009. "Is Modern Macro or 1978-Era Macro More Relevant to the Understanding of the Current Economic Crisis?" Unpublished manuscript. http://faculty-web.at.northwestern.edu/economics/gordon/GRU_Combined_090909.pdf

Greenspan, Alan. 2007. *The Age of Turbulence.* New York: Penguin Press.

Gregory, T. E. 1924. "Recent Trends Currency Reform," *Economica,* no. 11, 163–175.

———. 1925. *The Return to Gold.* London: E. Benn.

———. 1926. *The First Year of the Gold Standard.* London: E. Benn.

Grimes, William W. 2001. *Unmaking the Japanese Miracle: Macroeconomics Politics, 1985–2000,* Ithaca, NY: Cornell University Press.

Grossman, Richard S. 2013. *Wrong: Nine Economic Policy Disasters and What We Can Learn from Them.* New York: Oxford University Press.

Group 2001. 1994a. "Kisei kanwa to iu akumu" [A nightmare called deregulation]. *Bungei Shunju,* August, 134–147.

———. 1994b. "Kisei kanwa to iu akumu II" [A nightmare called deregulation II]. *Bungei Shunju,* November, 318–330.

Guajardo, Jaime, Daniel Leigh, and Andrea Pescatori. 2011. "Expansionary Austerity: New International Evidence." IMF Working Paper. International Monetary Fund, Washington, DC. http://www.imf.org/external/pubs/ft/wp/2011/wp11158.pdf

Haidar, Jamal Ibrahim, and Takeo Hoshi. 2014. "Implementing Structural Reforms in Abenomics: How to Reduce the Cost of Doing Business in Japan." http://iis-db.stanford.edu/pubs/24643/Haidar%26Hoshi-JapanDBrankJune252014.pdf

Hall, Thomas E., and J. David Ferguson. 1998. *The Great Depression: An International Disaster of Perverse Economic Policies.* Ann Arbor, MI: University of Michigan Press.

Hamada, Koichi, and Akiyoshi Horiuch, eds. 2004. *Ronso nihon no keizai kiki: Choki Teitai no shinin wo kaimei suru* [Controversy on Japan's economic crisis: Investigating a true cause of the persistent stagnation].Tokyo: Nihon Keizai Shimbunsha.

Hamada, Koichi, Motoshige Ito, Kikuo Iwata, Keiichi Ohmura, and Hiroshi Yoshikawa. 2003. "Roundtable Discussion Kozo Kaikaku: Do Naru Nihon Keizai." In *Gendai keizaigaku no choryu 2003*, edited by Yoshiyasu Ono, Mikio Nakayama, Shinichi Fukuda, and Yuzo Honda, 251–273. Tokyo: Toyo Keizai Shimposha.

Hamada, Koichi, Anil K Kashyap, and David E. Weinstein, eds. 2011. *Japan's Bubble, Deflation, and Long-term Stagnation*. Cambridge, MA: MIT Press.

Hamada, Koichi, and Asahi Noguchi. 2005. "Preconceived Ideas in Macroeconomic Policy: Japan's Experience in Two Deflationary Episodes." *International Economy and Economic Policy* 2:101–126.

Hamada, Koichi, and Yasushi Okada. 2009. "Monetary and International Factors behind Japan's Lost Decades." *Journal of the Japanese and International Economies* 23:200–219.

Handbury, Jessie, Tsutomu Watanabe, and David E. Weinstein. 2013. "How Much Do Official Price Indexes Tell Us about Inflation?" NBER Working Paper 19504. National Bureau of Economic Research, Cambridge, MA.

Hara, Miwako. 2010. "Shinto Suru Kakusa Ishiki" [Sense of inequality is creeping in]. *Hoso Kenkyu to Chosa*, May, 56–73.

Harada, Yutaka. 2003. *Nihon no "Daiteitai" ga Owaru Hi* [The day that Japan's Great Stagnation ends]. Tokyo: Nihon Hyorosha.

Harrigan, James, and Kenneth Kuttner. 2005. "Lost Decade in Translation: Did the US Learn from Japan's Post-bubble Mistakes?" In *Reviving Japan's Economy*, edited by Takatoshi Ito, Hugh Patrick, and David E. Weinstein, 79–106. Cambridge, MA: MIT Press.

Hatoyama, Yukio. 2009a. "Watashi no seiji tetsugaku" [My political philosophy]. *Voice*, September, 132–141.

———(2009b). "A New Path for Japan," *New York Times*. http://www.nytimes.com/2009/08/27/opinion/27iht-edhatoyama.html?pagewanted=1&_r=0

Hatta, Tatsuo. 2009. *Micuro keizaigaku II* [Microeconomics II]. Tokyo: Toyo Keizai Shimposha.

Hausman, Joshua K., and Johannes F. Wieland. 2014. "Abenomics: Preliminary Analysis and Outlook." *Brookings Papers on Economic Activity*, Spring, 1–76. http://www.brookings.edu/~/media/Projects/BPEA/Spring%202014/2014a_Hausman.pdf

Hayami, Masaru. 2005. *Tsuyoi Yen, Tsuyoi Keizai* [The strong yen, the strong economy]. Tokyo: Toyo Keizai Shimposha.

Hayasaka, Tadashi, and Kimihiro Masamura. 1974. *Sengo Nihon no Keizaigaku* [Economics in postwar Japan]. Tokyo: Nikkei Shinsho.

Hayashi, Fumio, ed. 2006. "Special Section: Aspects of Japan's Prolonged Slump," *Japan and the World Economy* 16 (4): 357–463.

———. 2007. *Keizai Teitai no Gennin to Seido* [Causes and institutions of the economic stagnation]. Tokyo: Keiso Shobo.

Hayashi, Fumio, and Edward Prescott. 2002. "The 1990s in Japan: A Lost Decade." *Review of Economic Dynamics* 5 (1): 206–235.

Hetzel, Robert L. 1999. "Japanese Monetary Policy: A Quantity Theory Perspective." *Economic Quarterly* 85 (1). http://199.169.211.101/publications/research/economic_quarterly/1999/winter/pdf/hetzel1.pdf

———. 2004. "Price Stability and Japanese Monetary Policy and Deflation." *Monetary and Economic Studies* 22 (3): 1–24.

———. 2012. *The Great Recession: Market Failure or Policy Failure?* Cambridge: Cambridge University Press.

Higgs, Robert. 1987. *Crisis and Leviathan: Critical Episodes in the Growth of American Government.* New York: Oxford University Press.

Hijikata, Seibi. 1929. *Kin Kaikin* [Lifting the embargo on gold]. Tokyo: Nihon Hyorosha.

Hirano, Tomohiro, and Noriyuki Yanagawa. 2010. "Asset Bubbles, Endogenous Growth, and Financial Frictions." CARF Working Paper F-223. University of Tokyo.

Hirata, Keiichiro, Saichi Tadashi, and Minomatsu Izumi, eds. *Showazeisei no kaiko to tenbo* [Retrospect and prospect of the Showa tax system]. Tokyo: Okura Zeimu Kyokai.

Hiscox, Michael J. 2006. "Through a Glass and Darkly: Attitude toward International Trade and the Curious Effects of Issue Framing." *International Organization* 60 (3): 755–780.

Horioka, Charles Yuji. 2006. "The Causes of Japan's 'Lost Decade': The Role of Household Consumption." *Japan and the World Economy* 18:378–400.

Horioka, Charles Yuji, Takatoshi Ito, Yasushi Iwamoto, Fumio Ohtake, Etsuro Shioji, and Fumio Hayashi. 2007. "Macuro Keizaigaku ha 'Ushinawareta Junen' kara Nani wo Mananda ka" [What lessons macroeconomics has learned from the Lost Decade]. In *Gendai keizaigaku no choryu 2007* [Currents of contemporary economics 2007], edited by Hidehiko Ichimura, Hideshi Ito, Kazuo Ogawa, and Koichi Futagami, 217–261. Tokyo: Toyo Keizai Shimposha.

Hoshi, Takeo. 1998. "Kakucho teki Kinyu Seisaku koso Yuko na Shohosen" [Expansionary monetary policy is the effective remedy]. *Ronso Toyo Keiza,* September, 76–83.

———. 2006. "Economics of the Living Dead." *The Japanese Economic Review* 57 (1): 30–49.

Hoshi, Takeo, and Anil Kashyap. 1999. "The Japanese Banking Crisis: Where Did It Come From and How Will It End?" *NBER Macroeconomics Annual* 14:129–201.

———. 2011. "Why Did Japan Stop Growing?" NIRA (National Institute for Research Advancement). http://nira.or.jp/pdf/1002english_report.pdf

———. 2012. "Policy Options for Japan's Revival." NIRA. http://nira.or.jp/pdf/1202english_report.pdf

Hylton, Keith N., and Fei Deng. 2007. "Antitrust around the World: An Empirical Analysis of the Scope of Competition Laws and Their Effects." *Antitrust Law Journal* 74 (2): 271–342.

Iida, Yasuyuki. 2013. "Zaisei seisaku ha Yuko ka" [Is fiscal policy effective?]. In *Rifure ga nihon keizai wo fukkatsu saseru* [Reflation resurrects the Japanese economy], edited by Koichi Hamada, Kikuo Iwata, and Yutaka Harada, 177–203. Tokyo: Chuo Keizaisha.

Iida, Yasuyuki, and Tatsuyoshi Matsumae. 2009. "The Dynamic Effects of Japanese Macroeconomic Policies: Were There Any Changes in the 1990s?" ESRI Working Paper 209. Economic and Social Research Institute, Tokyo.

Ikeo, Aiko. 2014. *A History of Economic Science in Japan: The Internationalization of Economics in the Twentieth Century*. Abingdon, UK: Routledge.

Ikeo, Kazuhito. 1985. *Nihon no Kinyu Shijo to Soshiki* [Financial markets and organizations in Japan]. Tokyo: Toyo Keizai Shimposha.

———. 2003. *Ginko wa Naze Kawarenainoka* [Why banks cannot change]. Tokyo: Chuo Koronsha.

———. 2006. *Kaihatsu shugi no boso to hoshin: kinyu shisutemu to Heisei keizai*. Tokyo: NTT Shuppan.

Inoue, Junnosuke. 1929. *Kin Kaikin: Zenn Nihon ni Sakebu* [Lifting the embargo: A call for the nation]. Tokyo: Senshinsha.

———. 1930. *Sekai Fukeiki to Waga Kokumin no Kakugo* [The world recession and our nation's resolution]. Tokyo: Keizai Chishikisha.

Inoue, Tomoo, and Tatsuyoshi Okimoto. 2008. "Were There Structural Breaks in the Effects of Japanese Monetary Policy? Re-evaluating Policy Effects of the Lost Decade." *Journal of the Japanese and International Economies* 22 (3): 320–342.

Irwin, Douglas A. 2010. "Did France Cause the Great Depression?" NBER Working Paper 16350. National Bureau of Economic Research, Cambridge, MA.

———. 2011a. "Anticipating the Great Depression? Gustav Cassel's Analysis of the Interwar Gold Standard." NBER Working Paper 17597. National Bureau of Economic Research, Cambridge, MA.

———. 2011b. *Peddling Protectionism*. Princeton, NJ: Princeton University Press.

Irwin, Neil. 2013. *The Alchemists: Three Central Bankers and a World on Fire*. New York: Penguin Press.

Ishibashi, Tanzan. 1970–1972. *Ishibashi Tanzan Zenshu* [The works of Tanzan Ishibashi]. 15 vols. Tokyo: Toyo Keizai Shimpo Sha.

Ito, Masanao. 1989. *Nihon no Taigai Kinyu to Kinyu Seisaku, 1914–1936* [Japan's external finance and monetary policy, 1914–1936]. Nagoya: Nagoya Daigaku Syuppankai.

Ito, Motoshige, Kazuharu Kiyono, Masahiro Okuno-Fujiwara, and Kotaro Suzumura. 1988. *Sangyo Seisaku no Keizai Bunseki*. Tokyo: Tokyo Daigaku Shuppan. Translated as *Economic Analysis of Industrial Policy* (San Diego: Academic Press, 1991).

Ito, Takatoshi. 2013. "War and Peace among Currencies: Spillover of Monetary Policy in the Age of Quantitative Easing." Paper read at the ESRI conference, May 2013. http://www.esri.go.jp/jp/workshop/130530/data/4_1_1Ito_takasoshi.pdf

Ito, Takatoshi, and Motoshige Ito. 1998. "Mokuhyo Infure Ritsu 3 kara 4 % Ryoteki Kanwa de Kano ka" [Inflation target 3% to 4%: Is it achievable with quantitative easing?]. *Ronso Toyo Keizai*, September, 84–90.

Ito, Takatoshi, Hugh Patrick, and David E. Weinstein, eds. 2005. *Reviving Japan's Economy*, Cambridge, MA: MIT Press.

Ito, Takatoshi, and Hiroshi Yoshikawa. 2003. "Keizaigakusha Group Kinkyu Teigen" [Urgent proposal by a group of economists]. *Nikkei Shimbun*, March 9.

Ito, Yukako. 2013. *Shohizei nikki* [Diaries on the consumption tax hike].Tokyo: Presidentsha.

Iwata, Kazumasa, ed. 2014. *Ryoteki Sitsuteki Kinyu Kanwa* [Quantitative and qualitative monetary easing]. Tokyo: Nihon Keizai Shimbunsha.

Iwata, Kazumasa, and Ikuko Fueda-Samikawa. 2013. "Quantitative and Qualitative Monetary Easing Effects and Associated Risks: Financial Research Report: General Remarks." *Japan Financial Report*. http://www.jcer.or.jp/eng/pdf/kinyu20131213.pdf

Iwata, Kikuo. 1998. *Kinyu Hotei* [Financial trial]. Tokyo: Nihon Keizai Shimbunsha.

———. 2001. *Defure no Keizaigaku* [The economics of deflation]. Tokyo: Toyo Keizai Shimposha.

———, ed. 2003. *Mazu Defure o Tomeyo* [Stop deflation first]. Tokyo: Nihon Keizai Shimbunsha.

———, ed. 2004. *Showa Kyoko no Kenkyu* [Studies on the Showa Great Depression]. Tokyo: Toyo Keizai Shimposha.

———, ed. 2013. *Nihon Keizai Saisei Mazu Defure o Tomeyo* [Reviving the Japanese economy: Stop deflation first]. Tokyo: Nihon Keizai Shimbunsha.

———. 2014. "Japan's Growth Potential and Quantitative and Qualitative Monetary Easing." Remarks at a panel discussion at the Bank of Korea International Conference 2014, June 3. http://www.boj.or.jp/en/announcements/press/koen_2014/data/ko140603a2.pdf

Iwata, Kikuo, and Tsutomu Miyagawa, eds. 2004. *Ushinawareta Jyunen no Shinin ha Nanika* [What is a true cause of the Lost Decade?]. Tokyo: Toyo Keizai Shimposya.

Iwata, Kikuo, Yasushi Okada, Seiji Adachi, and Yasuyuki Iida. 2008. "Lessons from the Inoue Zaisei and the Takahashi Zaisei." *Gakushuin Daigaku Keizai Ronso* 45 (3): 157–182. http://www.gakushuin.ac.jp/univ/eco/gakkai/pdf_files/keizai_ronsyuu/contents/4503/4503iwata/4503iwata.pdf

James, Harold. 2001. *The End of Globalization: Lessons from the Great Depression*, Cambridge: Harvard University Press.

Jinushi, Toshiki. 2007. *Amerika no Kinyu Seisaku* [The monetary policy of the United States]. Tokyo: Toyo Keizai Shimposha.

Johnson, Chalmers A. 1982. *MITI and the Japanese Miracle: The Growth of Industrial Policy, 1925–1975*. Stanford, CA: Stanford University Press.

Jonung, Lars. 2009. "The Swedish Model for Resolving the Banking Crisis of 1991–93: Seven Reasons Why It Was Successful." European Economy, Economic Paper 360. European Commission, Brussels, Belgium.

Kamikawa, Ryunoshin. 2005. *Keizai Seisaku no Seijigaku* [The politics of economic policy]. Tokyo: Toyo Keizai Shimposha.

———. 2010. *Koizumi Kaikaku no Seijigaku* [The politics of the Koizumi reforms]. Tokyo: Toyo Keizai Shimposha.

Kane, Edward. 1993. "What Lesson Should Japan Learn from the Deposit Insurance Mess." *Journal of the Japanese and International Economies* 7 (4): 329–355.

Karube, Kensuke, and Tomohiko Nishino. 1999. *Kensyo Keizai Shissei* [Examining economic policy mistakes]. Tokyo: Iwanami Shoten.

Kasuya, Yasutaka. 2005. "Kinyukiki Taio no Hikaku Bunseki—1990 Nendai Zenhan no Sweden to Nihon" [Comparative analysis of financial crisis management: Sweden and Japan in the early 1990s]. in *Heisei Baburu sakiokuri no kenkyu* [Studies in forbearance in the Heisei bubble], edited by Michio Muramatsu. 313–338. Tokyo: Toyo Keizai Shimposha.

Kataoka, Goushi. 2010. *Nihon no "Ushinawareta 20 nen"* [Japan's Lost Two Decades]. Tokyo: Fujiwara Shoten.

———. 2013. *Abenomikusu no Yukue* [Whither Abenomics]. Tokyo: Kobunsha.

Kataoka, Goushi, and Masazumi Wakatabe. 2011. "The Great Inflation in Japan: How Economic Thought Interacted with Economic Policy." TCER Working Paper, E-36. Tokyo Center for Economic Research. http://www.tcer.or.jp/wp/pdf/e36.pdf

Kato, Junko. 1994. *Problem of Bureaucratic Rationality: Tax Politics in Japan*. Princeton, NJ: Princeton University Press.

Kato, Ryo. 2003. "Zaisei Seisaku Josu no Nichibei Hikaku" [Comparison of Japanese and American fiscal multiplier]. Bank of Japan Working Paper Series 03-J-4, Tokyo.

Kato, Sota, and Keiichiro Kobayashi. 2001. *Nihon Keizai no Wana* [The trapped Japanese economy]. Tokyo: Nihon Keizai Shinbunsya.

Katsuta, Teiji. 1929. *Kin Kaikin Chokugo no Zaikai* [The economy after the return to the gold standard]. Tokyo: Syunyudo.

———. 1930. *Doitsu Zaikai no Kiko* [The system of the German business]. Tokyo: Chikura Shobo.

Katsuta, Teiji, and Kamekichi Takahashi. 1931. *Kin Yushutsu Saikinshi Zehi no Ninin Ronso* [Two debates on the desirability of the resuspension]. Tokyo: Shunyodo.

Katz, Richard. 1998. *Japan, the System That Soured: The Rise and Fall of the Japanese Economic Miracle*. Armonk, NY: M. E. Sharpe.

———. 2008. "A Nordic Mirror: Why Structure Reform Has Preceded Faster in Scandinavia Than in Japan," CJEB Working Paper 265. Center on Japanese Economy and Business, Columbia Business School, New York. http://www4.gsb.columbia.edu/filemgr?file_id=3536

Keizai Kaikaku Kenkyukai. 1993. *Keizaikaikaku ni Tsuite* [On economic reforms]. http://www.esri.go.jp/jp/prj/sbubble/data_history/5/makuro_kei12_1.pdf

Keizai Kikakucho. 1993. *Nenji Kaizai Hokoku Heisei 5-nen Ban* [The annual economic report, 1993]. Tokyo: Government Printing Office.

———. 1994. *Nenji Kaizai Hokoku Heisei 6-nen Ban* [The annual economic report, 1994]. Tokyo: Government Printing Office.

Keynes, John Maynard. 1923. *A Tract on Monetary Reform*. London: Macmillan and Co., Ltd. Vol. 4 of *The Collected Writings of John Maynard Keynes IV*. edited by E. Johnson and D. E. Moggridge. London: Macmillan.

———. 1925. *The Economic Consequences of Mr. Churchill*. London: Hogarth. Vol. 9 of *The Collected Writings of John Maynard* Keynes, 207–230. edited by E. Johnson and D. E. Moggridge. London: Macmillan.

———. 1971–1989. *The Collected Writings of John Maynard Keynes*, edited by E. Johnson and D. E. Moggridge. London: Macmillan.

Kindleberger, Charles P. 1973. *The World in Depression, 1929–1939*. Berkeley: University of California Press.

Kiyotaki, Nobuhiro, and John Moore. 1997. "Credit Cycles." *Journal of Political Economy* 105, (2): 211–248.

Klamer, Arjo, and Jennifer Meehan. 1999. "The Crowding Out of Academic Economics: The Case of NAFTA." In *What Do Economists Know? New Economics of Knowledge*, edited by Robert F. Garnett Jr., 65–85. London: Routledge.

Kobayashi, Keiichiro, and Masaru Inaba. 2005. "Debt Disorganization in Japan." *Japan and the World Economy* 17 (2): 151–169.

Komiya, Ryutaro. 1986. "Nichibei Keizai Masatsu to Kokusai Kyocho" [Japan-US trade disputes and international coordination]. *Shukan Toyo Keizai*, June 7 and June 14.

Komiya, Ryutaro, Masahiro Okuno, and Kotaro Suzumura, eds. 1984. *Nihon no Sangyo Seisaku*, Tokyo: Tokyo Daigaku Suppankai. Translated as *Industrial Policy of Japan* (San Diego: Academic Press, 1988).

Komiya, Ryutaro, and Yoshio Suzuki. 1977. "Inflation in Japan." In *Worldwide Inflation: Theory and Recent Experience*, edited by Lawrence B. Krause and Walter S. Salant, 303–348. Washington, DC: The Brookings Institution.

Kondo, Kenji. 1999. *Puraza Goi no Kenkyu* [A study on the Plaza Accord]. Tokyo: Toyo Keizai Shimposha.

Krugman, Paul. 1996. "Stable Prices and Fast Growth: Just Say No." *Economist*, August 31, 19–21.

———. 1997. *The Age of Diminished Expectations*. 3rd ed. Cambridge, MA: MIT Press.

———. 1998a. "It's Baaack! Japan's Slump and the Return of the Liquidity Trap." *Brookings Papers on Economic Activity*, no. 2, 137–205.

———. 1998b. "Japan: Still Trapped." http://web.mit.edu/krugman/www/japtrap2. html

———. 2001. "Reckonings; A Leap in the Dark." *New York Times*, July 8. http:// www.nytimes.com/2001/07/08/opinion/reckonings-a-leap-in-the-dark.html

———. 2012a. *End This Depression Now!* New York: Norton.

———. 2012b. "Filters and Full Employment." *Conscience of a Liberal* (blog). *New York Times*, July 11. http://krugman.blogs.nytimes.com/2012/07/11/filters-and-full-employment-not-wonkish-really/

———. 2012c. "Magneto Muddles." *Conscience of a Liberal* (blog). *New York Times*, July 12. http://krugman.blogs.nytimes.com/2012/07/12/magneto-muddles/

———. 2013a. "Is Japan the Country of the Future Again?" *Conscience of a Liberal* (blog). *New York Times*, January 11. http://krugman.blogs.nytimes.com/2013/01/11/ is-japan-the-country-of-the-future-again/

———. 2013b. "The Japan Story," *New York Times*, February 5, 2013.

———. 2013c. "Shizo and the Helicopters [Somewhat Wonkish]." *Conscience of a Liberal* (blog). *New York Times*, January 18.

Kume, Ikuo. 2002. "Koteki shikin tonyu wo meguru yoron Seiji" [Public opinion and politics over the injection of public funds]. In *Heisei baburu no kenkyu* [Studies on the Heisei bubble]. Tokyo: edited by Michio Muramatsu and Masahiro Okuno, 109–156. Toyo Keizai Shimposha.

———. 2009. "Koteki shikin tonyu wo meguru seiji katei" [The political process over the injection of public funds]. In *Baburu/Defure ki no nihon no keizai to keizai seisaku* [The Japanese economy and economic policy during the bubble to deflation period]. edited by Naikakufu Keizaishakai Sogo Kenkyusho, 215–249. Tokyo: Naikakufu Keizaishakai Sogo Kenkyusho.

Kuroda, Haruhiko. 2005. *Zaisei Kinyu Seisaku no Seiko to Shippai* [Successes and failures in fiscal and monetary policies]. Tokyo: Nihon Hyoronsha.

Kuttner, Kenneth, and Adam Posen. 2001. "The Great Recession: Lessons for Macroeconomic Policy from Japan." *Brookings Papers on Economic Activity*, no. 2, 93–185.

Laidler, David. 1981. "Monetarism: An Interpretation and an Assessment," *Economic Journal* 91:1–28.

———. 1999. *Fabricating the Keynesian Revolution: Studies of the Inter-war Literature on Money, the Cycle, and Unemployment.* Cambridge: Cambridge University Press.

———. 2003. "The Role of the History of Economic Thought in Modern Macroeconomics." In *Monetary History, Exchange Rates and Financial Markets*, edited by P. Mizen, 12–29. Cheltenham, UK: Edward Elgar.

Lange, Oskar. 1935. "Marxian Economics and Modern Economic Theory." *Review of Economic Studies* 2 (3): 189–201.

Leigh, Daniel. 2009. "Monetary Policy and the Lost Decade: Lessons from Japan." IMF Working Paper WP/09/232. International Monetary Fund, Washington, DC.

Leighton, Wayne A., and Edward J. López. 2012. *Madmen, Intellectuals, and Academic Scribblers: The Economic Engine of Political Change.* Stanford, CA: Stanford University Press.

Lincoln, Edward J. 2001. *Arthritic Japan: The Slow Pace of Economic Reform.* Washington, DC: Brookings Institution Press.

Lucas, Robert E., Jr. 1993. "Making a Miracle," *Econometrica* 61 (2): 271–341.

Mabuchi, Masaru. 1997. *Naze Ohkura-sho ha Oitsumeraretanoka* [Why was the MOF was cornered]. Tokyo: Chuko Shinsyo.

Malmendier, Ulrike, and Stefan Nagel. 2011. "Depression Babies: Do Macroeconomic Experiences Affect Risk-Taking?" *Quarterly Journal of Economics* 126 (1): 373–416.

Mankiw, N. Gregory. 2009. *Macroeconomics.* 7th ed. New York: Worth Publishers.

Mata, Tiago, and Steven Medema, eds. 2014. *The Economist as Public Intellectual.* Durham, NC: Duke University Press.

Matsukata, Kojiro. 1926. *Eikoku Kin Yushutsu Kaikin ni Taisuru Hyoron wo Tsujite Waga Keizai Seisaku ni Oyobu* [Our economic policy with commentary on the return to the gold standard in Britain]. Tokyo: n.p. Matsushima, Shigeru, and Harukata Takenaka eds. 2011. *Nihon keizai no kiroku: Jidai shogenshu oraru hisutori [Records of the Japanese economy: An Oral History].* Tokyo: Naikakufu Keizaishakai Sogo Kenkyusho.

McLannahan, Ben. 2013. "Japan Hits Top of Asian IPO Chart," *Financial Times*, March 18, 2013.

McCullum, Bennett. 2001a. "Japanese Monetary Policy." Shadow Open Market Committee, April 30, 2001. http://wpweb2.tepper.cmu.edu/faculty/mccallum/JapanMonPol2.pdf

———. 2001b. "Japanese Monetary Policy Again." Shadow Open Market Committee, October 15, 2001. http://wpweb2.tepper.cmu.edu/faculty/mccallum/Japanese%20MP%20Again2.pdf

McKinnon, Ronald, and Kennichi Ohno. 1997. *Dollar and Yen: Resolving Economic Conflict between the United States and Japan.* Cambridge, MA: MIT Press.

Melzer, Allan H. 1999. "Comments: What More Can the Bank of Japan Do?" *Monetary and Economic Studies* 17 (3): 189–191.

———. 2001. "Monetary Transmission at Low Inflation: Some Clues from Japan in the 1990s." *Monetary and Economic Studies* 19 (S-1): 13–34.

Mikuriya, Takashi, and Takafusa Nakamura, eds. 2005. *Kikigaki Miyazawa Kiichi Kaikoroku* [Memoires Kiichi Miyazawa: An oral history]. Tokyo: Iwanami Shoten.

Mikuriya, Takashi, and Yoichi Serizawa. 2014. *Nihon Seiji Hizautchi Mondo* [Chatting on Japanese politics]. Tokyo: Nihon Keizai Shinbunsha.

Mirowski, Philip. 2013. *Never Let a Serious Crisis Go to Waste: How Neoliberalism Survived the Financial Meltdown.* London: Verso.

Mitani, Taichiro. 2009. *Woru Sutorito to Kyokuto: Seiji ni Okeru Kokusai Kinyu Shihon* [The Wall Street and the Far East: International Financial Capital in Politics]. Tokyo: Tokyo Daigaku Shuppankai.

Miwa, Yoshiro. 2004. *State Competence and Economic Growth in Japan.* London: RoutledgeCurzon.

Miwa, Yoshiro, and Mark Ramseyer. 2006. *The Fable of the Keiretsu: Urban Legends of the Japanese Economy.* Chicago: University of Chicago Press.

Miyao, Ryuzo. 2006a. *Makuro Kinyu Seisaku no Jikeiretsu Bunseki* [Time series analysis of macroeconomic monetary policy]. Tokyo: Nihon Keizai Shimbunsha.

———. 2006b. "Nihon Keizai no Hendo Yoin: Seisansei Shock no Yakuwari" [Causes of Fluctuations of the Japanese Economy: Roles of Productivity Shocks]. Bank of Japan Working Paper 06-J-1, Tokyo.

Miyao, Takahiro. 1992. "Fukyo Akka no Seisaku Sekinin wo Tou" [The Current Policy Is Responsible for Worsening Recession]. *Shukan Tokyo Keizai*, December 12.

———. 1995. *Keizai Haisenkoku Nihon: Defure Dakkyaku eno Shin Gyokakuron* [Economically Defeated Japan: New Administrative Reform for Ending Deflation]. Tokyo: Toyo Keizai Shimposha.

Modeled Behavior. 2012. "Curious Case of Japan in the 21st Century." *Forbes*, August6.http://www.forbes.com/sites/modeledbehavior/2012/08/06/the-curious-case-of-japan-in-the-21st-century/

Morris-Suzuki, Tessa. 1989. *A History of Japanese Economic Thought.* London: Routledge.

Murakai, Yasusuke. 1992. *Han Koten no Keizaigaku.* Tokyo: Chuo Koron. Translated as *An Anticlassical Political-Economic Analysis: A Vision for the Next Century* (Stanford, CA: Stanford University Press, 1996).

Muramatsu, Mithio, ed. 2005. *Heisei baburu sakioku no Kenkyu* [Studies on forbearance during the Heisei bubble economy]. Tokyo: Toyo Keizai Shimposha.

Muramatsu, Michio, and Masahiro Okuno, eds. 2002. *Heisei baburu no kenkyu* [Studies on the Heisei bubble]. Tokyo: Toyo Keizai Shimposha.

Naikakufu. 2011. *Keizai Seicho to Zaisei Kenzenka ni Kansuru Kenkyu Hokokusyo* [Research report on economic growth and fiscal consolidation]. http://www5.cao.go.jp/keizai2/keizai-syakai/k-s-kouzou/shiryou/k-s-3kai/pdf/2.pdf

————. 2013. *Heisei 23 Nendo Nenji Keizai Zaisei Hokoku* [Annual report on the Japanese economy and public finance 2011]. Tokyo: Government Printing Office.

————. 2012. *Heisei 24 Nendo Nenji Keizai Zaisei Hokoku* [Annual report on the Japanese economy and public finance 2012]. Tokyo: Government Printing Office.

Naikakufu Keizaishakai Sogo Kenkyusho, ed. 2009. *Baburu/Defure ki no nihon no keizai to keizai seisaku* [The Japanese economy and economic policy during the bubble to deflation period]. Tokyo: Naikakufu Keizaishakai Sogo Kenkyusho.

————, ed. 2011. *Nihon Keizai no Kiroku* [Records of the Japanese economy]. 3 vols. Tokyo: Naikakufu Keizaishakai Sogo Kenkyusho.

Nakagawa, Hidenao. 2006. *Ageshio no Jidai* [The age of Rising Tide]. Tokyo: Kodansha.

Nakahara, Nobuyuki, with Yoshihiro Fujii. 2006. *Nichigin ha dare no monoka* [Whose BOJ?]. Tokyo: Chuo Koronsha.

Nakatani, Iwao. 1996. *Nihon keizai no rekishiteki tenkan* [Historic transformation of the Japanese economy]. Tokyo: Toyo Keizai Shmposha.

————. 2008. *Shihon syugi ha naze jikai shitanoka* [Why capitalism self-destructed]. Tokyo: Shueisha Intanashonaru.

Nakatani, Iwao, and Takatoshi Ito. 1994. "Kisei kanwa ha 'akumu' ka 'fukuin' ka" [Is deregulation a nightmare or a gospel?]. *Ekonomisuto*, August 30, 46–54.

Nakatani, Iwao, and Hiroko Ohta. 1994. *Keizai kaikaku no bijon: Hiraiwa repoto o koete* [Vision for economic reforms: Beyond the Hiraiwa report]. Tokyo: Toyo Keizai Shmposha.

Nihon Ginko Chosa Kyoku, ed. 1968. *Nihon Kinyushi Shiryo* [Historical documents of money and finance in Japan]. Vols. 20–23. Tokyo: Nihon Ginko.

Nihon Ginko Seisaku Iinnkai. 2001a. Kinyu Seisaku Kettei Kaigo Gijiroku (Transcript of the Monetary Policy Meetings), August 13–14, 2001. (http://www.boj. or.jp/mopo/mpmsche_minu/record_2001/gjrk010814a.pdf).

————. 2001b. Kinyu Seisaku Kettei Kaigo Gijiroku (Transcript of the Monetary Policy Meetings), September 18, 2001. (http://www.boj.or.jp/mopo/mpmsche_ minu/record_2001/gjrk010918a.pdf).

Nihon Keizai Shinbunsha, ed. 2001. *Kensyo Baburu: Hanni naki Ayamachi* [Examining the bubble economy: Unpremeditated wrongdoings]. Tokyo: Nihon Keizai Shinbunsha.

————. 2012. "'Kinyu kanwa wa fujyubun,' Jimin sosai, nichigin hihan" ['Monetary easing is not enough,' the LDP leader criticizes the BOJ] *Nihon Keizai Shimbun*, November 11, 2012, 4.

————. 2013. "Syusho chinage wo yosei" [The prime minister asks business leaders for a wage raise]. February 12, 2013, evening edition, 1.

Nikkei Business. (2014). "Kensetsu gemba ga abunai" [Construction in danger], *Nikkei Business*, June 9, 2014, 44–48.

Nishino, Tomohiko. 2001. *Kensyo Keizai Meiso* [Examining the economy in disarray]. Tokyo: Iwanami Shoten.

————. 2003. *Kensyo Keizai Annun* [Examining the gathering economic storm]. Tokyo: Iwanami Shoten.

Noah, Timothy. 2012. "What Happened to Japan." *Noahpinion* (blog), August 3. http://noahpinionblog.blogspot.jp/2012/08/what-happened-to-japan.html

Noguchi, Asahi. 2000. "External Liberalization and 'Industrial Structural Policy'." [In *Japanese*]. *Economics and Economists since 1945*, edited by Aiko Ikeo, 254–280. London: Routledge.

———. 2005–2006. "Heisei Keizai Ronso" [Economic debates of the Heisei period]. *The Keizai Seminar*, April 2005–March 2006.

———. 2014. "Controversies Regarding Monetary Policy and Deflation in Japan from the 1990s to the early 2000s." In *The Development of Economics in Japan*, edited by Toichiro Asada, 93–133. London: Routledge.

Noguchi, Asahi, and Hidetomi, Tanaka. 2001. *Kozo Kaikaku Ron no Gokai* [Misunderstood structural reform]. Tokyo: Toyo Keizai Shimposha.

Noguchi, Yukio. 1992. *Baburu no Keizaigaku* [The economics of the bubble]. Tokyo: Nihon Keizai Shinbunsha.

———. 1995. *1940 Nen-taisei* [The 1940 system]. Tokyo: Toyo Keizai Shimposha.

———. 1998. "The 1940 System: Japan under the War Economy," *American Economic Review: Papers and Proceedings* 88 (2): 404–407.

Noguchi, Yukio, and Eisuke Sakakibara. 1977. "Okurasho-Nichigin Ohcho no Bunseki [Analysis of the MOF-BOJ Dynasty]," *Chuo Koron*, August, 96–150.

North, Douglass C. 2005. *Understanding the Process of Economic Change*. Princeton, NJ: Princeton University Press.

Obstfeld, Maurice. 2011. "Time of Troubles." In *Japan's Bubble, Deflation, and Long-Term Stagnation*, edited by Koichi Hamada, Anil K Kashyap, and David E. Weinstein, 51–103. Cambridge, MA: MIT Press.

OECD. 2008. *Growing Unequal? Income Distribution and Poverty in OECD Countries*. Paris: OECD.

———. 2014. *Economic Policy Reforms 2014*. Paris: OECD.

Ogawa, Kazuo. 2003. *Dai Fukyo no Keizai Bunseki* [The economic analysis of the Great Stagnation]. Tokyo: Nihon Keizai Shimbunsha.

Ogiue, Chiki. 2012. *Kanojyo tachi no Baishun* [Her prostitution]. Tokyo: Fusosha.

Ogura, Seitaro, ed. 1955. *Toyo Keizai Shimpo Gennron Rokujyu-nen* [Sixty years of journalism by Toyo Keizai Shimpo Sha]. Tokyo: Toyo Keizai Shimposha.

Ohtake, Fumio. 2005. *Nihon no Fubyodo: Kakusa Shakai no Genso to Mirai* [Inequality in Japan: Illusions and future of disparity society]. Tokyo: Nihon Keizai Shimbunsha.

———. 2010. *Kyoso to Koheikan* [Competition and the sense of fairness]. Tokyo: Chuo Koronsha.

Okada, Yasushi, and Yasuyuki Iida. 2004. "Showa Kyoko to Yoso Infure-ristu no Suikei" [The Showa Great Depression and an empirical investigation into the real interest rate]. In *Showa kyoko no kenkyu* [Studies on the Showa Great Depression], edited by Kikuo Iwata, 187–217. Tokyo: Toyo Keizai Shinpousha.

Okimoto, Daniel I., and Thomas P. Rohlen, eds. 1988. *Inside the Japanese System: Readings on Contemporary Society and Political Economy*. Stanford, CA: Stanford University Press.

Okina, Kunio. 1992a. "'Nichigin Riron' ha Machigatte Inai" [The BOJ theory is right]. *Syukan Toyo Keizai*, October 10.

———. 1992b. "Seisaku Rongi wo Konran Saseru Jitsumu heno Gokai" [Misunderstandings about the practice confuses the monetary policy discussion]. *Syukan Toyo Keizai*, November 26.

———. 1993. *Kinyu Seisaku* [Monetary policy]. Tokyo: Toyo Keizai Shimpo Sha.

———. 2011. *Posuto Monetarism no Kinyu Seisaku* [Monetary policy after monetarism]. Tokyo: Nihon Keizai Shimbun Shuppansha.

———. 2013. *Nihon Ginko* [The Bank of Japan]. Tokyo: Chikuma Shinsho.

———. 2014. "Zero Kinri Seiyakuka deha Kinyu Seisaku de Bukka ha Kontororu Dekinai" [Under the zero interest rate monetary policy cannot control the price level]. In *Tettei Bunseki Abenomics* [Abenomics analyzed], 1–21. Tokyo: Chuo Keizaisha.

Okita, Yoichi. 2010. *Sengo Nihon Keizai Ron* [The postwar Japanese economy]. Tokyo: Toyo Keizai Shmposha.

Onaran, Yalman. 2011. *Zombie Banks: How Broken Banks and Debtor Nations Are Crippling the Global Economy*. New York: Bloomberg Press.

Ono, Nobukatsu. 2005. *Takenaka Heizo no Senso* [Heizo Takenaka's battle to tackle banking reform in 730 days]. Tokyo: PHP.

Ono, Yoshiyasu. 1994. *Fukyo no Keizaigaku* [The economics of recession]. Tokyo: Nihon Keizai Shinbunsha.

———. 2001. "A Reinterpretation of Chapter 17 of Keynes's *General Theory*: Effective Demand Shortage under Dynamic Optimization." *International Economic Review* 42 (1): 207–236.

———. 2007. *Fukyo no Mecanizumu* [The mechanism of recession]. Tokyo: Chuo Koronsha.

Ozawa, Ichiro. 1993. *Nihon Kaizo Keikaku*. Tokyo: Kodansha. Translated as *Blueprint for a New Japan* (New York: Kodansha International, 1994).

Patrick, Hugh T. 1971. "The Economic Muddle of the 1920s." In *The Dilemmas of Growth in Prewar Japan*, edited by J. W. Morley, 211–266. Princeton, NJ: Princeton University Press.

Pescatori, Andrea, Damiano Sandri, and John Simon. 2014. "Debt and Growth: Is There a Magic Threshold?" IMF Working Paper. WP/14/34. International Monetary Fund, Washington, DC. http://www.imf.org/external/pubs/ft/wp/2014/wp1434.pdf

Pesek, William. 2014. *Japanization: What the World Can Learn from Japan's Lost Decades*. Singapore: Wiley.

Petri, Peter, and Michael G. Plummer. 2012. "The Trans-Pacific Partnership and Asia-Pacific Integration: Policy Implications." Peterson Institute for International Economics Policy Brief, Washington, DC.

Piketty, Thomas. 2014. *Capital in the Twenty-First Century*, Cambridge: Belknap Press of Harvard University Press.

Pilling, David. 2014. *Bending Adversity: Japan and the Art of Survival*. London: Allen Lane.

Posen, Adam. 1998. *Restoring Japan's Economic Growth*. Washington, DC: The Brookings Institution.

———. 2003a. "Is Germany Turning Japanese?" IIE. http://www.iie.com/publications/wp/03-2.pdf

———. 2003b. "Japanese Macroeconomic Policy: Unusual?" IIE, Unpublished manuscript.

Prestowitz, Clyde V. 1993. *Trading Places: How We Are Giving Our Future to Japan and How to Reclaim It.* New York: Basic Books.

Quiggin, John. 2012. *Zombie Economics: How Dead Ideas Still Walk among Us.* Princeton, NJ: Princeton University Press.

Rajan, Raghuram. 2010. *Fault Lines: How Hidden Fractures Still Threaten the World Economy.* Princeton, NJ: Princeton University Press.

———. 2011. "Money Magic." Project Syndicate, June 8. http://www.project-syndicate.org/commentary/rajan18/English

Rajan, Raghuram, and Luigi Zingales. 2003. *Saving Capitalism from the Capitalists: Unleashing the Power of Financial Markets to Create Wealth and Spread Opportunity.* Princeton, NJ: Princeton University Press.

Reinhart, Carmen M., and Rogoff, Kenneth S. 2009. *This Time Is Different: Eight Centuries of Financial Folly.* Princeton, NJ: Princeton University Press.

———. 2010. "Growth in a Time of Debt." *American Economic Review: Papers & Proceedings* 100 (2): 573–578.

Robertson, Dennis H. 1937. "Is Another Slump Coming?" *The Listener*, July 28, 174–175.

Robinson, Joan. 1942. *An Essay on Marxian Economics.* London: Macmillan.

———. 1971. *Economic Heresies: Some Old Fashioned Questions in Economic Theory.* New York: Basic Books.

———. 1972. "The Second Crisis of Economic Theory." *American Economic Review* 62 (2): 1–10.

Robinson, Joan, and John Eatwell. 1973. *An Introduction to Modern Economics.* New York: McGraw-Hill.

Rodrik, Dani. 2014. "When Ideas Trump Interests: Preferences, World Views, and Policy Innovations." *Journal of Economics Perspectives* 28 (1): 189–208.

Rogoff, Kenneth. 2008. "Embracing Inflation." *The Guardian*, December 2.

Romer, Christina D. 2009. "Lessons from the Great Depression for Economic Recovery in 2009." Policy speech at the Brookings Institution, March 9. http://www.brookings.edu/~/media/events/2009/3/09%20lessons/0309_lessons_romer.pdf

———. 2013a. "Lessons from the Great Depression for Policy Today." Teach-In on the Great Depression and World War II, University of Oklahoma, March 11. http://eml.berkeley.edu/~cromer/Lessons%20from%20the%20Great%20Depression%20for%20Policy%20Today%20Written.pdf.

———. 2013b. "It Takes a Regime Shift: Recent Developments in Japanese Monetary Policy through the Lens of the Great Depression." Speech presented at the NBER Annual Conference on Macroeconomics, April 12. http://eml.berkeley.edu/~cromer/It%20Takes%20a%20Regime%20Shift%20Written%20(Second%20Revision).pdf

————, and David Romer 2013. "The Most Dangerous Idea in Federal Reserve History: Monetary Policy Doesn't Matter". *American Economic Review: Papers & Proceedings*, 103(3): 55–60.

Rosenzweig, Phil. 2007. *The Halo Effect: . . . and the Eight Other Business Delusions That Deceive Managers*. New York: Free Press

Sachs, Jeffrey. 2012. "Move America's Economic Debate out of Its Time Warp." *Financial Times*, July 12.

Saito, Tetsushi. 2013. "Kisei Kaikaku no Keiken kara Nani wo Manabuka" [What should be learned from experiences of regulatory reform]. NIRA Monograph Series 38. National Institute for Research Advancement, Tokyo.

Sakakibara, Eisuke. 2003. *Kozo Defure no Seiki* [The century of structural deflation]. Tokyo: Chuo Korosha.

Sargent, Thomas. 1982. "The End of Four Big Inflations." In *Inflation: Causes and Effects*, edited by Robert Hall, 41–97. Chicago: University of Chicago Press.

Sasaki, Minoru. 2013. *Shijo to Kenryoku* [Market and power]. Tokyo: Kodansha.

Sato, Toshiki. 2000. *Fubyodo Shakai Nihon: Sayonara Sochuryu* [Unequal society Japan: Good-bye to the middle class mentality]. Tokyo: Chuo Koronsha.

Sawada, Yasuyuki, Michiko Ueda, and Tetsuya Matsubayashi. 2013. *Jisatstu no nai Shakai he* [Toward evidence-based suicide prevention]. Tokyo: Yuhikaku.

Scheiber, Noam. 2012. "Exclusive: The Memo That Larry Summers Didn't Want Obama to See." *The New Republic*, February 22. http://www.newrepublic.com/article/politics/100961/memo-Larry-Summers-Obama

Scheve, Kenneth F., and Matthew J. Slaughter. 2001. *Globalization and the Perceptions of American Worker*. Washington, DC: Institute for International Economics.

Shibamoto, Masahiko, and Masato Shizume. 2014. "Exchange Rate Adjustment, Monetary Policy and Fiscal Stimulus in Japan's Escape from the Great Depression." RIEB Discussion Paper Series DP2014-12. http://www.rieb.kobe-u.ac.jp/academic/ra/dp/English/DP2014-12.pdf

Shibata, Akihisa, and Satoshi Hanabuchi. 2010. "Nihon Keizai Gakkai 75 Syunenn Jigyo: Gakkaiin ni taisuru Anketo Chosa ni tsuite" [The 75th Anniversary Memorial Event of the Japan Economic Association: On the questionnaire to the members]." In *Gendai keizaigaku no choryu 2010* [Trends in contemporary economics 2010], edited by Shinsuke Ikeda Masao Ogaki, Akihisa Shibata, Takatsohi Tabuchi, Yasuo Maeda, and Ryuzo Miyao, 265–284. Tokyo: Toyo Keizai Shimposha.

Shibata, Kei. 1933. "Marx's Analysis of Capitalism and the General Equilibrium Theory of the Lausanne School." *Kyoto University Economic Review* 8 (1): 107–136.

Shiller, Robert J. 1997. "Why Do People Dislike Inflation?" In *Reducing Inflation: Motivation and Strategy*, edited by Christina Romer et al., 13–65. Chicago: University of Chicago Press.

Shimizu, Masato. 2007. *Keizai zaisei senki* [Rising Tide vs. Fiscal Hawks]. Tokyo: Nihon Keizai Shimbunsha.

————. 2013. *Shohizei sei to kan tono "junen senso"* [The reform of the tax system wars in Japan: Document for ten years]. Tokyo: Shichosha.

Shioji, Etsuro. 2013. "The Bubble Burst and Stagnation of Japan." In *Routledge Handbook of Major Events in Economic History*, edited by Randall E. Parker and Robert Whaples, 316–329. London: Routledge.

Shirakawa, Masaaki. 2009a. *Gendai no Kinyu Seisaku* [Modern monetary policy]. Tokyo: Nihon Keizai Shimbun-sha.

———. 2009b. "Way out of Economic and Financial Crisis: Lessons and Policy Actions." Speech at Japan Society in New York, April 23. http://www.boj.or.jp/en/announcements/press/koen_2009/ko0904c.htm/

———. 2012a. "Deleveraging and Growth: Is the Developed World Following Japan's Long and Winding Road?" Lecture at the London School of Economics and Political Science (Cohosted by the Asia Research Centre and STICERD, LSE), January 10. https://www.boj.or.jp/en/announcements/press/koen_2012/data/ko120111a.pdf

———. 2012b. "Toward Sustainable Growth with Price Stability." Speech at the Kisaragi-kai Meeting in Tokyo, November 12, 2012. https://www.boj.or.jp/en/announcements/press/koen_2012/ko121112a.htm/

———. 2013. Press Briefing on January 22, 2013. https://www.boj.or.jp/announcements/press/kaiken_2013/kk1301a.pdf

Shizume, Masato. 2009. *Sekai Kyoko to Keizaiseisaku* [The world depression and economic policy]. Tokyo: Nihon Keizai Shimbun Shuppannsha.

———. 2011. "Sustainability of Public Debt: Evidence from Japan before the Second World War." *Economic History Review* 64 (4): 1113–1143.

Smethurst, Richard J. 2007. *From Foot Soldier to Finance Minister: Takahashi Korekiyo, Japan's Keynes*. Cambridge, MA: Harvard University Asia Center.

Stigler, George J. 1971. "The Theory of Economic Regulation." *Bell Journal of Economics* 2 (1): 3–21.

Stiglitz, Joseph E. 2012. *The Price of Inequality*. New York: Norton.

———. 2014. "On the Wrong Side of Globalization." *Opinionator* (blog), *New York Times*, March 15. http://opinionator.blogs.nytimes.com/2014/03/15/on-the-wrong-side-of-globalization/?_php=true&_type=blogs&_r=0

Straumann, Tobias, and Ulrich Woitek. 2009. "A Pioneer of a New Monetary Policy? Sweden's Price Level Targeting of the 1930s Revisited." *European Review of Economic History* 13:251–282.

Strumthal, Adolf Fox. 1944. *The Tragedy of European Labor, 1918–1939*. London: V. Gollancz.

Sumner, Scott. 2009. "Now That's the Price Stability." Wall Street Pitt, October 17. http://wallstreetpit.com/11288-bank-of-japan-got-exactly-what-they-aimed-for

———. 2010. "Rooseveltian Resolve." The Money Illusion, January 5. http://www.themoneyillusion.com/?p=3587

Svensson, Lars. 2003. "Escaping from a Liquidity Trap and Others: The Foolproof Way and Others." *Journal of Economic Perspectives* 17 (4) 145–166.

Sveriges Riksbank. 1993. "The Riksbank's Target for Monetary Policy", January 15, 1993. http://www.riksbank.se/Upload/Dokument_riksbank/Kat_publicerat/Pressmeddelanden/930115e.pdf.

Tachibanaki, Toshiakira. 1998. *Nihon no Keizai Kakusa: Shotoku to Shisan kara Kangaeru* [Economic disparity in Japan: Considerations on income and wealth]. Tokyo: Iwanami Shoten.

Takahashi, Kamekichi. 1930a. *Kabushiki Kaisha Bokoku Ron* [Corporations are ruining our country]. Tokyo: Banrikaku Shobo.

Takahashi, Kamekichi. 1930b. *Kinyusyutsu Sai Kinshi Ron* [Reembargo of the gold exports]. Tokyo: Senshin Sha.

Takahashi, Kamekichi. 1931. *Keiki ha do naru* [What is happening to the recession?]. Tokyo: Chikura Shobo.

Takahashi, Kamekichi Takahashi. 1954–1955. *Taisho Showa Zaikai Hendo Shi* [History of economic changes during the Taisho and Showa era]. Tokyo: Toyo Keizai Shimpo Sha.

Takahashi, Korekiyo. 1936. *Takashi Korekiyo Keizairon* [Korekiyo Takahashi on the economy]. Tokyo: Chikura Shobo.

Takahashi, Yoichi. 2000. "Furyo Saiken Syori Shippai no Honshitsu" [The bad loan problem: The nature of failure]. *Voice*, March.

———. 2003. "Will Japan Go Bankrupt? If Japan Goes Bankrupt, What Should Be Done?" *Waseda Economic Papers*, no. 42, 25–112.

———. 2007. *Zaisei Kaikaku no Keizaigaku* [The economics of the fiscal investment and loan program reform]. Tokyo: Toyo Keizai Shimposha.

———. 2008. *Saraba Zaimusho* [Farewell to the Ministry of Finance]. Tokyo: Kodansha.

Takemori, Shumpei. 2002. *Keizai Ronsen ha Yomigaeru* [Economic controversy revives]. Tokyo: Nihon Keizai Shinbunsha.

Takenaka, Harukata. 2014. *Failed Democratization in Prewar Japan: Breakdown of a Hybrid Regime*. Stanford, CA: Stanford University Press.

Takenaka, Heizo. 1984. *Kenkyu Kaihatsu to Setsubi Toshi no Keizaigaku* [Economics of R&D and investment]. Tokyo: Toyo Keizai Shimposha.

———. 1993. *Nihon Kenkokuron* [Founding wiser Japan]. Tokyo: Dentsu.

———. 1999. *21-seikigata Minpuron* [Wealth of people in the 21st century]. Tokyo: Nihon Hoso Shuppan Kyokai.

———. 2006. *Kozo Kaikaku no Shinjitsu: Takenaka Heizo Daijin Nisshi* [Truths of structural reform: The diary of Minister Takena Heizo]. Tokyo: Nihon Keizai Shinbunsha.

———. 2014. "Kokka Senryaku Tokku wo Kaikaku no Kibakuzai ni" [The national economic special zone to the ignition of reform]. In *Tettei Bunseki Abenomics* [Abenomics analyzed], 161–176. Tokyo: Chuo Keizaisha.

Takenaka, Heizo, Haruo Horioka, Ayako Tejima, and Hisae Takahashi. 2001. "90 Nendai no Keizai Ronso to Seisaku Kettei" [Economic controversies and policymaking during the 1990s]. In *Seisaku Kiki to Nihon Keizai* [Policy crises and the Japanese economy], edited by Kazuo Ogawa and Heizo Takenaka, 191–224. Tokyo: Nihon Hyoronsha.

Takeshita, Noboru. 1991. *Syogen Hosyu Seiken* [Testimony on the conservative government]. Tokyo: Kodansha.

Takita, Yoichi, and Kashima Heiwa Kenkyujyo, eds. 2006. *Nichibei Tsuka Kosho* [Japan-US currency negotiations]. Tokyo: Nihon Keizai Shimbunsha.

Taylor, John B. 2001. "Low Inflation, Deflation, and Policies for Future Price Stability." *Monetary and Economic Studies* 19 (S-1): 35–52.

———. 2007. *Global Financial Warriors: The Untold Story of International Finance in the Post-9/11 World.* New York: Norton.

———. 2009. *Getting off Track: How Government Actions and Interventions Caused, Prolonged, and Worsened the Financial Crisis.* Stanford, CA: Hoover Institution Press.

———. 2012. *First Principles: Five Keys to Restoring America's Prosperity.* New York: Norton.

Temin, Peter. 1976. *Did Monetary Forces Cause the Great Depression?* New York: Norton.

———. 1989. *Lessons from the Great Depression*, Cambridge, MA: MIT Press.

Temin, Peter, and Barrie A. Wigmore. 1990. "The End of One Big Deflation," *Explorations in Economic History* 27 (4): 483–502.

Tett, Gillian. 2003. *Saving the Sun: A Wall Street Gamble to Rescue Japan from Its Trillion-Dollar Meltdown.* New York: Harper.

———. 2013. "Forget the Fed, Watch Out for a Japanese Taper." *Financial Times*, December 13.

Teulings, Coen. 2012. "Fiscal Consolidation and Reforms: Substitutes, not Complements." Vox, September 13. http://www.voxeu.org/article/fiscal-consolidation-and-reforms-substitutes-not-complements

Teulings, Coen, and Richard Baldwin, eds. 2014. *Secular Stagnation: Facts, Causes, and Cures.* London: CEPR Press. http://www.voxeu.org/article/secular-stagnation-facts-causes-and-cures-new-vox-ebook

Thorndike, Edward L. 1920. "A Constant Error in Psychological Ratings." *Journal of Applied Psychology* 4 (1): 25–29.

Tobin, James. 1977. "How Dead Is Keynes." *Economic Inquiry* 15 (4): 459–468.

Todo, Yasuyuki. 2013. "TTP no Seicho Koka Suikei" [Estimates on the growth effects of the TPP]. RIETI Special Report. http://www.rieti.go.jp/jp/special/special_report/060.html

Tokyo Daigaku Keizaigakubu, ed. 1976. *Tokyo Daigaku Keizaigakubu Gojunenshi* [The fifty years of the Department of Economics, University of Tokyo]. Tokyo: University of Tokyo Press.

Tokyo Shogyo Kaigisyo. 1927. *Kin Yushyutsu Kaikin Mondai ni Kansuru Sanko Shiryo* [Briefs on the lifting the embargo on gold problem]. Tokyo: Tokyo Shogyo Kaigisyo.

Tsuru, Shigeto. 1971. "In Place of Gross National Product." In *Kutabare GNP*, edited by Asahi Shimbun Keizaibu, xxi–xxxii. Tokyo: Asahi Shimbun.

Uchihashi, Katsuhito, and Group 2001. 1995. *Kisei Kanwa to iu Akumu* [A nightmare called deregulation]. Tokyo: Bungei Shunjusha.

Ueda, Kazuo. 2012. "Deleveraging and Monetary Policy: Japan since the 1990s and the United States since 2007." *Journal of Economic Perspectives* 26 (3): 177–202.

Umeda, Mitchinobu. 2011. *Nichigin no Seisaku Keisei* [Monetary policymaking at the BOJ]. Tokyo: Toyo Keizai Shimposha.

Vogel, Ezra. 1979. *Japan as Number One: Lessons for America.* Cambridge, MA: Harvard University Press.

Volcker, Paul A., and Toyoo Gyohten. 1992. *Changing Fortunes: The World's Money and the Threat to American Leadership.* New York: Times Books.

Von Staden, Peter. 2012. "Fettered by the Past in the March Forward: Ideology as an Explanation for Today's Malaise in Japan." *Asia Pacific Business Review* 18 (2): 187–202.

Wakatabe, Masazumi. 2005. "Was the Great Depression the Watershed of Macroeconomics? The Impact of the Great Depression Reconsidered." Unpublished manuscript.

———. 2009. *Kiki no Keizai Seisaku* [Economic crises and policy responses]. Tokyo: Nihon Hyoronsha.

———. 2011. "Central Banking, Japanese Style: Economics and the Bank of Japan, 1945–2010." Paper presented at the Workshop on Economic Theories and Policies: A Historical Perspective, 1945–2002, Roma Tre University, September 21–22.

———. 2012. "Turning Japanese? Lessons from Japan's Lost Decade to the Current Crisis," Center on Japanese Economy and Business, Columbia University, December. http://academiccommons.columbia.edu/download/fedora_content/download/ac:155609/CONTENT/WP_309.pdf

———. 2013. "Central Banking, Japanese Style: Economics and the Bank of Japan, 1945–1985." *History of Economic Thought and Policy* 2 (1): 141–160.

———. 2014a. "Is There Any Cultural Difference in Economics? Keynesianism and Monetarism in Japan." In *The Development of Economics in Japan*, edited by Toichiro Asada, 134–154. London: Routledge.

———. 2014b. "'The Lost Thirteen Years': The Return to the Gold Standard Controversy in Japan, 1919–1932." In *The Development of Economics in Japan*, edited by Toichiro Asada, 13–38. London: Routledge.

Wapshott, Nicholas. 2011. *Keynes Hayek: The Clash That Defined Modern Economics.* New York: Norton.

Watanabe, Tsutomu, and Tomoyoshi Yabu. 2011. "The Great Intervention and Massive Money Injection: The Japanese Experience 2003–2004." CARF Working Paper F-266. University of Tokyo. http://www.carf.e.u-tokyo.ac.jp/pdf/working-paper/fseries/277.pdf

Watanabe, Tsutomu, Tomoyoshi Yabu, and Arata Ito. 2008. "Seidojoho wo Motiita Zaisei Josu no Keisoku" [Estimation of fiscal multiplier using institutional information]. Understanding Inflation Dynamics of the Japanese Economy Working Paper Series 28.

Weil, David N. 2013. *Economic Growth.* 3rd ed. Boston: Pearson.

Wessel, David. 2009. *In Fed We Trust: Ben Bernanke's War on the Great Panic.* New York: Crown Business.

White, Lawrence H. 2008. "Did Hayek and Robbins Deepen the Great Depression?" *Journal of Money, Credit and Banking* 40:751–768.

———. 2012. *Clash of Economic Ideas.* Cambridge: Cambridge University Press.

White, William R. 2012. "Ultra Easy Monetary Policy and the Law of Unintended Consequences." Working Paper 126. Federal Reserve Bank of Dallas,

Globalization and Monetary Policy Institute. http://dallasfed.org/assets/documents/institute/wpapers/2012/0126.pdf

Wolf, Martin. 2013. "Why Abenomics Will Disappoint." *Financial Times*. December 17.

Yamamoto, Kozo. 2010. *Nichigin ni tsubusareteta Nihon keizai* [The Japanese economy was crashed by the Bank of Japan]. Tokyo: First Press.

Yamazaki, Seijun. 1929a. *Kin Yushutsu Kaikin Mondai* [The lifting the embargo on gold problem]. Kyoto, Japan: Ritsumeikan Daigaku Shuppanbu.

———. 1929b. *Kokumin Keizai no Tatenaoshi ka Hakai ka* [The national economy, reconstruction or destruction]. Tokyo: Shubunkaku.

Yano, Koiti, Yasuyuki Iida, and Hajime Wago. 2010. "Fiscal Policy and the Share of Non-Ricardian Households: A Monte Carlo Particle Filtering Approach." Paper read at Econometric Society World Congress. Shanghai, China.

———, Yasuyuki Iida, Goushi Kataoka, Tae Okada, and Yasushi Okada. 2014. "The End of One Long Deflation: An Empirical Investigation," Unpublished manuscript.

Yomiuri Shimbun. 2014. "Jimin assho 'tato yori mashi' 65 %" ['there is no choice but to elect the governing' said 65 % of the respondents]. *Yomiuri Shimbun*, December 16, 2014. http://www.yomiuri.co.jp/election/shugiin/20141216-OYT1T50123.html?from=tw

Yoshikawa, Hiroshi. 1999. *Tennkan ki no nihon Keizai*. Tokyo: Iwanami Shoten. Translated by Charles H. Stewart as *Japan's Lost Decade* (Tokyo: International House of Japan, 2002).

———. 2013. *Deflation*. [In Japanese]. Tokyo: Nihon Keizai Shimbunsha.

Yoshikawa, Hiroshi, and Tsusho Sangyo Kenkyujo. 2000. *Makuro Keizai Seisaku no Kadai to Soten* [Macroeconomic policy: Agenda and issues]. Tokyo: Toyo Keizai Shimposha.

Yoshitomi, Masaru. 1965. *America no Daikyoko* [The Great Depression in the United States]. Tokyo: Nihon Hyoronsha.

———. 1991. "Watashi no Keiki Jikkan—Schumpeter-teki Keizai to Churitsuteki Zaisei Kinyu Seisaku" [My take on the current economy—the Schumpeterian economy and the neutral fiscal and monetary policy]. *Shukan Tokyo Keizai*, December 7.

Young, Louise. 1998. *Japan's Total Empire: Manchuria and the Culture of Wartime Imperialism*, Berkeley: University of California Press.

Zaimusho Shukei Kyoku 2009, "Heisei 21 nendo kuni no zaimusyorui" [Balance sheet of Japanese government FY 2009], http://www.mof.go.jp/budget/report/public_finance_fact_sheet/fy2009/national/2009_01c.pdf.

Zingales, Luigi. 2012. *A Capitalism for the People: Recapturing the Lost Genius of American Prosperity*. New York: Basic Books.

Websites

Asahi Shimbun: http://database.asahi.com/library2/

Bank of Japan: http://www.boj.or.jp/

European Central Bank: https://www.ecb.europa.eu/home/html/index.en.html
Federal Reserve Board: http://www.federalreserve.gov/
Mainichi Shimbun: http://mainichi.jp/contents/edu/maisaku/
Nihon Keizai Shimbun: http://t21.nikkei.co.jp/
Sankei Shimbun: http://db.g-search.or.jp/g_news/QSKS.html
Yahoo Finance: http://finance.yahoo.com/
Yomiuri Shimbun: https://database.yomiuri.co.jp/rekishikan/

Index

Lightning Source UK Ltd.
Milton Keynes UK
UKOW06n1817220515

252127UK00004B/59/P

9 781137 438843